Risk Management
for Accountants

Risk Management
for Accountants

Barlow, Lyde & Gilbert

Editor

Andrew Scott

Principal Contributor

Charlotte Hart

abg
professional
information

40 Bernard Street
London
WC1N 1LD
Tel: +44(0) 20 7920 8991
Fax: +44(0) 20 7920 8992
E-mail: info@abgpublications.co.uk
Website: www.abgweb.com

ISBN 1 85355 954 7

British Library Cataloguing-in-Publication Data

A catalogue record for this book is available from the British Library.

Typeset by Marksbury Multimedia Ltd, Midsomer Norton, Bath
Printed by Bell & Bain, Glasgow

Foreword

Effective Risk Management by accountancy practices is in both the public interest and the practitioners' interest. In the public interest because it leads to clarity in the expectations of clients, closer meeting of those expectations and higher quality advice. In practitioners' interest because it improves their professional reputation and reduces their exposure to court action and to professional disciplinary investigation. The Institute of Chartered Accountants in England and Wales sets the professional scene through its bye-laws, regulations and ethical and other guidance. This excellent book takes the issues to the next, intensely practical stage giving clear guidance on how to get it right and what to do if it goes wrong.

The days of clients and the public saying 'tell me' and accountants simply saying 'trust me' and that being enough are long gone. Our future as individual practitioners, as firms and as a profession depends on us earning our reputation and demonstrating our merits on a daily basis. The advice and information in this book will be invaluable in helping accountants to achieve these ends.

Graham Ward
President
Institute of Chartered Accountants in England and Wales

Preface

The explosion of negligence claims against accountants in the 1980s and 1990s has inevitably caused much greater attention to be devoted to risk management. The larger firms, and increasingly many smaller ones, have devoted considerable resources to devising and enhancing procedures designed to reduce the risk of claims.

At the most general level, risk management for the accountancy profession, as in all other areas of business life, is about delivering a quality product. In the accountant's case that means one that is provided on time and at a reasonable cost and one which, above all, provides the appropriate information or advice. But quality control, though fundamental, is not the end of the story. Risks can arise in many other ways: through taking on the wrong client or the wrong job; through responding inappropriately to requests for assistance from people who are not clients; through creating or preserving material that is unnecessary or unhelpful; or by failing to observe basic precepts of independence or confidentiality. It is the management of risk of this nature that forms the basic subject-matter of this book.

Inevitably, of course, things do sometimes go wrong. The problems that can then arise also need to be managed. With this in mind we have also included chapters on insurance, on handling complaints and claims, and on the disciplinary and litigation processes. A final chapter offers a short and hopefully accessible guide to the law relating to professional negligence claims.

In preparing the more specifically legal material, the overriding aim has been to be practical rather than definitive. This, coupled with the fact that fine distinctions are all too often the essence of the law, means that the book should not be treated as more than a general guide: when important or complex legal issues arise, specific legal advice, responsive to the particular circumstances, should always be sought. Within those limits, however, we hope that those who refer to it will find it helpful and practical.

The following have played various but always important parts in the production of the book: Giles Adams, David Arthur, Jenny Brown,

Clare Canning, Susan Collett, Helen Cormack, Anna Fleming, Andrew Forsyth, Stuart Hall, Claire Harradine, Oscar Harrison-Hall, Simon Judd, Francis Kean, Rosemary Norton, Julian Randall, Jane Scott, David Smyth and Gill Young. But far and away the biggest contribution came from Charlotte Hart, without whose particular combination of enthusiasm, energy and patience the project could not have succeeded. It is inevitable that despite the best endeavours of all of these individuals, some errors or omissions will remain: for these I claim sole responsibility.

Andrew Scott

Contents

Table of Cases

Table of Statutes

Table of Statutory Instruments

1 Independence and confidentiality

1.1 Introduction

This Chapter looks at issues connected with independence (including conflicts of interest) and confidentiality. The following matters are covered:

- Section 1.2 covers the general principle of independence.

- Section 1.3 covers the general principle of confidentiality.

- Section 1.4 considers recent cases concerning independence and confidentiality and the practical lessons to be drawn from them.

- Section 1.5 deals briefly with the situation in which the accountant receives confidential information without its owner's consent.

1.2 Independence

The general principle is that an accountant is expected to act with integrity, objectivity and independence when performing his engagement. Such an expectation arises by reason of his professional status and the tasks that he is required to perform. The precise extent of independence required will vary depending on the task or function for which the accountant is engaged. Generally, he should not undertake an engagement in circumstances where he has some conflict of interest, either between himself and his client, or as a result of competing interests of different clients, which affects or threatens to affect his integrity, independence or objectivity.

The general principle is stated in the Fundamental Principles of the ICAEW in the following terms:[1]

'1. A member should behave with integrity in all professional dealings and business relationships. Integrity implies not merely honesty but also fair dealing and truthfulness.

2. A member should strive for objectivity in all professional and business judgements. Objectivity is the state of mind which

---

[1] *ICAEW Members' Handbook 2000*, 1.200; and see generally ICAEW Statement 1.201 ('Integrity, Objectivity and Independence').

has regard to all considerations relevant to the task in hand but no other.'

As a matter of law, the need for independence and the avoidance of conflicts will be the subject of, or will result from:

- an express or implied term of the engagement contract;
- a fiduciary or other equitable obligation;
- a statutory or regulatory requirement.

1.2.1 Acting as a fiduciary

The independence requirement is enhanced where the accountant acts as a fiduciary. A fiduciary is someone who has undertaken to act for, or on behalf of, another in a particular matter in circumstances that give rise to a relationship of confidence and trust.[2] In such circumstances the following specific obligations arise:

(i) The 'no conflict rule'. The fiduciary must not place himself in a position where his own interest conflicts with that of his client, the beneficiary.

(ii) The 'no profit' rule. A fiduciary must not profit from his position at the expense of his client, the beneficiary.

(iii) The 'undivided loyalty' rule. A fiduciary owes undivided loyalty to his client, the beneficiary, not to place himself in a position where his duty towards one client conflicts with a duty that he owes to another client. A consequence of this duty is that a fiduciary must make available to a client all the information that is relevant to the client's affairs.

(iv) The 'duty of confidentiality'. A fiduciary must only use information obtained in confidence from his client, the beneficiary, for the benefit of the client and must not use it for his own advantage, or for the benefit of any other person.

An accountant will generally be a fiduciary wherever he acts as trustee or agent for his client. However, general obligations of independence and confidentiality will arise in any event, regardless of whether in a strict sense the accountant is acting as a fiduciary.

---

[2]*Bristol and West Building Society v Mothew* [1998] 1 CH 1at p.18 (approved by the Privy Council in *Arklow Investments Ltd v Maclean* [2000] 1 WLR 594).

1.2.2 Other specific independence requirements

When undertaking some engagements, the accountant may be subject to or affected by specific statutory or other independence requirements. It is not practical to set out an exhaustive list of these requirements, which can include foreign statutory or regulatory requirements (for example, those of the US Securities and Exchange Commission ('SEC')), but the following constitute familiar examples:

- In providing a statutory audit opinion on the accounts of a company, an accountant is required to provide an independent opinion.[3]

- An accountant who is an officer or employee of a company (or a partner or employee of such accountant) cannot act as the auditor of that company.[4]

- An expert in legal proceedings owes a duty to the Court to provide an independent opinion.[5]

1.2.3 Remedies for breach

The remedies for any breach of the independence requirement will vary depending upon the nature of the precise duty owed and the identity of the complainant. In the context of a client, this may result in proceedings in which the client seeks:

- an injunction to restrain any further infringement of duty;[6]

- damages for breach of contract or any statutory or fiduciary duty if the client has suffered loss as a result of the breach;

---

[3]See Companies Act 1985, s235; Companies Act 1989, s24 and Sch 11.

[4]Companies Act 1989, s27 and Sch 11, paras 6 and 7.

[5]CPR Rule 35.3.

[6]In *United Pan-Europe Communications NV v Deutsche Bank AG* (CA May 2000), cable communication company UPC dealt with Deutsche Bank and provided them with confidential information in relation to a possible acquisition of cable service provider Tele Columbus Group. Deutsche Bank subsequently acquired TC in preference to a joint bid by UPC and PrimaCom AG. UPC sought an injunction restraining Deutsche Bank from disposing of its TC shares, a declaration that the shares be held on constructive trust for UPC and damages for breach of the fiduciary duty of loyalty and the misuse of confidential information arising from their commercial relationship. An interim injunction was granted by the Court of Appeal on the basis that there was a serious issue to be tried.

- where the accountant has profited from breach of a fiduciary duty, an account of those profits.

1.3   Confidentiality

The general principle is that an accountant owes a duty of confidence[7] to his client not to disclose information that is confidential to his client without the client's consent.

This principle is reflected in ICAEW Statement 1.205 ('Confidentiality'), which states:

> 'Information confidential to a client or employer acquired in the course of professional work should not be disclosed except where consent has been obtained from the client, employer, or other proper source, or where there is a legal right or duty to disclose.'[8]

Coupled to this is a requirement not to make improper use of information:

> 'A member acquiring or receiving confidential information in the course of his or her professional work should neither use, nor appear to use, that information for his personal advantage or for the advantage of a third party.'[9]

As a matter of law, a duty of confidence can arise:

- at common law as an express or implied term of the accountant's contract of engagement or retainer;

- in equity, including where the accountant is acting in a fiduciary capacity towards his client (see **1.2** above);

- as a result of statutory or regulatory provision.[10]

---

[7]A duty of confidence arises when confidential information comes to the knowledge of a person (the confidant) in circumstances where he has notice, or is held to have agreed, that the information is confidential, with the effect that it would be just in all the circumstances that he should be precluded from disclosing the information to others.

[8]Para 1.0.

[9]Ibid., para 2.0.

[10]Such as under the Banking Act 1987.

1.3.1 Extent of the duty

Subject to any express agreement to the contrary, the duty of confidence is unqualified. The duty to preserve confidentiality continues even after the end of an engagement or a client relationship and until the information is no longer confidential.

In the light of this it may be necessary to give consideration to issues of confidence when preparing the engagement letter, or to have in place structures and procedures for minimising the risk of disclosure or misuse of confidential information such as Chinese walls.

1.3.2 What is confidential?

What actually comprises confidential information can sometimes be in dispute. In general:

● The information must be of a confidential nature.

● The information should have some intrinsic value and not be trivial or useless – in other words it must be objectively worth protecting. It is not always easy to conclude that information is trivial.

If the information is published or accessible in the public domain it cannot be, or cannot continue to be, confidential.

In many cases what is, or is not, confidential information will be self-evident. In some instances, there may be specific provisions dealing with confidentiality. For example, SAS 230 provides that auditors should adopt procedures for maintaining the confidentiality (and safe custody) of their working papers. There are also occasions when the accountant will be under a statutory duty of confidentiality such as under the Banking Act 1987. However, there will be many times when the position is not so clear. If there is any uncertainty, it would be prudent to seek specific legal advice before making use of or disclosing information, or risking its inadvertent disclosure. In general, an accountant is advised to treat all his client's affairs as being confidential.

1.3.3 Exceptions to the duty of confidence

There are occasions when the accountant may be released from his duty not to disclose confidential information. Such a release may arise by:

● client consent (which may sometimes be implied);

- an overriding statutory duty to cooperate with a statutory (or regulatory) investigation (see **Chapter 5**);

- a Court Order;

- a statutory right, or duty, to 'whistleblow', or a general public duty to disclose or expose fraud.[11]

1.3.4   Remedies available to a client whose confidence is, or is threatened to be, breached

Where the accountant has breached or seems to be about to breach his duty of confidence, the client may have a claim for breach (or threatened breach) of that duty of confidence. The precise cause of action (and remedies) may vary depending upon whether the duty arises in contract (common law), as a result of a fiduciary duty (in equity), or in some other way. It is generally open to the client to commence proceedings seeking appropriate relief, which will usually include at least some of the following:

- an injunction restraining any breach or further breach of confidence;

- associated injunctions seeking return of confidential documents or putting in safeguards to ensure that risk of further breach is avoided;

- damages for breach of contract or fiduciary duty if financial loss has been suffered as a result of the accountant's breach;

- an account for any profits made by the accountant as a result of the breach of an equitable duty.

The response that the accountant gives when threatened with any such proceedings will depend on the circumstances, but generally any such threat should be treated as if it were a potential claim and the procedures suggested in **8.2** below followed so far as appropriate.

In many circumstances where the accountant has breached confidence, it will be sensible for him to minimise costs and avoid a contested application for an injunction by volunteering to abide by restrictions over the use or return of the material. This is done by offering an 'undertaking' (a formal promise) such as not to use the information

---

[11]Detailed guidance on this aspect is to be found in the *ICAEW Members' Handbook 2000*, 1.306 ('Professional Conduct in Relation to Defaults or Unlawful Acts') and in the more specific material there referred to. Section 1.306 also covers the accountant's ability to disclose confidential information in his own interests in limited circumstances (see para 19).

further and to return any documents obtained in breach of confidence (together with any photocopies which have been taken). An undertaking incorporated in a Court Order is binding in the same way as an injunction. In other words, if the accountant does not honour his undertaking he may be guilty of Contempt of Court.[12] The Court may consider it necessary to go to some lengths to prevent the risk of a breach of confidence. For example, the Court may require the accountant to cease to act for a particular client if by acting there is a real risk that another client's confidentiality could be misused.

1.3.5 Possession of another client's confidential information which is relevant to an engagement

It is sometimes said that fiduciaries must make available to a client all the information that they have which is relevant to the client's affairs. This can give rise to difficulties – for example, if use or disclosure of the information would put the fiduciary in breach of a duty of confidence owed to another client, or former client. In such circumstances, the fiduciary arguably could not meet his fiduciary obligations to his client without risking a breach of another obligation. Generally, although preferably this situation will be covered in the engagement letter, a Court is likely to solve this problem by implying a term that an accountant is not obliged to breach the confidence of another client when performing an engagement.[13]

There may be situations, however, where an accountant's knowledge of another client's confidential information affects whether or not he can continue his engagement, notwithstanding any express or implied term. Consider, for example, the discovery during an audit that a client has not revealed a material transaction which the auditor knows of from another confidential source. The auditor would have difficulty saying outright that he knew of the transaction for fear of breaching the other client's confidence. However, it may be appropriate to use the information at least to the extent of asking questions which ought to result in the first client disclosing the transaction. If that client still does not disclose the transaction the auditor will then be in a better position to consider the options, including whether he should resign.

---

[12]Contempt is punishable by committal to prison, by fine or by sequestration of assets (in the case of a company).

[13]*Kelly v Cooper* [1993] AC 205; *Clarke Boyce v Mouat* [1994] 1 AC 428; *Prince Jefri* p.235 B.

1.3.6 Imputed knowledge?

In some cases the confidential information may be known to one partner but not to the partner actually performing the engagement. This may lead to the question being raised whether the knowledge of one partner should be imputed (or attributed) to the firm as a whole for the purposes of carrying out an engagement so that the engagement partner is deemed to have knowledge of it even though he does not have actual knowledge. In general terms, knowledge will not be imputed in this way: for every partner to be deemed to have the knowledge of every other partner in a firm would be inconsistent with the principles of confidentiality and would mean that Chinese walls could never work.[14]

1.4 Recent cases and practical guidance

Confidentiality and conflicts of interest and the efficacy of Chinese walls have been the subject of some recent, well-publicised Court decisions. Two of these in particular concerned forensic accountants: *Prince Jefri Bolkiah* v *KPMG and Young* v *Robson Rhodes*. These cases illustrate that confidentiality and the risk of inadvertent disclosure can have enormous implications for a firm.

Prince Jefri Bolkiah v KPMG[15]

Prince Jefri, a brother of the Sultan of Brunei, was for many years the Chairman of the Brunei Investments Agency ('BIA'). KPMG were the auditors to BIA. Between 1996 and 1998, the firm's forensic department were instructed by Prince Jefri to act for him personally in major litigation. That retainer came to an end and shortly thereafter the firm was approached by the Government of Brunei to investigate the activities of BIA and in particular certain transfers. This was to be a major forensic investigation, rather than a natural extension of the audit.[16] It was to be

---

[14]*Prince Jefri* p.235F: 'there is no cause to impute or attribute the knowledge of one partner to his fellow partners. Whether a particular individual is in possession of confidential information is a question of fact which must be proved or inferred from the circumstances of the case'. See also *Northumberland Insurance Limited (in liquidation) v Alexander & Ors* [1984] 8 ACLR p.882.

[15][1999] 2 AC 222.

[16]An injunction may not have been granted if it had been a natural extension of the audit. In this respect, Prince Jefri knew that BIA was an existing audit client of KPMG. The Court may have concluded that he had consented to them continuing to act in that capacity and hence took the risk of any inadvertent disclosure of confidential information which went along with their continuing so to act.

conducted by members of the same forensic accounting department that had carried out the engagement for Prince Jefri. It was clear at around the time that the engagement was accepted that it was partly adverse to Prince Jefri's interests and that information confidential to him might be of relevance.

KPMG took the view that they could properly accept the new instructions because Prince Jefri was no longer a client and thus no question of a conflict of interest arose.[17] This view was upheld by the House of Lords. However, recognising that they might owe a continuing duty of confidentiality, KPMG took steps to set up a Chinese wall to preserve the Prince's confidentiality:

- No one who was in possession of information confidential to Prince Jefri was to work on the new engagement.

- Physical barriers were put in place in order to separate the team from the rest of the department.

- Arrangements were put in place to restrict access to information which was confidential to Prince Jefri by depositing files relating to work for him with the firm's solicitors, deleting any such information from the computer servers and using separate file servers for the new team.

The firm did not seek their former client's consent to their acting for BIA and when Prince Jefri found out he applied for an injunction to restrain KPMG from carrying out the investigation. The injunction was granted by the High Court, discharged by the Court of Appeal, and reinstated by the House of Lords. Having regard to the extensive nature of KPMG's role in interviewing witnesses and other evidence-gathering, the House of Lords approached the position as if KPMG had been acting as solicitors.[18] The following can be extracted from the judgment.

A professional firm is restricted from acting for a client whose interests conflict with those of an existing client. The restriction is not absolute and can be overcome by the consent of each client.[19] In the case of accountants acting in relation to litigation, the consent must be informed and expressly given, but in some other situations consent may be

---

[17]The House of Lords accepted this reasoning as a matter of law although the decision might have given rise to ethical issues.

[18]In the light of this, the obligation imposed on them to preserve confidentiality was perhaps at the extreme end of the scale, though whether it is realistic to suppose that the equivalent duty imposed on forensic accountants whose only role is to provide an expert's report for use in litigation is any less is debatable.

[19]*Prince Jefri*, p.235B.

inferred. The House of Lords gave auditors of competing audit clients as one example of where clients with competing interests can be deemed to have consented to the firm acting for a competitor, although it is still necessary for the auditors to keep information obtained from their respective clients confidential.

Where the complainant is no longer a client, the position is different because it is no longer a question of acting for two different clients with competing interests as one has ceased to be a client. The issue is then no longer one of conflict, but of confidentiality.[20] The duty of a forensic accountant to preserve confidentiality is unqualified. The former client is entitled to prevent his former forensic accountant from exposing him to any avoidable risk.

A party who seeks to restrain his former accountant from acting for another client must first show:

(i) that the accountant is in possession of information that is confidential to him and to the disclosure of which he has not consented, and

(ii) that the information is or may be relevant to the new matter in which the interest of the other client is or may be adverse to his own.

The Court should intervene on the part of the former client unless it is satisfied that there is no risk of disclosure or misuse of confidential information. This is not a balancing exercise but the risk must be real, and not merely fanciful or theoretical; however, it need not be substantial.[21] The onus is then on the professional to show that there is no risk of disclosure or misuse.[22] Lord Millet expressed the view that, without the consent of his former client, no forensic accountant should accept instructions unless, viewed objectively, his doing so will not increase the risk that information which is confidential to the former client may come into the possession of a party with an adverse interest.

Their Lordships confirmed that there was no rule of law that Chinese walls or other arrangements of a similar kind are insufficient to eliminate the risk of confidential information being disclosed. However, the

---

[20]*Prince Jefri*, p.235C.

[21]*Prince Jefri*, p.237A.

[22]The fact that Prince Jefri might ultimately have to disclose this information was not regarded as a reason not to grant the injunction. The question of whether public policy outweighed any confidentiality issue was not debated.

starting point is that unless special measures are taken, information moves within a firm. The Court was prepared to adopt the formulation that it would restrain the firm from acting for the other client unless it was satisfied on the basis of clear and convincing evidence that all effective measures had been taken to ensure that no disclosure would occur.

The House of Lords concluded that good practice requires there to be established institutional arrangements designed to prevent the flow of information between separate departments.[23] The establishment of the ad hoc barriers which KPMG had put in place within a single department were not regarded as being sufficient and the Court held that KPMG could not continue to act in the new engagement.[24]

Young v Robson Rhodes[25]

The claimants were Names at Lloyd's and members of a Lloyd's syndicate. Another firm, Pannell Kerr Forster ('PKF') were the former auditors to the syndicate. The syndicate had incurred large losses and had brought an action against PKF alleging breach of contract and negligence. In this context they instructed a partner at Robson Rhodes to act as experts.

---

[23]For this purpose the Court considered that Chinese walls should have the following features:
(i)   The physical separation of departments in order to insulate them from each other. (This may involve housing the departments in different buildings or parts of the same building and can extend to restricting business and social arrangements between members of different departments. It will also involve ensuring that access to records whether in hard or computerised form is restricted.)
(ii) An educational programme to ensure that employees are aware of the importance of not improperly using or inadvertently disclosing confidential information.
(iii) Defined procedures for dealing with situations where it is appropriate to cross the Chinese walls and ensuring that records are kept of where this occurs.
(iv) Monitoring by compliance officers of the effectiveness of the walls.
(v)   Disciplinary sanctions where there has been a breach of the wall.

[24](*Prince Jefri*, p.238C.) See also City Disputes Panel Review of Conflicts and Duties in Relation to Confidential Information – April 2000.

[24]The case law (concerning solicitors) suggests that it may be quite difficult to persuade the courts that a Chinese wall is sufficiently 'soundproofed'; see *Supasave Retail Ltd v Coward Chance* [1990] 3 WLR 1278.

[25][1999] 3 All ER 524.

Subsequently Robson Rhodes and PKF entered into merger negotiations. The Names were informed by Robson Rhodes that if they merged they would have to cease to act. The Names, who by that stage had paid or owed substantial fees to Robson Rhodes, sought undertakings that the merger would not go ahead until after the trial of their action against PKF. When this undertaking was not given they commenced proceedings seeking to prevent the merger until after the trial. They relied on the fact that if the merger went ahead Robson Rhodes could not continue to act as experts and that there was a risk that confidential information would be passed to PKF.

The Court held that Robson Rhodes' refusal to carry on work was a breach of contract but was not prepared to grant injunctions preventing the merger. As regards the confidential information, the issue was whether measures could be put in place which would provide the Names with adequate protection. It was argued that ad hoc arrangements could never work, but the judge did not agree:

> 'The crucial question is "will the barriers work?" If they do, it does not matter whether they were created before the problem arose or are erected afterwards. It seems to me that all Lord Millett was saying was that Chinese walls which have become part of the fabric of the institution are more likely to work than those artificially put in place to meet a one-off problem.'

In the event, the judge concluded that sufficient measures had been put in place to maintain confidentiality and refused to restrain the merger. These measures included:

- confidentiality undertakings;

- deletion of confidential information from Robson Rhodes' computers;

- the placing of Robson Rhodes' relevant documents with solicitors to which access would not be given without the Names' consent; and

- Robson Rhodes' expert team were to work in a building separate from any of PKF's personnel connected with the litigation and were not to have any professional (rather than social) contact with them until after the trial.

1.4.1 Practical implications

In each of the *Prince Jefri* and *Robson Rhodes* cases a large amount of money was turning on the decision and there were also tactical implications for the underlying litigation. Similar issues might apply to any number of situations in which a firm might find itself. Comparisons can be made with merchant banks and other professional advisers where injunctions have been sought – though not always successfully – in particular situations. Thus, issues of independence and confidentiality can have significant commercial implications. This can be so in any area of practice and not just in the particular situations addressed in the Prince Jefri and Robson Rhodes cases.

So far as independence is concerned, safeguards should be put in place to ensure that possible independence or conflicts problems are spotted, prevented and managed. Not every situation will prevent the accountant from acting. There may be occasions where he will be prevented from doing so either by statute, by regulation, or by reason of the particular relationship with the client, but in many circumstances it will be possible to act with the informed consent of the client, or clients, concerned. Sometimes consent will be implied. In practice, some issues can be managed by appropriate engagement letters and often by having in place structural and procedural measures to minimise the risk of independence, conflicts, or confidentiality issues such as institutionalised Chinese walls.

More generally, the accountant will be well advised to cover independence, conflicts of interest and confidentiality issues as much as possible in the engagement letter. For example, in those practice areas where problems are more likely to occur, particularly corporate finance or forensic accountancy, it will be sensible to accept an engagement on condition that:

- both during and after the engagement it is open to the firm to act for existing and future clients with conflicting, competing, or adverse interests subject to preserving the client's confidential information;

- any information confidential to other past, current, or future clients will not be used for the purposes of the engagement;

- reasonable steps will be taken to preserve and keep confidential any confidential information provided by, or on behalf of the client, except as in accordance with legal, regulatory, or disciplinary requirements;

- reasonable steps will be those which the firm deems appropriate.[26]

---

[26]Sample clauses to this effect for inclusion in an engagement letter appear in Tech 4/00 'Conflict of Interest and Confidentiality Guidance', issued in January/May 2000 by the Business Law Committee of the ICAEW.

1.5 Receipt of confidential information without the consent of the party to whom the confidence belongs

Situations sometimes arise in which an accountant is passed confidential information which belongs to a third party in circumstances where there is doubt as to whether the third party authorised or intended the disclosure. Sometimes, the passing on of the information will be deliberate – for example, where an accountant performing an investigation into a company is offered information by his client or by a third party (such as an employee of the company being investigated), which has been taken without the company's consent. In other cases, the disclosure may be inadvertent – for example, where a fax is sent to the wrong recipient in error.

Great care needs to be taken in situations of this type. If the accountant receives information which he knows or ought to realise is confidential and has been passed on without authorisation, he himself comes under the duty of confidence. In such circumstances, he too will be liable to the owner of the information if he discloses or uses it: a claim for an injunction or damages could follow.[27]

The accountant cannot be held to be in breach of duty where he uses information which he does not know and has no reason to know is confidential. However, if the content of the material (or its source or the way it is received) raises suspicions in the accountant's mind, it would be wise to follow these up promptly and for the documents and information to be quarantined in the meantime.

Where what has happened appears to be the result of inadvertent disclosure, ascertaining the true position will generally be straightforward: a check can be made with the person responsible for the disclosure. In other situations, however, the accountant may suspect that material which has been deliberately passed to him by his client for example, should not have been. His first step then should be to seek explicit confirmation from his client or other information provider of the status of the material. If this is not forthcoming, the accountant should proceed with great circumspection: he will need to balance the need to get the job done for his client against the risk of an action for breach of confidence by the owner of the information. In some instances it may be wiser not to proceed with the work for the client: it is unlikely that where the client

---

[27]See, for example, *English and American Insurance Company Limited v Herbert Smith* [1988] FSR 232, a case concerning solicitors.

has surreptitiously passed on another's confidential material the accountant could be compelled to complete the engagement, if to do so would involve him in acting unlawfully *vis-à-vis* another. In other cases, where the associated risks are lower, it may be possible to find a way forward on the basis that the client provides an indemnity to the accountant against any adverse consequences of doing so. In all these situations, however, it would be wise to take legal advice before proceeding.

2 Accepting engagements

2.1 Introduction

In this Chapter we consider a number of different issues connected with accepting engagements:

Section 2.2 examines procedures for assessing what work should be declined because the risks posed by the client and/or the engagement are unacceptably high.

Section 2.3 looks at how engagement letters should be drafted so as to maximise the risk protection they offer.

Section 2.4 considers the extent to which it is possible to exclude or limit liability to the client.

2.2 Assessing new work

Commercial pressures may mean that firms are tempted to accept all available work. There are, however, clients or engagements that bring with them an unacceptably high risk and which the accountant would be much better advised to turn down. Many firms now recognise this and have introduced routine procedures for assessing the level of risk posed both by the client and the engagement. We outline below a number of factors which a firm's procedures should be designed to pick up.[1]

2.2.1 The client

Indications which should cause the accountant to think twice before accepting a particular piece of work include the following:

The client's relationship with other professionals

Is there a history of frequent changes of auditors/other advisers or a tendency to be litigious? This may be a sign that the client has unrealistic

---

[1] Consideration should also be given to identifying potential conflicts of interest: see Chapter 1.

expectations. If so, the likelihood is that he will feel as disappointed in your firm as with all his other advisers. Alternatively, relations with his former advisers may have collapsed because they are pressing for answers or assurances that the client is unwilling to give. Since it will clearly put the new adviser at a disadvantage if he accepts the instructions without fully understanding the background, the client should be required to consent to access to his former advisers and their files. This should ensure that a reasonably accurate picture emerges about the reasons for the decision to change adviser.

The client's reputation for honesty and integrity

Is there any hint of sharp practice or a desire to tie the hands of advisers by keeping them in the dark? One danger sign is the client who instructs a different firm of accountants or solicitors for each transaction or, sometimes, for different elements of the same transaction. An honest client is more likely to want to use a firm that is familiar with and has a good understanding of his business. A dishonest one knows he is safer when the professional has a limited amount of information and will be careful to maintain this.

The dominant individual as client

Recent experience has shown the dangers that can be associated with dominant and powerful entrepreneurs. Firms and the individuals within them can be less impervious to the charm and bullying of powerful individuals than they like to imagine, and the higher the level of fees involved the greater the risk of a loss of independence. Any indication that there is a significant imbalance of power in the company's management structure should give pause for thought. Equally, it is important to consider the structure of the business. For example, is it apparent where the beneficial interest lies? Is the accountant being asked to act in the interests of a 'controlling mind' to the detriment of other legal rights and responsibilities?

The client's solvency

Screening procedures should try to identify those clients who cannot or are known to be unwilling to pay for professional services. A frequent tactic of the client who cannot afford to pay the accountant's fees is to complain about the standard of the services provided. If the accountant sues to recover unpaid fees, he may well find himself the subject of a counterclaim alleging negligence. For this reason, the accountant should always think very carefully before pursuing proceedings for unpaid fees. Even with a weak counterclaim, the client will be able to drag the accountant into a legal process that requires him to spend considerable time and money in defending his good name. Many such clients successfully gamble that the accountant will reduce or waive his fees, to avoid such litigation.

Where there is some doubt about the client's ability to pay, one option is to accept the engagement on the understanding that work will only continue as long as the accountant's interim bills are paid. Whilst in theory this answers the problem, there may be difficulties in carrying through the arrangement. First, if the accountant and his team are under pressure, it is easy to let billing procedures slip. The time involved in frequent billing and chasing for payment can be considerable. Second, once the accountant and his client are engaged in a joint enterprise or the accountant has assumed statutory responsibilities, it is very difficult to 'pull the plug'. For example, the client who already owes fees may involve the accountant in further work aimed at securing extra funding on the understanding that once this is available, the outstanding fees will be paid. The accountant agrees, knowing that if he does not do so the client's business may fail and then he most definitely will not be paid.

The nature and history of the client's business

The accountant is far more likely to be sued by a client whose business is in trouble, or, once it has failed, by its liquidator, who will be keen to swell the assets available to creditors. There are certain business sectors that can be regarded as 'high risk' both in absolute terms and at different stages of the economic cycle. Extra caution is needed when assessing the stability of such clients. Unfortunately, it is sometimes much easier to spot a high risk sector with hindsight, than to appreciate the dangers at the time. For example, the Lloyd's litigation had a major adverse impact on firms operating in the insurance sector, but the particularly high nature of the Lloyd's market risk was not appreciated either by the insurance market or by their advisers at the time when the work – which was to become the subject matter of major litigation – was undertaken.

Leaving aside the risks involved in particular business types, the accountant should make an effort to find out the business histories of the principal players. Who are the directors and are any of them known to have been involved in businesses that have failed in the past? Have any of them been disqualified as directors at some stage in the past? This area naturally overlaps with the need to enquire into the integrity and reputation of the client. For the purposes of screening clients and their businesses, it is important to take account of past mistakes and difficulties.

2.2.2 The engagement

The nature of the engagement

There are some types of engagement that carry inherently more risk than others. For example, engagements without a guaranteed or clear outcome are more likely to result in client dissatisfaction and thus to lead to litigation. Such projects would include reviews of the client's taxation arrangements, where it may not be known whether savings can be achieved until the project is well under way and fees have been incurred. Similarly, corporate finance and due diligence work suffer from the same disadvantage in that it will not be clear whether the proposed transaction will go through until late in the day. Due diligence reports are particularly high risk because, for example, what the accountant is able to find out about the target may determine, or be perceived to determine, whether an acquisition goes ahead. The client may well have an unrealistic belief that, irrespective of the actual scope of the accountant's investigations, the accountant is promising to uncover all and any problems and is, therefore, effectively underwriting the commercial risks of the transaction. Such a belief is likely to become more certain in hindsight if problems arise following an acquisition.

It is important for the level of risk inherent in the engagement to be judged in conjunction with the risks particular to the client so that the cumulative risk is appreciated and a decision can be taken whether, looking at the position in the round, it would in fact be better to decline the work.

The firm's resources and skills

Key to the management of risk is the management of a client's expectations.

The risk of client dissatisfaction can be reduced by ensuring that a clear explanation has been given about what results can realistically be expected from the engagement. Firms may be tempted to promise the earth when tendering for work, putting to the back of their minds that they may be creating unrealistically high expectations. Firms need to take an honest view about what can be achieved and whether this is likely to satisfy the client. The accountant should consider whether there is anything that is wholly unrealistic in what is expected either in the results that the client is hoping for, the level of fees involved, or the time that the project will take. If there are differences in expectations which cannot be resolved, the accountant would be wiser not to proceed.

Firms also need to be realistic about their own skills and resources. Again, the temptation may be to secure the promise of work, without really considering whether sufficient resources and expertise are available to perform the engagement competently and within the agreed deadline. Projects embarked upon without an honest assessment of skills and resources are far more likely to end in litigation. It is important, therefore, that a system exists to enable a realistic assessment of the abilities within the firm and the suitability of partners and managers for a particular engagement.[2]

2.3 The engagement letter

2.3.1 Introduction

The relationship between accountant and client is based on contract.[3] This is so even if they have not drawn up a contract in writing. It is recommended practice, however, to create written evidence of the terms agreed in the form of an engagement letter. This is usually drafted by the accountant and countersigned by the client[4] to indicate his acceptance of the terms.

There is a legal presumption that where contractual terms are recorded in writing, what is written down constitutes the whole of the parties' agreement. Whilst there are a number of ways in which this presumption may be overridden, it avoids legal gymnastics to operate on the basis that the engagement letter will bind the parties and the letter should contain comprehensive details of what has been agreed. It is no exaggeration to say that a well drafted letter can be an indispensable tool for minimising risk, whilst the absence of an engagement letter or a badly drafted one can be very damaging and may expose the accountant to liability unnecessarily.

---

[2]Regard should also be had in this context to the ICAEW's Fundamental Principle 3: 'A member should not accept or perform work which he or she is not competent to undertake unless he obtains such advice and assistance as will enable him competently to carry out the work' (*ICAEW Members' Handbook 2000*, 1.200).

[3]The accountant also owes his client a concurrent duty of care in tort. The significance of this lies in the fact that the client may be able to claim for some losses under contract which he cannot under tort and vice versa. In this Chapter we focus on the contractual relationship since the Court is likely to have regard to the contractual terms which have been agreed between the parties when deciding the extent of the accountant's tortious duty to take reasonable care and skill.

[4]Where the client is not an individual, the accountant should ensure that the person signing the letter is someone with the authority to bind the client, such as the finance director.

This point was illustrated in the case of *Keith Fawkes-Underwood* v *Hamiltons & Hereward Philips.*[5] The claimant was a Lloyd's Name who had participated in a number of syndicates which had proved heavily loss-making. He claimed compensation from his accountants who had provided advice and assistance in relation to his involvement as a Name. The claimant alleged that the scope of the retainer had included advice on which syndicates he should participate in. The accountants denied that this was any part of their agreed responsibilities. However, since there was no engagement letter covering the advice and assistance aspect of the accountant's work, the Court was forced to decide the scope of the retainer by reference to other evidence. In the light of a conflict of oral evidence, the Court was thrown back on the available documents, such as the narratives of the accountant's bills. The accountants were held liable. Had there been a well-drafted engagement letter, liability might have been avoided.

2.3.2 Professional guidance

Engagement letters are dealt with in detail in the *ICAEW Members' Handbook* ('Managing the Professional Liability of Accountants' at 1.311). There is also direction for auditors in SAS 140 ('Engagement Letters'). These make it clear that the accountant is expected to prepare an adequate engagement letter and provide considerable guidance about what is required for particular types of engagement. Our intention is to set out the broader principles which apply to their drafting rather than to focus on the needs of specific types of engagement.[6]

2.3.3 Contents

It is easy to overlook the care that is required to draft a 'good' engagement letter – in other words, one that will provide maximum protection against future criticism or claims. The most fundamental requirement from a risk management perspective is that the letter sets out the scope of the work to be done and clearly defines the responsibilities of both accountant and client. A significant number of professional negligence claims arise not because of shortcomings in the

---

[5] 24 March 1997, unreported.

[6] Regard should also be had to applicable professional requirements such as the need to specify how fees will be calculated (ICAEW Statement 1.210, 'Fees', para 2.0) and to advise clients of how they may make a complaint about bad service, including their right to complain to the ICAEW (Disciplinary Bye-law 11(1)).

work, but as a result of uncertainty or misunderstanding about these basic issues. To put it bluntly, if a dispute about these issues arises, the recollection of the parties may well be tainted with hindsight and influenced by the litigation. If the accountant can produce contemporaneous written evidence of what was agreed, this evidence will be compelling.

In defining the scope of the engagement, regard should be had to any written proposals produced when tendering for the work. Not unnaturally, the client's expectations will be affected by what was said at this stage. Firms, however, sometimes regard proposals as disposable marketing documents that lose their significance once the work is secured. If there is a dispute, evidence of what was said at the tendering stage may well be relevant in assessing the accountant's contractual obligations. It is therefore important to ensure that documents produced (and indeed verbal representations made) during tendering will not cause problems for those drafting the engagement letter, or at least are brought to their attention.

It is also important to record the scope of the engagement in detail so that a clear definition of the project is always available. This can be useful, for example, where there is a turnover of the client's staff and the accountant finds himself reporting to someone new. The engagement letter provides an easy way of explaining the parameters of the engagement, so that realistic expectations are maintained.

2.3.4 Defining the scope of the engagement

In order to define the scope of the engagement effectively, the engagement letter should:

(i) Outline clearly the tasks to be undertaken and the purpose of the engagement. Even with 'standard' engagements it is safer to state the obvious. For example, an audit engagement letter should set out the statutory responsibilities of both auditors and directors. It should also be made clear that the work should not be relied upon for any other than the stated purpose. If the engagement is defined in this way, there is much less chance that the client will have an unreasonable or unclear expectation of what is going to be achieved or, indeed, of his own responsibilities.

(ii) It should be made clear what type of report the firm is going to produce and to whom the firm is prepared to release it. This is important in limiting the accountant's liability to parties other than his client. For practical purposes, it is safe to assume that where the accountant is aware that a party will receive and may rely on his work, he can expect to be liable to that party for any negligence in performing that work.[7]

(iii) It can be as important to set out what is not going to be done or what information is not available as to describe what is. Tasks which might commonly be undertaken by an accountant but which are not to be performed on a particular occasion should be explicitly excluded.

(iv) Where, for example, the accountant is commenting on the forecasts generated by a new company, he should draw attention to the lack of past results upon which to rely. Equally, the accountant should spell out, if the information is available, the tasks he will not be doing, but that to his knowledge other professionals or the client will be doing. For example, it is quite common on a due diligence engagement for the accountant to be responsible for the 'financial' due diligence while others, often the client, undertake 'commercial' due diligence. In such circumstances, the accountant should state in the engagement letter that the client (or other) is assuming responsibility for the commercial side of the due diligence exercise. Beyond identifying tasks that would usually be performed and tasks that are to the accountant's knowledge being performed by others, it is likely to be impossible to identify and list everything that is not going to be done. All the possibilities will never be contemplated. Indeed, any attempt to produce such a list opens the way to an allegation that the client expected a particular transaction to be performed because it was not on the list of tasks not being undertaken. Apart, therefore, from drawing attention to obvious omissions and the responsibilities of other professionals and the client, it is safer not to try to produce a definitive list of what the engagement does not involve.

(v) The letter should state the information and assumptions upon which the engagement is to be based. This includes specifying the sources for the information to be used and whether the accountant is going to verify that information. If assumptions provided by the client are to be used, these should be set out in full so that there can be no misunderstanding about them.

(vi) The letter should indicate whether the accountant is to update his work on receipt of subsequent information. This is particularly important when it is known that further relevant information

---

[7]The issue of when the accountant owes a legal duty to a party with whom he has no contractual relationship is a complex one. See Chapter 3.

is going to become available fairly shortly after completion of the engagement.

(vii) It should also make clear how far the client has accepted responsibility for determining the scope of the engagement. This is another issue upon which professional negligence cases often turn and we discuss it in greater detail in the next section.

2.3.5 Defining responsibilities

It follows from the passage above that it is very important to set out in detail what the responsibilities of the accountant, client and any third parties involved are to be.

The client or the agent of the client will frequently be providing information upon which the accountant's work is based, such as management accounts or assumptions. Several steps should be taken therefore:

(i) The information or assumptions being provided should be listed in the engagement letter.

(ii) Any deadline which has been agreed for the provision of information should be recorded. This may offer some protection if the accountant comes under unreasonable pressure to complete the engagement within the original deadline because of delay on the part of the client or another of the client's advisers. Negligence can frequently be traced back to unrealistic time pressure. Where possible, therefore, the accountant should negotiate and be clear about what is a reasonable time frame. Indisputable evidence of the client's responsibility for any delay, in the event of one, is likely to be helpful.

(iii) The extent to which the client is responsible for the accuracy of the information or to which the accountant is to verify it should be recorded. Evidence of this can be crucial in resolving any later dispute.

(iv) Where staff employed by the client or other advisers are to have an involvement in the engagement, the letter should be clear about the extent of their input and their respective responsibilities. The extent to which one adviser is to rely on the work of another should be made explicit.

(v) It should be made clear how far the client is responsible for determining the procedures and scope of the work to be performed. In some situations, the accountant takes full responsibility for deciding which investigations are required to fulfil the engagement.

In others, the client instructs the accountant to perform specific tasks. In the latter case, the engagement letter should state that the client accepts responsibility for ensuring that the steps to be taken are sufficient for their needs, since a subsequent claim may allege that the accountant was negligent in failing to point out the dangers of omitting certain procedures. It is probably the case that the accountant should not in any event remain silent in the face of a glaring omission in the work being undertaken on a particular project, but his position will be much stronger if it is clear that he did not assume responsibility for determining the nature or extent of the work involved.[8] It is also advisable, therefore, for the engagement letter to record any reservations that the accountant has expressed about the nature and scope of the work undertaken.

2.3.6 Limitation of liability

If the accountant has negotiated any exclusion or limitation of his liability to his client this should, of course, be recorded in full. Similarly, any term which the accountant has negotiated excluding liability arising from any wrongful behaviour on the part of their client, such as fraud, wilful default or misrepresentation must also be recorded. Limitation of liability is dealt with in detail at **2.4** below.

2.3.7 Other points to note

Work of a specialist nature

Where the accountant is instructed because he has specialist experience or expertise (for example, about a particular area of business, market or type of transaction), it is important that there is no misunderstanding between client and accountant as to the extent of his expertise. Where the accountant has specialist knowledge that the client does not have, there is a risk that the client will perceive the accountant to be taking full responsibility for the transaction, so that if something goes wrong a claim will almost inevitably follow.

The accountant should consider whether 'specialist' expertise is in fact relevant to the engagement and resist the temptation to 'talk up' his expertise in the engagement letter (or anywhere else) if this is not really

---

[8]Much can depend on the relative experience of accountant and client, the extent of the accountant's information about his client's affairs and the adequacy (or otherwise) of the procedures proposed by the client.

necessary. The significance of this is that in the context of a dispute it may be argued against the 'specialist' accountant that he has assumed a higher duty of care. Equally, the accountant should be cautious about engagements that have a specialist element in which he has inadequate expertise. His lack of specialist knowledge should be referred to in the engagement letter (or he should decide against taking on the engagement).[9]

Timing

Where practicable it is sensible to prepare the engagement letter and have it countersigned as early as possible. There are, however, many occasions where the scope of the engagement is initially unclear – for example, where it is not known what can be achieved because it is not clear precisely what information is going to be available to the accountant. An engagement letter finalised without this knowledge is likely to be either so vague as to be dangerous in the context of litigation or at least misleading when compared with the work subsequently completed and therefore valueless. In such cases, a framework engagement letter may be used. This can be updated as the engagement develops. It may be possible to divide the engagement into discrete phases, which are listed in a framework engagement letter. A detailed engagement letter would then be prepared at the start of each phase.

Equally, in practice, engagement letters are often being negotiated with a client at the same time as the work is being undertaken. This is particularly true of corporate finance engagements where time may be of the essence. The important practical point to remember is that the engagement letter should be finalised and signed before any work product is delivered. This will be the time at which the accountant has maximum bargaining power and will ensure that the work is only delivered on agreed terms.

There may also be circumstances in which it is practically difficult to secure the return of a signed engagement letter from the client. To maximise the protection for the accountant, it is sensible to include in the letter a statement to the effect that silence on the part of the client on receipt of the engagement letter will be taken as acceptance of its terms.

Review

Once the engagement letter has been countersigned, it should not be filed away and forgotten. It may need to be reviewed as the engagement develops, either because of changes in what the parties feel is necessary

---

[9]See 2.2.2 above.

or because of the imposition of new legal or professional requirements. If, for example, the letter records an intention to carry out tasks which are subsequently not performed, it is important that this change should be agreed by the parties and recorded in writing to avoid a later suggestion that the accountant simply omitted the work.

Some engagements develop significantly during the course of the project and confusion can easily arise about the work done if these changes are not recorded in writing. Where there are a number of alterations, the best course is to ask the client to countersign a fresh engagement letter, rather than to record changes piecemeal in correspondence. Similarly, where the accountant performs repeat engagements for a client (such as an annual audit), the engagement letter should be reviewed and re-signed before the start of each engagement.[10]

It is not only a change in the scope of the work that can make the re-signing of the letter desirable. Major changes to the client's business, such as changes in the senior management with whom the accountant is dealing or changes to the structure of the client organisation or its commercial objectives and strategy, often make it desirable to check that the client continues to accept the original terms.

This type of review is also important at the end of the engagement when it is important to ensure that the report (or other work product) produced is consistent with the engagement letter. For example, if the introduction of the report contains a summary of its purpose and the work undertaken, time should be taken to check that this accords with the engagement letter. To the extent that it does not, the changes to the project need to be discussed with the client whose acceptance of the situation should in some way be recorded in writing – most usually in the text of the report itself.

One letter per engagement

To avoid unnecessary confusion, it is sensible to draft a separate letter for each engagement, even where they are simultaneous. Different requirements may apply to the different engagements, as in the situation where the accountant is acting both as statutory auditor and as tax adviser.

Who should sign?

Thought may need to be given to the question of the identity of the client and who within the client firm has the authority to enter into the

---

[10]SAS 140.2.

contract of engagement and/or vary it. In some circumstances, a number of companies will be involved and a director from each company may need to sign a copy of the engagement letter. Alternatively, it may be more appropriate to prepare a separate letter for each.

Dispute resolution

Firms often include information about complaint procedures in their engagement letters. Today, engagement letters increasingly contain a provision obliging the parties to try to resolve any dispute by Alternative Dispute Resolution ('ADR') rather than through the courts. This approach is increasingly common in commercial disputes because ADR can offer a much cheaper and speedier solution than the courts depending on the nature and quantum of a dispute. Since a resolution is only reached by consensus, there is also a much better chance of preserving the client relationship. Thought needs to be given to whether it is preferable to commit to ADR at the outset of an engagement or to keep one's options open. Attempts may also be made to control the accountant's exposure to litigation by including a time limit within which the client agrees to pursue any grievance (whether through the courts or otherwise). However, it should not be assumed that such attempts will always be effective. These issues are discussed in more detail at **2.4** below.

International

If the engagement is in any way of an international nature, it is sensible to include a term about jurisdiction and choice of law. This can provide that any litigation arising from the engagement will be decided under English Law in the courts of England and Wales.

Situations in which this may be appropriate include engagements where:

- the client is a foreign entity;
- the assets being reported on are based outside the UK; and
- the engagement involves the accountant in working with a firm of accountants or other advisers based abroad. This applies whether or not the other accountants are from the same or an unrelated firm.

Where work is to be performed by an associated office, it is sensible to ensure that both firms have engagement letters that make clear the extent of their responsibilities. Care needs to be taken that the letters are consistent. In addition, there should be clarity over whether either firm is taking responsibility for reviewing the other's work.

Fees

It is usual practice to include details of the basis on which the accountant's fees will be calculated and any arrangements for interim billing. The engagement letter provides a good opportunity to set out unambiguously various 'trigger points' at which fees are to be paid and the consequences if they are not paid. Friction about when fees are due will only tend to increase the chance of subsequent litigation.

Ownership of work product and protecting intellectual property rights

A report prepared for the client will usually belong to the client, but, as previously mentioned, the accountant should specify the parties who are authorised to rely upon his work. Increasingly, the report or advice produced may make use of computer software generated by the firm. In such cases, the engagement letter needs to address the issue of the ownership of the intellectual property rights in any such software. This will usually be a matter of negotiation with the client concerned and will depend upon the ultimate use of any software.

Confidentiality

Similarly, where engagements involve commercially sensitive client information, the accountant may come under pressure to agree to a clause ensuring that the client's confidentiality is maintained. Potentially, this is a complex topic involving the consideration of fiduciary and other duties.[11] The most important practical guidance for the accountant is to ensure he is not committed to maintaining a confidentiality that it is practically impossible to maintain and that distinction is drawn between information that can be characterised as belonging to the client, information and know-how that is the accountant's, and information that is within the public domain in any event.

Clients with opposing commercial interests

We have already seen that where an accountant is acting in a fiduciary capacity, neither he (nor his partner) may act for another client with an opposing interest without the consent of both clients.[12] Where possible, wording dealing with this can be included in the engagement letter of both clients, but if that is not possible their express written consent should be obtained separately. In many instances the accountant will not

---

[11]See Chapter 1.

[12]See Chapter 1.

be acting strictly in a fiduciary capacity. Nevertheless, a potential conflict of interest may still arise. Here it is also desirable to obtain the clients' consent through the engagement letter. It may not always be possible to deal with this overtly; the mere fact of referring to the firm's involvement on behalf of another client may be a breach of confidentiality. In these circumstances the engagement letter can make it clear that the accountant is not undertaking to act exclusively for that client in relation to the transaction.

Consent may therefore often be forthcoming. It may also in some situations be inferred. For example, the Court has acknowledged that auditors often act for competing clients whose identity is publicly acknowledged. The clients are taken to consent, provided that the information obtained from each is kept confidential.[13]

2.4 Excluding and limiting liability

2.4.1 Introduction

When accepting an engagement the accountant should consider whether he wishes to try to exclude or restrict his liability to his client for any shortcomings in his work. Such agreements are becoming increasingly common as a reaction to the rapid increase in claims against accountants which occurred in the 1980s and early 1990s. By the 1990s a number of firms faced claims that had the potential to bankrupt them. This fundamentally changed the attitude of the large firms to restricting liability. Smaller firms, who generally face fewer and lower value claims, remain less concerned to limit their liability. Indeed, some of these firms may well see an advantage in being able to market themselves as not doing so.

2.4.2 Types of limitation

There are a number of different ways in which accountants can seek to limit or exclude liability for negligence:

- by agreeing a financial cap which fixes a maximum amount for the accountant's liability;

- by excluding liability for fraud, misrepresentation or wilful default on the part of the client or his employees;

---

[13]Per Millett LJ in *Prince Jefri Bolkiah v KPMG* [1999] 2 AC 222 p. 235B.

- by limiting or excluding liability for certain types of loss, such as loss of profit, loss of opportunity or punitive damages;

- by agreeing a shorter limitation period for commencing proceedings than that provided by the Limitation Act. In most cases, the effect of the Act is to enable claims to be commenced at any time up to six years from the time the course of action accrued;[14]

- by introducing proportionate liability. This might be used where the accountant is working in conjunction with others and wishes to oust the principle of joint and several liability in favour of an agreement that the accountant will only be liable to the extent of his culpability.

The first two of these are most commonly in use and do not attract criticism in the ICAEW's guidance on 'Managing Professional Liability'.

Any exclusion or limitation which is negotiated should of course be included in the engagement letter. This prevents any suggestion at a later stage that the client did not agree to the restriction or limitation or that it was imposed part way through the engagement. It is always sensible to obtain legal advice on the precise wording of any limitation, since the client will certainly try to exploit any ambiguity if a dispute arises.

2.4.3   Restrictions on limiting liability

Statute currently imposes two main restrictions on the accountant's ability to limit his liability to his client:

- Companies Act 1985, s310; and

- Unfair Contract Terms Act 1977 ('UCTA').

Companies Act 1985, s310

Companies Act 1985, s310 prevents the auditor of a company from limiting his liability to his client by any agreement to exempt or indemnify the auditor from liability for any breach of duty in relation to the company. Under s310 any such agreement is void.

There is some uncertainty as to how far s310 extends. It is certainly possible that a restriction on the scope of the retainer would fall within its ambit.Thus, the common practice of agreeing the scope of audit testing to be performed would be unlikely to provide any defence to a claim in negligence if it were found that the extent of the work was inadequate

---

[14]More information on the operation of the Limitation Act can be found in Chapter 11.

to support a competent opinion in compliance with the auditor's statutory duties.

Section 310 only relates to a company regulated by the Companies Act and it would therefore seem that it is possible to limit liability in relation to the audit of other entities (such as charities or pension schemes) provided that this is not prevented by other statutory provisions relevant to such work.[15]

Although s310 only applies to audits, some care should be taken by auditors who perform additional work for the company which is based upon or makes use of the knowledge acquired during the audit. In the event of a dispute it may be suggested that any restriction of liability which was agreed is rendered void by s310. Whilst such an argument would probably fail, it is not something that the courts have yet been called upon to decide. The best way for the accountant to protect himself would be to deal specifically with the point in the engagement letter or, ideally, to prepare a separate engagement letter for the non-audit work. The accountant should also make sure that the term 'auditor' is used only in the context of work performed specifically for the audit.

In recent years there has been lobbying on the part of some of the profession for the repeal of s310.[16] Its reform was one of the matters considered in the 'Feasibility Investigation into the Reform of Joint and Several Liability' conducted jointly by the DTI and the Law Commission and concluded in December 1995. They formed 'an initial tentative view' that reform of s310 was 'probably justified', provided that there were adequate safeguards to protect shareholders from the possibility of collusion between directors and auditors.[17] It was acknowledged, however, that without amendments to UCTA the enforceability of such arrangements was uncertain. It also seems

---

[15]Of course, it is possible that a Court asked to judge whether a limitation of liability in respect of the audit of such an entity was reasonable under UCTA would draw a comparison with the protection afforded to a company under s310 and refuse to uphold the limitation.

[16]Those urging reform point to the position in some other jurisdictions. For example, the equivalent provision in New Zealand, Companies Act 1955, s204, was amended in 1993, and in Germany there has been a statutory cap on the liability of auditors for many years.

[17]It was suggested that this might be achieved by allowing a limit on liability to be agreed (subject to a statutory floor), provided that the restriction was approved by the shareholders in general meeting.

increasingly unlikely that legislation will, in the short term, result from the feasibility investigation.

UCTA

In relation to non-audit work, the accountant will generally be free to exclude or limit his liability to his client, subject to the provisions of UCTA. The effect of this Act is that any limitation or exclusion of the accountant's duty to take reasonable skill or care is only effective in so far as the restriction 'satisfies the requirement of reasonableness'.[18]

For a restriction in the contract between accountant and client to be reasonable:

> '...it shall have been a fair and reasonable one to be included having regard to the circumstances which were, or ought reasonably to have been, known to or in the contemplation of the parties when the contract was made.'[19]

It should be noted that reasonableness is assessed as at the time when the contract was made, rather than by considering whether the circumstances existing at the time when the term is relied upon are such as make it reasonable to uphold the restriction. Furthermore, that where there is a dispute about whether a restricting term should be upheld, the burden of showing that it meets the 'fair and reasonable' test will fall upon the accountant.[20]

The great difficulty with any restriction which is enforceable subject to the reasonableness test is the lack of certainty about whether the Court will uphold the restriction or not in the event of a claim.[21] There are only a limited number of cases in which the courts have been called upon to comment on the reasonableness test and they have been keen to preserve the principle that each case will be considered on its own peculiar facts. The result is that whilst those cases which have come before the courts have provided some guidance, it is impossible to identify from them a framework of principles which the accountant

---

[18]UCTA, s2(2).

[19]UCTA, s11(1).

[20]UCTA, s11(5).

[21]There is now a further potential hurdle to overcome in the form of the EC Directive on Consumer Protections, which came into effect on 1 January 1995. Since the protections apply only to 'natural persons' and not to corporations, this will only affect the position in relation to individual clients.

could be confident would be consistently applied in assessing reasonableness.[22]

Nevertheless, clauses seeking to restrict liability are worth including despite the real uncertainty about whether they will be upheld by the courts. For example, a reduction in the time limit within which the client must pursue any claim is likely to provide some encouragement to clients to come forward with any grievances promptly, regardless of whether or not it is enforceable in law. Equally, clauses seeking to cap liability provide a significant lever in negotiating the settlement of any claim. Of course, the more 'reasonable' the clause the better. The more likely the clause is to be enforced by the courts, the more convincingly it can be relied upon in settlement negotiations.

A limited amount of guidance as to how 'reasonableness' is to be interpreted is provided by the Act itself. Schedule 2 of the Act provides a list of factors to be taken into account in applying the reasonableness test. These factors do not expressly apply to the type of contract that exists between client and accountant but, in practice, a number of them would probably be treated as relevant by a Court assessing reasonableness. The factors are:

- the relative strength of the bargaining positions of accountant and client;

- any alternative means available by which the client could have achieved its objective, including the option of instructing an alternative firm without accepting a similar term; and

- whether the client received any inducement to enter the contract or accept the restriction.

These factors were echoed and expanded in *Smith v Eric Bush*,[23] in which the House of Lords considered together two cases concerning clauses purporting to exclude the liability of surveyors for negligence.[24] Lord Griffiths, whilst maintaining that it was impossible to draw up an

---

[22]For example, in *George Mitchell (Chesterhall) Ltd v Finney Lock Seeds Ltd* [1983] 2 All ER 737 at 747 Lord Bridge said of the decision as to the reasonableness test, 'There will sometimes be room for a legitimate difference of judicial opinion as to what the answer should be, where it will be impossible to say that one view is demonstrably wrong and the other demonstrably right.'

[23][1989] 2 All ER 514.

[24]In both cases the surveyors were instructed by third parties to perform a survey on domestic property and had attempted to exclude liability to the prospective purchasers, even though they knew that they were effectively paying for the survey and would probably rely on it.

35

exhaustive list of factors that must be taken into account by a Court in assessing reasonableness, outlined a number of factors which he believed should always be considered. These were:

- Were the parties of equal bargaining power? Where the party on whom the restriction is placed has no effective power to object, it will be more difficult to show reasonableness.

- Would it have been reasonably practicable to obtain the advice from another source, taking into account considerations of cost and time?

- How difficult is the task for which liability is being restricted? A restriction of liability in relation to a very difficult task with a high risk of failure would be more likely to be reasonable than such a restriction in relation to a task which presents no difficulty provided it is undertaken with reasonable skill and care.

- What are the practical consequences of the decision on the question of reasonableness? This includes the sums of money potentially at stake and the ability of the parties to bear the loss involved. It was relevant that the loss was one which was likely to be covered by the surveyor's insurance and would be 'unlikely to cause significant hardship' to the surveyor, whilst it was 'quite possible that it will be a financial catastrophe for the purchaser'.

The emphasis on equality of bargaining power means that it is likely that it will be more difficult for the accountant who deals with an inexperienced client (such as an individual or small company) to restrict his liability than for the accountant who deals with a substantial commercial client. It also suggests that any restriction that appears to have been imposed by the accountant as a matter of common practice (for example, if contained within standard terms and conditions[25]) rather than being individually negotiated with the client, is less likely to be enforced, since the lack of negotiation will suggest inequality of bargaining power. We shall discuss this further in the context of caps below.

Lord Griffiths made it clear that he did not consider it unreasonable for professionals to exclude or limit their liability in negligence for all circumstances. He stated that:

> 'Some breathtaking sums of money may turn on professional advice against which it would be impossible for the adviser to obtain adequate insurance cover and which would ruin him if he were to

---

[25] See *South West Water v International Computers Limited* (1999) BLR 420 in which, amongst other things, the defendant's use of standard terms and conditions was found to be fatal to the clause limiting liability.

be held personally liable. In these circumstances it may indeed be reasonable to give the advice on a basis of no liability or possibly of liability limited to the extent of the adviser's insurance cover.'

This provides weak comfort for the professional, as it might be taken to suggest that a complete exclusion of liability is unlikely to be enforced and that it may not be considered reasonable to attempt to limit liability below the level at which insurance cover is available.

This last point is particularly relevant to the enforceability of liability caps and could be criticised for ignoring what are in practice grey areas. For instance, it fails to address the issue of whether (and at what point) the accountant can reasonably refuse to acquire cover which is available but only at a premium that is considered excessive. Nor does it address the fact that the accountant will not necessarily know when he negotiates a cap what cover will be available in the event of a claim, as this may depend on how many other claims are made on the policy during a particular policy period.

It should be noted that Lord Griffiths' guidance amounts only to comment and is not binding on other judges. It is not clear therefore how far it would be followed in other cases. Nevertheless, his comments are of some importance to accountants, given that both of the cases being considered concerned attempts to exclude liability for negligent professional advice. The situation of the accountant and his client is not exactly parallel, however, since it is based on contract and in many cases the client will have commercial experience.

Finally, it should be noted that UCTA prohibits excluding liability for death or personal injury resulting from negligence.[26] Care should be taken to avoid drafting exclusions which could be construed as extending to such liability, as this might bring into question the effectiveness of the entire exclusion.

Practical steps

Given the importance that the Court will put on the circumstances surrounding the negotiation and agreement of the restriction of liability, firms which agree such terms with their clients should ensure that they have procedures in place which encourage the negotiation of clauses individual to that engagement and which preserve evidence of these negotiations. Such procedures will greatly increase the chance of having the term upheld. A standardised checklist might include:

---

[26]Section 2(1)

- an assessment of the risks and rewards of the engagement for client and accountant;

- details of the factors which the accountant took into account in deciding what restriction on liability was appropriate (for example, the amount of monetary cap);

- evidence of the information given to the client. This should include the factors mentioned above;

- evidence of any negotiations with the client. If, for example, there is correspondence attaching drafts of the term and amendments by the client, these should be kept;

- equally, evidence of the client taking independent legal advice and being advised to do so should be recorded;

- in relation to inexperienced clients (particularly where they are individuals), evidence that the term was fully explained to the client, understood by him and accepted, and evidence of a recommendation to the client that he might wish to seek legal advice.

The other purpose of having procedures of this kind is to provide guidance for the members of the firm about the restrictions being used by their colleagues and, in the long term, to build a picture of the 'success rate' of different types of restriction, i.e., whether the clause has been challenged and the outcome of that challenge.

Since market practice is also relevant to reasonableness, firms should gather as much information as possible about the approach of other firms, in addition to collecting the information available within their own firm.

2.4.4 Liability caps

The liability cap currently seems to be the most common method used by firms to restrict liability and the reasonableness test in UCTA applies as much to a financial cap as to any other limitation of liability. In addition, the Act provides that in assessing the reasonableness of a cap, the Court must consider two further matters beyond those set out at p35 above:

- the resources which the accountant could expect to have available to him to meet a claim if liability arose, and

- how far it was open to the accountant to cover his liability by insurance.[27]

---

[27]UCTA, s11(4)

In practice, this seems to add little, given that both of these are factors which Lord Griffiths identified as indispensable in *Smith*.

A practical consideration in deciding upon a monetary cap is to remember that, if unreasonable, the whole clause will fall away. It would seem sensible, therefore, in setting a cap, to work on the basis of erring on the side of generosity rather than to risk losing the entire clause as a result of an unreasonably low cap.

Different types of cap

A cap can either take the form of a specified amount of money or it can be expressed as a multiple of the accountant's fees.

A transactional cap is to be preferred where possible, since there are a number of potential drawbacks to caps based on a multiple of fees:

(1) The fees may not be quantified at the time the cap is agreed (even though the basis of charging will have been made clear to the client). This leaves open the possibility that the client will later challenge the validity of the cap on the basis that, at the time of the contract, the amount of the cap was not sufficiently certain to enable the client to fully assess whether to accept the proposed limitation.

(2) If a firm applies the multiple across the board, the cap is likely to be interpreted as having been imposed as part of the firm's routine practices and will therefore be likely to fail the reasonableness test.

(3) Where the engagement is ongoing or repeated, care needs to be taken that it is clear exactly to what fees the multiple is to be applied.

(4) The multiple of fees basis is more likely to lead to a situation where the agreed cap is less than the firm's compulsory insurance level, which, as already outlined, renders the cap much less likely to be upheld.

(5) There is some doubt as to how far a Court would regard the level of fees as a persuasive or relevant factor.

2.4.5 Caps and the reasonableness test

Whilst it is always uncertain whether the reasonableness test will be satisfied if a cap is challenged, there are steps that a firm can take to increase the chances of the term being upheld:

• Each cap should be individually set to reflect the risks and rewards of the particular engagement. A cap which is set without any regard to the level of difficulty for the accountant in performing the engagement and the losses which the client is likely to suffer if the accountant is negligent is much less likely to be enforced as fair and reasonable. For this reason it is important to avoid adopting a 'standard' level of or approach to caps.[28] There is obviously a limit to the resources that a firm can afford to devote to setting caps, but it is worth drawing up a fairly detailed policy on the factors which partners should take into account in fixing a cap. For practical purposes, some form of 'sliding scale' approach is useful, including the imposition of a minimum cap as a matter of firm policy. Such minimum cap should take into account the firm's financial strength, commercial power and available insurance cover.

- The cap is more likely to be upheld if there is written evidence that the clause has been negotiated with the client. Evidence of negotiation is important in establishing that there was some equality of bargaining power between the parties. It is to the accountant's advantage if the client suggests changes to the proposed cap and some of these changes are accepted (where feasible). It is also important to bear in mind that the stronger the bargaining position of the accountant, the more generous he should be in negotiating the cap.

- If the engagement is renewed, care should be taken to ensure that the cap is renegotiated at each renewal. If caps are to be used it is vital that they are kept up to date.

- If a particular engagement involves more than one client, thought should be given to how a cap will operate. It should be made clear if the cap is a total cap to all liability to all the clients concerned, in which case each client's express agreement will be needed.

The extent to which caps are successful may in part depend on the lengths firms are prepared to go to in order to introduce them and to 'police' their introduction and the level of resistance put up by clients. Our experience suggests that many clients these days accept the principle of limitation by cap, but may argue about the quantum.

2.4.6 Excluding liability to third parties

The relationship between accountant and client is based on contract. As a general rule, a contract cannot confer rights or obligations on someone who is not a party to the contract (the doctrine of privity of contract). An accountant who is negligent may, nevertheless, be liable to a third party if he has assumed a duty of care to that party.[29]

---

[28]See *South West Water v International Computers Limited* (1999) BLR 420.

[29]The circumstances in which such liability may arise are discussed in Chapter 3.

Similar considerations apply to any limitations in the contract of the accountant's liability. As a result of privity, the third party is not a party to any such restrictions which are included in the engagement letter. Nevertheless, the accountant may successfully restrict any liability he has to the third party by ensuring he has notice of the limitation. A statement excluding or restricting liability for negligence will be effective against a person who has had notice of the statement, provided it is fair and reasonable to allow reliance on it.[30] There is a potentially significant difference in the way the UCTA reasonableness test is applied to a third party as opposed to a client. As far as the client is concerned, the Court will, as mentioned, consider whether the restriction of liability was reasonable as at the time it was made. As far as the third party is concerned, the relevant time is the time when liability arose (or would do but for its exclusion).[31]

In practical terms, this means that the accountant should ensure that any restrictions on the scope of his work or on his liability are brought to the attention of any third party who might rely on it. Further guidance on this is given in Chapter 3.

---

[30]UCTA, s2(2).

[31]UCTA, s11(3).

3 Avoiding duties & liabilities to third parties

3.1 Introduction

In this Chapter we consider the practical steps which the accountant can take to control the extent of his legal responsibilities to those with whom he has no contractual relationship. The law governing the accountant's responsibilities to these third parties is in a state of transition, but a variety of situations already exist in which the accountant may be liable for losses suffered as a result of the third party's reliance on either:

- Work performed by the accountant for his client which has been performed negligently, or

- A negligent misstatement (an erroneous statement of fact that is made without reasonable skill or care), which the accountant has made to the third party. The accountant may also be liable in respect of an expression of opinion (as opposed to one of fact) provided he implies that he has reasonable grounds for believing the opinion to be true when this is not the case.

The law has struggled in recent years to identify in precisely what circumstances a legal responsibility (known as a duty of care) will be owed to a third party, given the lack of a contractual relationship. The crux lies in the degree of relationship between the accountant and the third party and the extent to which the accountant is regarded as having assumed a responsibility towards the third party. Both of these depend very much on the individual circumstances that apply.

The purpose of this Chapter is to identify those situations in which auditors and accountants are most commonly at risk of being found liable to a third party and to set out the protections that can be adopted to avoid or minimise liability.

Many of the actions brought by third parties arise from their having relied upon audited accounts and we therefore start in **3.2** by identifying the duties that an auditor owes when he performs a statutory audit. These duties may, however, be extended and in **3.3** we look at the circumstances in which the auditor may owe wider duties to 'insiders', by which we mean to directors and shareholders of the audited company and to other companies within the same group. We also consider what steps can be taken by the auditor to protect against such wider responsibilities.

In **3.4** we examine a variety of circumstances in which an auditor may owe wider legal duties to 'outsiders', by which we mean those who are not directors or shareholders in the audited company. These 'outsiders' are most commonly lenders investors or acquirers. If the auditor provides the lender, investor or acquirer with information or assurances about the audited accounts, he may find that he has assumed a legal responsibility to the third party in respect of the information provided.

A third party who is contemplating an investment or takeover will often seek disclosure from the auditor of his working papers, usually so that they can be reviewed by the investigating accountant instructed to report on the proposed transaction. In **3.5** we consider how the risks involved for the auditor can be minimised by requiring the third party and his investigating accountant to sign a release or hold harmless letter. The auditor will also require his client to sign an authorisation letter consenting to the disclosure (which would otherwise breach client confidentiality). We shall consider the effective drafting of release and authorisation letters.

Accountants as well as auditors are at risk of being found liable for losses suffered by third parties. A common situation in which the accountant performing non-audit work may be exposed to risk is where his report or conclusions are published in securities documentation, such as listing particulars. In **3.6** we look at this risk and the safeguards that are available.

In reviewing the situations in which auditors and accountants are most likely to be found to owe a duty to a third party, we have relied heavily on the cases that have come before the courts. Although these provide the best available source of guidance each case was necessarily decided on its own particular facts. They can, therefore, provide no more than guidance and are certainly not an exhaustive description of the circumstances in which a duty may be owed. Indeed, the courts have acknowledged that these cases are particularly 'fact sensitive'[1] and that a fairly slight difference in circumstances may have a significant effect on the legal position. Thus, whilst the objective of this Chapter is to highlight when third party duties may commonly arise and increase the practitioner's ability to control his liabilities, it is not possible to outline a

---

[1] Per Lord Jusice Auld in *Electra Private Equity Partners & Ors v KPMG Peat Marwick & Ors* [2000] PNLR 247.

set of watertight rules, capable of removing the risk of unexpected liability to third parties.

In addition, many of the cases referred to in this Chapter have come before the courts only on an application to strike out the proceedings at an early stage, in which the accountant asks the Court to rule that all or part of the third party's claim should not be allowed to proceed further because the accountant owes the third party no duty of care. When hearing these applications the Court will consider little or no evidence. Instead, it assesses whether the facts alleged by the claimant would be sufficient to establish a duty of care if proved at a full trial. Provided that the Court is satisfied that the action is not bound to fail, it will be allowed to continue. As a consequence, the decisions resulting from these applications provide less certain guidance than those based on a full trial. Decisions resulting after a full trial are, however, relatively rare since the vast majority of civil cases eventually settle.

3.2 Duties in performing the statutory audit

3.2.1 Shareholders: the principle in *Caparo* v *Dickman*[2]

Where the auditor performs a statutory audit, he owes a duty of care to the audited company and to the company's shareholders in their role as supervisors of the management of the company. Beyond this he owes no duty of care unless special circumstances apply. Without such circumstances, the auditor has no legal responsibility to existing shareholders or others who choose to invest in the company in reliance on the audited accounts.

This principle was established by the House of Lords in the landmark case of *Caparo* v *Dickman* in which the claimant, Caparo Industries plc, purchased shares in Fidelity plc and ultimately acquired the company allegedly in reliance on the audited accounts. Following the takeover, Caparo sued the auditors of Fidelity alleging that the audited accounts had been negligently prepared and were misleading (in that they showed a profit when they should have recorded a loss). It was alleged that the auditors knew or should have foreseen that Fidelity was vulnerable to a takeover bid and that potential acquirers such as Caparo would rely on the audited accounts in deciding whether to proceed. The auditors denied that they owed Caparo any duty of care.

The House of Lords agreed, deciding that the auditor of a company owes no legal responsibility to 'members of the public at large who rely on the

---

[2] [1990] 1 All ER 568.

accounts in deciding to buy shares'. The fact that an auditor knew that it was highly probable that the company's shares would be attractive to investors was not sufficient to make the auditor liable.

The decision defined the auditor's duty by reference to the statutory purpose of the audit (to enable the shareholders to exercise their power to manage and control the company in an informed way) rather than by reference to any wider purpose for which the accounts were used. Accordingly, shareholders would be entitled to a remedy against the auditor if his negligence meant that they lost the opportunity to control the management of the company, but the auditor was not responsible for losses that resulted from reliance on the audited accounts as a source of investment information. Audits were not required to provide information for the purposes of individual speculation with a view to profit, nor were they inspired by the need to protect the public at large and investors in particular.

Caparo had been an existing shareholder, which had purchased additional shares in reliance on the audited accounts. The House of Lords made it clear that their decision would have been the same had Caparo been a new investor. If it was right that no duty was owed by the auditor to the general public, it would produce 'entirely capricious results' if such a duty arose from the same information simply because someone happened to be an existing shareholder.

3.2.2   Lenders: *Al Saudi Banque* v *Clark Pixley*[3]

Shortly before the House of Lords' decision, the same conclusion about the limits on the auditor's responsibility had been reached in a claim brought by a lender rather than a shareholder, *Al Saudi Banque* v *Clark Pixley*.

Various banks lent money to a company in reliance on its audited accounts. Some of the banks were new lenders and some were existing creditors, but both advanced loans in reliance on the accounts. The company was subsequently found to be insolvent. The banks sued the auditor alleging that the accounts, having negligently failed to reveal the insolvency, had not shown a true and fair view of the company.

The Court considered as a preliminary issue the question of whether the auditor owed the banks any duty of care. For this purpose, it was agreed that various facts would be assumed which the banks would have to

---

[3] [1989] 3 All ER 361.

prove at a full trial if the claim was allowed to proceed. First, it was assumed that the auditor must have (or ought to have) foreseen that the company would provide copies of the accounts and the audit report to the banks; second, that the banks would rely on them in considering whether to grant the loan facilities.

The Court held that the auditor owed the banks no duty of care. It was not enough that it was foreseeable that the banks might rely on the auditor's conclusions. Again, the Court made it clear that the position was the same whether or not the bank was an existing creditor.

The approach in *Al Saudi Banque* was approved by the House of Lords in *Caparo*, where it was said that it would be wrong to hold the auditor under a duty to anyone who might lend money to the audited company just because the auditor could or should foresee that it was highly probable that the company would borrow money in the year following publication of its audited accounts, and that lenders might rely on those accounts in deciding to lend.[4]

3.3 Extensions to the auditor's duty to 'insiders'

3.3.1 Introduction

Whilst *Caparo* and *Al Saudi Banque* provide some comfort for the auditor, they are only a starting point since there have been a number of cases in which the auditor has been deemed to owe a more extensive duty of care. The common theme in these cases is that the auditor performs a role beyond what is involved in a statutory audit. In so doing, he crosses a line beyond which the protection offered by *Caparo* is compromised and the extent of the auditor's duty may be widened.

In this section we consider circumstances in which the auditor may have an extended duty of care to 'insiders', by which we mean to the audited company's shareholders and/or its directors or to another company within the group. There are a variety of situations in which the auditor may acquire a wider legal responsibility towards an insider by performing tasks that go beyond his statutory functions. In terms of fee earning, this

---

[4] Per Lord Bridge. Banks are of course aware of these decisions and will often take steps designed to ensure that the necessary proximity of relationship is created between the bank and the borrower's auditor. This issue is addressed in the Auditing Practices Committee's Practice Note 4 'Reliance on Audited Financial Statements'. We consider this Practice Note further at 3.4.6 below.

is of course attractive, but as the performance of additional work may involve taking on extra legal responsibilities, the risks involved require to be weighed with the advantages.

3.3.2   Smaller businesses

A number of the cases which have come before the courts illustrate that crossing the line between auditor and accountant may not be so much a matter of choice as inevitable in some circumstances. Where the client is a small or inexperienced business, the auditor may have little choice but to guide the client by performing extra tasks. Otherwise, the client may not have the resources or knowledge necessary to prepare adequate draft accounts. However, in providing the service required by the smaller or less experienced client, the auditor runs the risk of widening his legal responsibilities, so that he owes a duty not only to the audited company, but also to its shareholders and directors. Two recent cases, *Coulthard & Others* v *Neville Russell* and *Siddell & Another* v *Smith Cooper & Partners*, illustrate the dangers in this area.

Coulthard & Ors v *Neville Russell*[5]

Neville Russell ('NR') were the auditors of both Dawes and Henderson (Agencies) Ltd ('D &H') and Hendal Ltd ('H'). The shares of D&H had all been acquired by H. The acquisition had been funded by a loan made to H by National Westminster Bank. This was originally intended to be repaid from dividends declared by D&H but it was later decided that D&H's payments to H should take the form of loans. D&H went into insolvent liquidation, following which steps were taken against D&H's directors to disqualify them under the Directors Disqualification Act 1986. One of the allegations against them was that the loans made by D &H to H amounted to providing financial assistance for the purchase of shares contrary to Companies Act 1985, s151.

D&H's former directors sued NR alleging that they had owed them a duty of care to warn them that the loans might breach s151,[6] but that NR had either said nothing about the proposed treatment or advised that it was unexceptional. NR applied to strike out the claim on the basis that they

---

[5][1998] BCC 359.

[6]For the purposes of the appeal it was accepted by the parties that a loan made contrary to s151 was unenforceable against the borrower and that, as a result, a balance sheet which showed such a loan as an asset of the lending company would fail to show a true and fair view.

had owed no such duty but failed both at first instance and in the Court of Appeal.

The Court of Appeal accepted that there was no legal obligation on the part of a statutory auditor to advise the directors on the way in which they should fulfil their responsibilities. The auditor's statutory responsibility was to give an opinion as to whether the balance sheet gave a true and fair view. It was the directors' responsibility to prepare the balance sheet. Strictly speaking, therefore, advice as to how controversial items (such as the payments to H) should be treated in the accounts would come within the role of the accountant, rather than the auditor. The claim against NR was nonetheless allowed to proceed because the complaint was not about NR's role as statutory auditor, but about their wider role in respect of which they allegedly owed a common law duty of care to the directors. They had allegedly breached that duty by not warning the directors that treating the payment as a loan would lead to a qualified audit report and was not, therefore, a path down which 'responsible directors could sensibly go' (at least not without first obtaining supportive legal advice).

Coulthard potentially demonstrates that with smaller companies the auditor may have little choice but to accept a legal responsibility which goes beyond that identified in *Caparo* as arising from his statutory responsibilities. Indeed, the role of auditor and accountant may be so entwined that the line between the two functions disappears altogether. In order to perform their audit, NR had to consider and discuss with the directors the treatment of the repayments to H. In doing so, they arguably acquired a legal duty to the directors.[7]

Siddell & Anor v Smith Cooper & Partners[8]

The claimants, Mr & Mrs Follows and Mr & Mrs Siddell were the shareholders and (at various times) the directors of Busyindex Ltd ('B Ltd'). Smith Cooper ('SC') were appointed as the auditors and accountants of B Ltd. After B Ltd went into liquidation, the Follows and the Siddells sued SC alleging that but for their negligent advice the

---

[7]Chadwick LJ considered that on the facts of this case the distinction between the role of the auditor and the accountant was immaterial since the auditor could be expected to inform the directors of the way in which they will regard the treatment of any controversial item. Once the auditor has done this, it was unlikely that the director would pursue a treatment which would lead to a qualification of the audit opinion.

[8][1999] PNLR 511.

claimants would not have paid off company borrowings of £120,000 by taking on personal debt secured on their homes.

The claimants alleged that SC's role had always been to advise not only B Ltd, but also the claimants in their personal capacities. It was alleged that B Ltd, with only four shareholders, was a 'quasi-partnership' and SC would or should have been aware that their advice would be relied upon not only by B Ltd, but also by the claimants both as directors and shareholders. In particular, it was said that SC knew that any advice as to how B Ltd should deal with its borrowings would be relied upon by the claimants for the particular purpose of deciding how to arrange their personal financial affairs.

SC denied the allegations and applied to strike out the claims on the basis that they disclosed no reasonable cause of action. At first instance SC succeeded, but the decision was reversed by the Court of Appeal, which accepted that the claim against SC was at least arguable. The Court of Appeal saw a clear distinction between these circumstances and those in *Caparo*. SC had not simply been acting as statutory auditor, but had been providing much broader services, including the provision of quarterly management accounts and the giving of advice. The Court indicated that whilst it should not be thought that the principles in *Caparo* were restricted to large companies, the question of whether a duty of care existed would depend on all the circumstances, including the size of the company and the type of shareholders and/or directors to whom a duty was said to be owed. Clearly, the Court of Appeal envisaged that it would not always be realistic to draw a distinction between shareholders and directors in their roles as custodians and managers of the company on the one hand and in their personal capacity as individuals on the other.

The decisions in *Coulthard* and *Siddell* can be seen as part of an increasing tendency by the courts to promote and protect the interests of individual, 'non-corporate' users of professional services. This reflects public expectations about protecting the consumer. In practical terms, the auditor or accountant should recognise that his legal responsibilities may be greater when he is acting for any client who may be regarded as being on an unequal footing with the auditor in terms of experience or resources. Clients obviously falling into this category are small organisations and individuals, particularly those who have limited experience of business.

As has been discussed elsewhere, where it is practicable to separate the performance of the statutory audit from other functions, it is preferable to arrange for separate engagement letters to be drawn up for each engagement.[9] This will assist in defining clearly the scope of the work being undertaken and, consequently, the duties being accepted by the firm.

3.3.3 Companies within the same group

The next category of cases in which the auditor may sometimes owe a wider duty is that in which the audited company is part of a group of companies. The two decisions relating to this both arise from somewhat unusual circumstances: the first is *Bank of Credit and Commerce International (Overseas) Ltd* v *Price Waterhouse (No.2)* and the second *Barings plc (in administration) & Another* v *Coopers & Lybrand (a firm) & Others*. The *BCCI* decision concerned a subsidiary alleging that it was owed a duty of care by the auditor of its parent company. The *Barings* decision addressed the reverse situation, with the parent company alleging that it was owed a duty by the auditor of a subsidiary.

Bank of Credit & Commerce International (Overseas) Ltd v *Price Waterhouse (No.2)*[10]

This decision arose out of the collapse of the BCCI group, which went into liquidation owing debts of US$11 billion. The claimants were BCCI (Overseas) Ltd ('Overseas') and BCCI (SA) Ltd ('SA'), both of which were wholly-owned subsidiaries of a holding company ('Holdings'). Price Waterhouse ('PW') had been the auditors of Overseas and Ernst & Whinney ('EW') the auditors of SA and Holdings.

After the group's collapse, Overseas and SA sued PW and EW alleging negligence in the performance of their audits and other work. It was contended that as a result of their negligence attention had not been drawn to the losses within the group, which had therefore continued to trade, when otherwise it would not have done. EW applied to strike out the claim of Overseas on the basis that since they were not that company's auditors, they owed them no duty of care. EW succeeded at first instance, but the decision was later reversed by the Court of Appeal.

The claimants' case was that, whatever the legal structure of the group, the reality was that the business of all three companies operated as a single bank. It was alleged that as a result an unusually high level of cooperation was required between the firms of auditors and that PW either did not or should not have conducted self-contained audits of Overseas, but were reliant on a good deal of information from EW. The

---

[9]See 2.3.7 above.

[10][1998] PNLR 564.

claimants alleged that in agreeing to audit Holdings and SA in the knowledge that the group operated as a 'single bank', EW had assumed a duty of care to Overseas.

The Court of Appeal considered that the Court of first instance had understated the level of liaison and mutual reliance between the auditors. A 'constant interchange of information' had been necessary between the two firms and in those unusual circumstances it was arguable that EW owed a duty of care to Overseas. The Court of Appeal emphasised, however, that the facts of the claim were 'most unusual' and the decision should not be taken as signalling a general widening of the circumstances in which liability would be imposed.

Barings plc (in administration) & Another v Coopers & Lybrand & Others[11]

This case arose out of the collapse of Barings Bank as a result of the massive losses incurred by Nick Leeson in unauthorised trading in futures and options on SIMEX (the Singapore Money Exchange) on behalf of Barings Futures Singapore Pte Ltd ('BFS'), a Singaporean-registered company within the group.

Barings plc (Barings), the English parent company of the group, had engaged Coopers & Lybrand (C&L) as their auditors. C &L instructed their associated firm in Singapore ('C&LS') to audit BFS. Baring's liquidators sued (amongst others) two partners in C&LS alleging that the firm owed them a duty of care as auditor and had also assumed a duty to them in relation to a report from subsidiary auditor to parent auditor. It was alleged that C&LS should have detected Leeson's fraud and that, had they done so, the insolvency of the group could have been averted. Instead, the consolidation schedules supplied by C&LS for incorporation into the group accounts showed BFS as profitable.

The claim was based on an assertion that there was a direct relationship between C&LS and Barings arising from the circumstances in which information was supplied by C&LS to Barings and C&L relating to the preparation of the consolidated group accounts. C&LS applied to set aside the proceedings on the basis that they owed no relevant duty of care.[12]

---

[11] [1997] 1 BCLC 427.

[12] It was also alleged (unsuccessfully) that any damage suffered could not be claimed by the parent company (which was only a shareholder in the subsidiary), but only by the subsidiary that suffered the damage. The submission made on behalf of C&L Singapore was that the shareholders of a company only suffered 'in concert' because the value of their shareholding had gone down.

They argued that the information which they were required to supply was obtained simply so that Barings' directors could comply with their obligation to prepare consolidated accounts. This could not, maintained C&LS, be the basis for a duty of care.

Both at first instance and on appeal C&LS' application was dismissed. It was enough that C&LS knew that their audit and the report on the consolidation schedules were required so that the directors of Barings could comply with their obligation to provide accounts which showed a true and fair view of the accounts of the group. The Court of Appeal reasoned that C&LS could not have supposed that so long as they provided the accounts of BFS, it did not matter whether they showed a true and fair view.

The decision seems to imply that it was possible for C&LS to acquire a duty to Barings simply as a result of submitting their consolidation schedules. If this is so, the principle is one of wide application. Wherever different firms are engaged to audit a parent company and subsidiary within the same group, the auditor of the subsidiary may well owe a duty of care to the parent company in respect of the information supplied for the purposes of the consolidated accounts.

The risks for the auditor created by such situations can be reduced by ensuring that there is a clear delineation of responsibilities between the firms and that it is clear what reliance each seeks to put on the work of the other. Both internal documents (such as audit planning memoranda) and external ones (such as reports from one auditor to another) can provide useful ammunition for a third party claimant unless they are expressed in a way that accurately reflects the responsibilities accepted by the firm. Similar care should be taken in the case of joint appointments.

3.4 Extending the auditor's duty to 'outsiders'

In this section we examine the circumstances in which the auditor may owe a legal responsibility to a third party who is an 'outsider', by which we mean those who are not shareholders in or directors of the audited company. Whether any legal duty is owed by the auditor very much depends on the particular circumstances, and the purpose of this section is to identify some situations in which there is a high risk of a legal duty arising and to examine ways of minimising this risk.

3.4.1 Auditors and acquirers, investors or lenders

As discussed in **3.2** the general principle that the auditor does not usually owe a legal duty to those who choose to invest in or lend to a company in reliance on the audited accounts is only a starting point. As a result, investors, acquirers and lenders who have suffered a significant loss may bring claims against the company's auditor formulated so as to overcome the hurdle set by *Caparo* that special circumstances must exist for such claims to succeed.

The courts have characterised the special circumstances that are needed in two principal ways. The first is that in order to succeed the claimant must convince the Court that the circumstances were such that the auditor assumed or is deemed to have assumed a duty of care to the investor/lender. The second formulation is that in the particular circumstances the relationship between the auditor and the investor was sufficiently 'proximate' to create a duty. Once such a duty on the part of the auditor is established he will be liable to the third party for any negligent misstatement in the audited accounts or in any other information that he provided.

3.4.2 Advising the third party in writing

The more direct the relationship between third party and auditor, the easier it will be to establish the existence of a duty of care. Thus, the third party will find it easier to establish a duty where the auditor has clearly performed work for the third party's benefit.

An example is provided by *Yorkshire Enterprises Limited* v *Robson Rhodes*,[13] where the claimants were venture capital companies that suffered losses as a result of investing in the audited company 'ML', and advancing it a loan. The auditors had undertaken various work in addition to performing ML's statutory audit, and in particular had provided a letter of advice quantifying ML's bad debts at the claimants' request. The Court decided that the auditors must have realised that the claimants would rely on the information in the audited accounts and on their assessment of ML's bad debts in deciding whether to proceed with the transactions. Further, the auditors were aware that the accuracy of their assessment of bad debts was highly material to the question of whether ML was insolvent and, accordingly, to whether the investment would be lost and the loan recovered. In these circumstances, the auditors were held liable for the negligent inaccuracies in the audited accounts and their letter of advice, which had resulted in the loss of the sums invested and loaned.

In situations such as those in *Yorkshire Enterprises*, the auditor can take steps to reduce the appearance of a direct relationship with the investor– for example, by ensuring that he responds only to instructions received

---

[13] *New Law Digest*, 19 June 1998; LTL, 14 September 1998.

from his client and that any written advice is addressed to the client rather than to the investor direct. Whilst such precautions are advisable, it would be wrong to assume that they will necessarily be enough to protect the auditor from liability. Rather than focusing on the outward appearance of the parties' relationship, the Court is likely to examine whether the auditor's work had any purpose other than to assist the investor and the auditor's awareness of the extent to which his work would be relied upon for this purpose.

3.4.3 Oral assurances

In contrast to the type of situation that arose in *Yorkshire Enterprises* where the auditor advises a third party in writing, there have in the last decade been a number of claims based on the allegation that the auditor is legally liable for assurances given to a potential investor in a meeting. The most well known of these oral assurance cases is that of *ADT* v *BDO Binder Hamlyn*, which resulted in a first instance judgment against the defendant of £65 million.

ADT v *BDO Binder Hamlyn*[14]

The defendant firm ('BDO') were the auditors of Britannia Security Group ('BSG'), which the claimant, 'ADT', was considering acquiring. During negotiations, a BDO partner was asked at short notice to attend a meeting with BSG and ADT. The partner was aware of the potential acquisition and was told that the meeting was a 'final hurdle' for ADT, which would proceed with the transaction if satisfied with the outcome. The partner had been told by BSG that ADT would be likely to ask about the last audited accounts, but knew nothing more detailed about the proposed content of the meeting. He was provided with no agenda and no written instructions.

At the meeting (which lasted for less than an hour), the BDO partner confirmed in answer to questions raised by ADT's finance director that he still stood by the accounts and that he was not aware of any change in BSG's financial position following the year end. ADT proceeded with the acquisition, but subsequently found that the audited accounts had shown a significantly higher profit than was justified. At trial, BDO were found to have assumed a duty of care to ADT and were ordered to pay damages of £65 million, being the difference between the price ADT had paid for BSG and that which would have been paid had the audited accounts shown the true position.

---

[14][1996] BCC 808.

The circumstances of the meeting did cause the trial judge to pause for thought. He hesitated first over whether the auditor could fairly be regarded as assuming a legal responsibility to the third party when the partner concerned was 'bounced into answering questions for which he had inadequate notice or time for preparation and where the potential additional liability he would assume was enormous'. The judge concluded that since the auditor could have taken steps to avoid liability, by declining to comment or issuing a disclaimer, it was reasonable to find that legal responsibility had been assumed.

Second, the trial judge considered whether it was fair that the duty of care that the auditor was deemed to have assumed towards the third party carried financial risks far in excess of those originally accepted to BSG or its shareholders in return for the audit fee. The trial judge concluded, however, that the hesitation he felt in finding that the auditor had accepted an onerous additional risk for no extra fee could not, in itself, provide a justification for deciding that the additional responsibility had not been assumed. The message of *ADT* is clear. If auditors choose to comment to third parties, they must accept the potential consequences.

Not surprisingly, the Court's willingness to hold BDO liable for such a large award of damages in these circumstances was greeted with alarm by the accountancy profession. Whilst, however, this is certainly an area of high risk, it is worth remembering that there have been other oral assurance cases where similar facts have not resulted in a finding of liability.[15]

Perhaps conscious of the apparent contradiction that the case law presents, trial judges in oral assurance cases have sought to justify decisions by a detailed analysis of the facts of each case. Whilst an analysis of these distinctions should assist in identifying more precisely the circumstances in which an auditor is at risk, this remains difficult, principally because many of the distinctions that can be drawn are fine ones or open to subjective interpretation. Some conclusions can, however, be drawn, which should assist the auditor in assessing the level of risk that he faces on a particular occasion.

3.4.4 Factors relevant to the risk of liability

The third party's experience and own investigations

Where the third party is experienced in business matters he will find it more difficult to persuade the Court that the auditor owed him a legal

---

[15]See *James McNaughton Group v Hicks Anderson & Co.* [1991] 1 All ER 134 and *Peach Publishing Ltd v Slater & Co.* [1998] BCC 139.

responsibility: he will be expected to have appreciated the need to reach his own assessment (where necessary assisted by his own advisers) before entering into a transaction at arm's length. The basic principle applicable to such transactions holds good: it is for the 'buyer to beware'. The third party cannot expect to rely on free advice from the target's auditor in place of his own investigations.

Thus, the third party will find it more difficult to establish his claim where he has had the benefit of independent advice, for example where he has instructed an investigative accountant who could have been expected to review the auditor's input. Similarly, where the third party would normally have been expected to make further enquiries, rather than relying on the auditor's assurances, but chooses not to, the Court may well decline to hold the auditor liable.

Having said this, there may be occasions when the third party and his advisers are not in a position to obtain the information they would need to verify the auditor's input. Alternatively, verification may be theoretically possible, but the auditor's input may have been provided at such a late stage that it self-evidently will not be subjected to independent review. Where the third party is of necessity required to take the auditor's input at face value, the chance that the auditor will be regarded as owing the third party a legal responsibility is greater. Thus in *ADT* the trial judge found that there was no possibility of ADT being able to instruct investigative accountants or inspect the target's records for themselves. The published accounts were, therefore, a 'primary source of information', and the auditor should have appreciated that no further substantial investigations would be performed after the meeting.

Warranties

Where the third party is an acquirer, the Share Purchase Agreement may well contain warranties, which give him the comfort of knowing that he may claim against the vendor(s) if the position is not as represented at the time of the transaction. Where a claim under the warranties is available the Court may have less sympathy for a third party who chooses instead to claim against the target's auditor.

Reliance

The extent to which the third party relied on the auditor's input and whether the auditor was or should have been aware of this will be an important factor in determining whether a duty of care is owed. Where, for example, the queries raised with the auditor were fairly general, he may reasonably contend that he had no reason to expect that he would be relied upon. By contrast, where the enquiries are detailed or it is made plain that a satisfactory response is a pre-condition to proceeding with the deal (as was the case in *ADT*), it is far more likely that the auditor will be deemed to have assumed a duty of care. Similarly, an auditor who is involved at one meeting at short notice with little prior notice is less at risk than the auditor who plays a larger part in the negotiations. As has been seen from *ADT* however, it is possible for an auditor in the former position to be deemed to have assumed a duty of care.

There is a temptation for the auditor to find out as much as possible about the transaction and the third party before providing the information or comment that has been requested. Whilst it may go somewhat against his instincts, this temptation should be resisted, since the clearer an idea the auditor has of the reliance being placed upon his input, the more likely he is to be deemed to have assumed a legal responsibility.

In addition to considering the nature of the enquiries put to the auditor, it may be relevant to consider the context in which they were raised. Questions raised in a formal meeting are more likely to be interpreted as having put the auditor on notice that his answers would be relied on than ones raised on a more casual occasion.

Also relevant to the issue of reliance is whether the view expressed by the auditor should have been understood to be provisional. Where, for example, the auditor comments on accounts that are known to be in draft form, it may be less reasonable for reliance to be placed upon them. Of course, much will depend on how much further work was required in order to express a final view on the question(s) asked.

Similarly, where there is evidence that no reliance has actually been placed on the auditor's work or on his assurances (for example,where it is clear that a definite decision had been made to proceed with the transaction in any event or where the third party doubts the quality of the auditor's work), the third party will not later succeed in complaining about the quality of that input.

3.4.5 Safeguards for the auditor asked to comment on his client's audited accounts

The fine nature of the distinctions that have been drawn lead to uncertainty. This is increased by the fact that many of these cases have come before the courts only as applications to strike out the claim on the basis that the claimant cannot succeed. The auditor argues that since he owes the claimant no duty of care, the claim is bound to fail. As previously mentioned, a refusal to strike out cannot be equated to a finding of liability after a full trial in which all the evidence has been examined. A dismissal of the auditor's application indicates no more than that the third party has a claim that can legitimately be pursued; it remains for the claimant to prove the facts he is alleging at full trial.

In consequence, the auditor who is subject to an oral assurance claim may well find it very difficult to assess the likely outcome of the trial. The number of oral assurance cases in recent years suggests that this is an area that loss-making third parties regard as ripe with potential.

The warning provided by *ADT* and other verbal assurance cases is clear. If the auditor (or in other circumstances, the accountant) chooses to comment on his work to a third party who clearly intends to rely on it for a specific known purpose, he may well be assuming a legal responsibility to that party. Every meeting with a potential acquirer carries the possibility of an expansion of the scope of the accountant's responsibilities. This is so even if the meeting is informal, brief or called at short notice. Seen from this perspective, it is apparent that the onus is firmly on the auditor to protect himself. There are various steps he can take to minimise the chances both of a claim being made and of its succeeding.

To comment or not to comment?

The only certain protection for the auditor lies in declining to comment. Where the auditor is asked to comment on financial statements that have been finalised, it is very likely that he will stand by his audit opinion. He would not, after all, have signed off on the accounts without believing his audit opinion to be justified. Therefore, unless he is aware of subsequent events that change his mind, it is inevitable that he will give the requested assurance.

This was the situation faced by the audit partner in *ADT* when asked whether he still stood by the accounts. The trial judge in that case suggested that the partner could have added some caveat along the lines of 'We stand by our opinion, but there were various difficulties in conducting the audit'. We doubt that this approach would have worked. A clean audit opinion had been signed. Since any problems that BDO were aware of at the time of the audit had not been sufficient to make them qualify or withhold their opinion, they could not credibly have relied on these at the meeting as a justification for not standing by the accounts.

What would happen in a transaction such as this if the auditor simply refused to comment? It is certainly possible that some deals would proceed regardless. Alternatively, the target might be forced to make concessions about the investigations that the acquirer could perform. Lastly, the auditor's lack of cooperation might scupper the deal. From a client relations point of view the last (and possibly the second) of these options would be uncomfortable. The auditor will obviously feel the need to balance risk management against the commercial pressure he will be under to cooperate with his client's wishes. The reality is that commercial pressures often triumph and dictate that cooperation is volunteered despite the risks.

The option of refusing to comment should not, however, be rejected out of hand. For example, if the likelihood is that further work from the client company is not on the cards, either because the company is failing or because once acquired a change of auditor is expected, there is little reason to risk a third party claim by agreeing to cooperate. Even where it is decided that some form of cooperation is required, it may be feasible to limit its scope. For example, the auditor may think it reasonable to refuse access to the audit working papers but to agree to answer specific enquiries or to allow access but without additional comment.

The disclaimer

Where the auditor agrees to comment on the audited accounts or provide information to a third party, he should only do so with great care. The best chance of avoiding liability is through the use of a disclaimer that makes it clear that the auditor accepts no legal responsibility to the third party. In *ADT*, it was clear that the trial judge considered that BDO could have avoided liability by the use of such a disclaimer and that he had limited sympathy where the auditor had chosen not to disclaim:

> 'If for commercial reasons those who give advice do not want to give disclaimers or otherwise limit their liability, then I see no reason why they should not live with the consequences.'

Indeed, given what has been said about the inevitability that BDO would in the circumstances stand by their accounts, only a disclaimer could have saved them from liability once they had decided to comment.

Wherever possible, therefore, the auditor should write to the third party (and copy the letter to his client) recording that the auditor accepts no responsibility to the third party for the information provided. An example of a disclaimer letter is shown at Figure 1 (see p 67). It would be inappropriate to use this as a precedent without adapting it to the particular circumstances of each case. The essentials are that the auditor makes clear that:

- any opinion expressed by the auditor or any information given by him is not intended to provide the basis of the third party's decision to invest or lend;

- no duty of care is being assumed; and

- no representations are being or will be made.

Whilst it is not essential for the third party to acknowledge acceptance of the terms of the disclaimer, it may avoid later argument if they do so. The easiest way of achieving this is by asking the third party to sign and return a copy of the disclaimer letter. In cases where it may be difficult to achieve this, the device used in **Figure 1** of stating that the third party's attendance at the meeting will be assumed to indicate acceptance should be used. This approach is preferable to being in a position where the third party forgets or refuses to countersign despite being asked.

On occasions, the pressure to comment without prior notice at a meeting or during a telephone conversation may be irresistible, with the result that the auditor has no opportunity to prepare a letter before commenting. In such situations, the accountant should give a clear, oral disclaimer and confirm this in writing as soon as possible.

As previously discussed,[16] the enforceability of a disclaimer is dependent on its satisfying the 'reasonableness test' imposed by the Unfair Contract Terms Act 1977. This requirement applies to disclaimers given to third parties as much as it does to exclusions of liability between contracting parties.[17] The burden of proving reasonableness is on the auditor. Given that there is no obligation to provide the third party with assistance, it should be much easier to establish reasonableness. This being so, the auditor should not ask for any payment in respect of the assistance given to the third party. This will create a contractual relationship under which it may be more difficult to satisfy the reasonableness test. It is, however, unlikely that the charging of reasonable expenses such as photocopying charges will have the effect of creating a contract between auditor and third party.

Another possible objection to the legality of the auditor's disclaimer is that it falls foul of Companies Act 1985, s310, which renders void any arrangement purporting to exempt the auditor from or indemnify him against any liability for negligence. Whilst it is probable that this provision only excludes the possibility of a disclaimer in relation to the performance of the statutory audit, rather than applying in any wider context, the issue has not yet been determined by case law.

---

[16]See 2.4 above.

[17]The test is not identical to that applied where there is a contract. Reasonableness is judged as at the time that liability to the third party arises rather than as at the time the contract is made.

Recording the advice given

Whether or not a disclaimer is in place, but particularly where one is not, the auditor should take a careful contemporaneous note of any telephone conversations or meetings at which he is asked to comment to the third party. He should ensure that any assurance or advice given is recorded in detail.

In addition, he should consider following up the conversation by sending to both the client and (with the client's permission) the third party an accurate and carefully worded written confirmation of what was said. This may take the form of a letter or a note of the meeting. The client and the third party should be invited to let the auditor know as soon as possible if they do not regard the written record as full or accurate.

3.4.6 Turning the third party into a client

In some circumstances where the accountant's relationship with a third party is such that there is a significant risk that the accountant would be found to owe the third party a duty of care, he may wish to consider whether to enter into a formal client relationship with the third party. The greatest advantage of this is that the accountant's duties can be clearly defined (and therefore limited) by a carefully drafted engagement letter. In addition, the accountant will also be able to ask for the information he needs from the third party about his business and the proposed transaction in order to advise properly. Where the accountant comments without much knowledge of the context in which his working papers and explanations are being relied on, he is far more likely to give inappropriate (and potentially negligent) advice that fails to fulfil the third party's needs. Lastly, the accountant will at least obtain some payment for the extra risk he is accepting.

The use of this approach is limited by the fact that it cannot be used where there is any possibility of a conflict of interest arising between the third party and the original client. Even where there is no conflict, it requires client consent (since it necessarily involves a breach of confidentiality).

This solution is most commonly used where a bank (or other lender) requires assurances from a company's auditor before agreeing to lend money. Its use has developed because of the high degree of awareness on the part of banks about the circumstances in which auditors will owe them a duty of care and their willingness to do what is necessary to ensure that their correspondence with the accountant demonstrates the existence of such a duty. For example, banks fairly commonly seek a written acknowledgement that the auditor consents to the accounts being relied upon. Where the bank's attempt to push the right legal buttons is convincing, it may be better for the accountant to agree to advise, but only under a contract. This issue is specifically addressed in the Auditing Practices Committee's Practice Note 4 'Reliance on Audited Financial Statements'.

Whether any duty is owed to the bank outside of a contract will of course depend on the particular circumstances. For example, the bank is far less likely to succeed in creating a legal duty in relation to possible future loans over an indefinite period of time, than if the lending is specific and the details are known to the auditor. Similarly, there is a greater risk to the auditor where the bank seeks to rely on a single audit opinion rather than on notifying an intention to rely on the company's audited financial statements generally.

Where the risk of a duty of care is less great, a disclaimer is likely to be sufficient. Practice Note 4 suggests various forms of disclaimer letter which can be issued and also suggests drawing the bank's attention to the joint statement prepared with the Committee of London and Scottish Bankers (which is attached to the Practice Note) and which sets out the positions of both the banks and the auditors.

Where, however, there is a greater likelihood of a duty of care arising, the best option may be to enter into a formal engagement with the bank. Practice Note 4 suggests that this is the appropriate course where the bank is seeking assurances about:

- audited financial statements;
- the adequacy of the client's systems of internal control or the efficiency of management;
- the possibility of illegal acts, such as fraud.

3.4.7　Regulators and others

Another category of third party 'outsider' to whom the auditor may be deemed to have assumed a duty are those who perform a regulatory or monitoring role towards the audited company and/or are responsible for the company's liabilities if it fails. Where the auditor is aware that this monitoring is based wholly or in part on a review of the company's financial statements, the Court may regard the auditor as owing the third party a duty of care. Two recent cases illustrate the point: *CAA* v *Kounnis Freeman* and *The Law Society* v *KPMG Peat Marwick & Others*.

CAA v *Kounnis Freeman*[18]

The claim arose from the collapse of Flight Company (UK) plc ('Flight'), which organised air travel. In this case the 'outsider' was the Civil Aviation Authority ('CAA'), which had issued Flight with an Air Travel Organiser's Licence ('the Licence'). The Licence provided assurance to consumers that should Flight collapse, the costs of repatriating stranded travellers and fulfilling forward bookings would be met.

Flight's Licence came up for renewal and was renewed by the CAA. Some three months later Flight ceased trading. Kounnis Freeman ('KF') were Flight's auditors. The CAA alleged that in renewing the licence it had relied upon statements made by KF. The question before the Court of Appeal was whether KF could be said to owe the CAA a duty of care in the preparation of Flight's financial statements, which were alleged to be inaccurate and misleading.

The CAA had refused an initial application for renewal, making it clear to Flight that there would be no renewal unless certain conditions were met. These included receiving confirmation of particular points and audited accounts. On the day that the audited accounts were signed, KF sent a copy direct to the CAA. The covering letter referred to the application to renew and confirmed the specific points raised by the CAA. The CAA alleged that KF must have been aware that the CAA was relying both on this confirmation and on the reliability of the audited accounts, without which there would have been no renewal. KF denied that in sending the audited accounts to the CAA they had assumed any legal responsibility to them. In particular, they pointed to the fact that the CAA had not expressly asked KF to confirm their audit report.

The Court of Appeal decided that KF were or should have been aware that the CAA would take the accounts as having been prepared with reasonable care and skill and would use them as a basis for their decision whether or not to renew. In this instance, a reasonable auditor (knowing that the deadline for renewal of the licence expired the day the accounts were sent) would have been aware that there was no reasonable opportunity for the CAA to organise an independent examination of the audited accounts. Nor would the auditor have reasonably regarded the accounts as separate and distinct from the confirmations sought on particular issues. From these facts it was reasonable to infer that a duty of care had been assumed.

---

[18][1999] 2 BCLC 641.

Whilst the circumstances in this case are somewhat unusual, they are by no means unique. Where a third party owes a financial responsibility to the general public for the company's liabilities if it collapses, the courts are likely to be more inclined to impose a duty on the auditor for reasons of public policy. This type of situation is distinct from that envisaged in *Caparo*, where the third party relies on the audited accounts as a source of investment advice.

The Law Society v KPMG Peat Marwick & Others[19]

This case provides a further example of the Court's willingness to find that an auditor owes a legal duty to a body with responsibilities towards the public. The body in this instance was the Law Society, which has responsibilities in connection with the regulation of solicitors in England and Wales and as a trustee of the fund set up to compensate clients defrauded by solicitors. Each firm of solicitors regulated by the Society is required by statute to forward an annual audit report on which the Society relies as providing an assurance that the firm has complied with accounting requirements intended to safeguard client money held by firms.

The Society issued proceedings against KPMG, who had been the auditors of a firm of solicitors who unknown to KPMG were involved in the misappropriation of client funds. KPMG had issued a clean audit report, which was forwarded to the Law Society in the usual manner. After the frauds came to light, the Society started proceedings alleging that they had relied on the audit report which amounted to a negligent misrepresentation and which had enabled the misappropriations to remain undetected. The question of whether the auditors owed a duty of care to the Society was considered as a preliminary issue.

The Court (at first instance) decided that it was foreseeable that the Law Society would rely on the report and that a failure to take care in its preparation might contribute to improprieties remaining hidden, with consequential losses to clients and calls on the compensation fund available to such victims. The Court was satisfied that there was a sufficient relationship between the auditor and the Society to found a duty of care and to make its imposition fair and reasonable. There was no reason why the auditor should not be responsible to the Society for any calls on the compensation fund that resulted from their alleged negligence. This decision has now been confirmed by the Court of Appeal.

---

[19][2000] PNLR 364.

The decision underlines the fact that where a regulator is known to be relying on the audit report to perform functions intended to protect the general public, the Court is willing to impose a duty of care even though there is little direct connection between the auditor and the regulator. The Society had no involvement in the appointment of the auditor, nor does it seem that there was any contact between them. The auditor would, however, have been aware that the Society would be receiving the report, which was required by statute for regulatory purposes. It seems that where the purpose of the regulation is the protection of the public, this is sufficient.

3.5 Disclosing working papers: release and authorisation letters

3.5.1 The risks involved in providing access to audit working papers

Where his client is involved in a potential transaction with a prospective acquirer, investor or lender, the auditor is often asked to give disclosure of his audit working papers. The third party will commonly instruct an investigating accountant to report on the proposed transaction and a review of the audit working papers is often the most cost-effective way of gaining an insight into the target company. The working papers and any further explanations or information provided by the auditor may well be one of, if not the only, major source of available information.

As in the situations discussed in **3.4**, there is a risk that where the investor or lender relies on the audit working papers in deciding whether to enter the transaction, he will pursue a claim against the auditor if the transaction subsequently results in a loss. The allegation will be that the information supplied by the auditor was negligently prepared and that the auditor knew or ought to have known that this would be relied upon by the third party in deciding to proceed with the transaction. The recent case of *Electra Private Equity Partners & Others* v *KPMG Peat Marwick & Others* illustrates the potential for a claim to arise where the auditor provides information or copy working papers to an investigating accountant instructed by a third party.

Figure 1

Prospective Purchaser

[c/o Merchant Bank if applicable]

Dear Sirs,

[client name & transaction reference]

We have been asked to attend a meeting with you on [date & venue]. We understand that the sole purpose of the meeting [of our attendance at the meeting] to be that we, as auditor of [client name] might assist you to gain an understanding of [prior year adjustments in the accounts of [client name] for the year/period ended as applicable].

The work performed by us in arriving at our audit opinion on these accounts was not carried out in the knowledge or context of any specific requirements that you may have as a prospective purchaser. Nor was it performed pursuant to any instructions from you.

Our attendance at a meeting such as you propose is unusual and we are only prepared to attend on the following terms:

1. Any information which is provided by us to you is not intended to and should not form the basis of any decision by you to [invest in/ purchase client].

2. No representation or warranty, express or implied, is or will be made by us in relation to any written or oral information or opinion which has been made or may be made available to you or your advisers.

3. We accept no duty of care and expressly disclaim any liability to you arising out of or in connection with the provision to you of any information or opinion.

4. In providing any information to you, we undertake no obligation to provide you with access to any additional information or update such information or correct any inaccuracies therein that become apparent.

It would also assist our preparation for the meeting if you would let us have a list of the queries that you wish to raise.

We shall assume that your presence at the meeting signifies your acknowledgement and acceptance of these terms.

Yours faithfully,

[firm name]

cc [client] [and purchaser's advisers *if applicable*]

Electra Private Equity Partners & Others v *KPMG Peat Marwick & Others*[20]

The claimants – venture capital fund managers – invested IR£10 million in loan stock in an Irish leasing company known as the Cambridge Group ('Cambridge'), thereby acquiring effective control. The entire investment was lost when Cambridge went into receivership some 18 months later. The claimants had instructed KPMG Peat Marwick ('KPMG') to prepare a report on the suitability of the proposed investment. This relied on information provided by Cambridge's auditors, SKC, a firm belonging to the KPMG international group. The claimants sued both KPMG and SKC alleging negligence. It was alleged against SKC that the claimants' decision to invest in Cambridge was made in reliance upon the audited accounts and SKC's unqualified audit opinion. The accounts were alleged to be misleading in showing a profit where they should have shown a substantial loss. SKC applied to strike out the claim against them on the basis that they did not owe the claimants any duty of care. SKC initially succeeded in striking out the claim against them, but this decision was subsequently reversed on appeal.

By the time of the appeal the claimants were seeking to change the emphasis of their allegations to focus on the information supplied by SKC to KPMG. The claimants contended that in supplying this information SKC had assumed a duty of care because SKC knew or ought to have known that KPMG would rely on it for the purpose of its report and that the claimants would in turn rely on that report in deciding to invest. SKC acknowledged that information had been supplied to KPMG, but maintained that this was no more than 'background material'. Further, that SKC neither knew nor ought to have known that KPMG or the claimants would rely upon it.

The Court of Appeal decided that this allegation disclosed a reasonable cause of action and the amended claim should be allowed to proceed to a full trial. The Court of Appeal did not accept the submissions made by SKC that their interaction with KPMG could not be relevant to determining the legal relationship between SKC and the claimants. It was considered possible that the close association between SKC and KPMG might be found to create a 'special relationship' between SKC and the claimants, giving rise to a duty of care.

Electra provides a good illustration of the potential risk that faces the auditor if he allows access to his working papers and/or agrees to

---

[20][2000] PNLR 247.

comment on them. Given this risk the auditor should bear in mind that his working papers belong to him[21] and that he is therefore entitled to refuse access.

Regardless of his legal rights, the auditor may feel compelled by commercial pressures to cooperate with his client (who will usually be in favour of disclosure). As a result, auditors commonly consent to access but minimise the risk of a claim by obtaining a release (or hold harmless) letter from the third party (and any adviser he has instructed), confirming their acceptance that no liability will attach to the auditor in relation to the disclosure. The auditor will also obtain an authorisation letter from his client consenting to the breach of confidentiality involved in the disclosure and agreeing to indemnify the auditor in respect of any claims that arise in connection with it. The *ICAEW Members' Handbook* makes it clear that whilst practitioners may sometimes experience reluctance on the part of the third party and/or the client to the use of a release letter, this is not unreasonable and should be insisted upon. Indeed, as the *Handbook* points out, the greatest resistance may arise where the auditor is most at risk.

Given that release and authorisation letters are routinely used, it is noteworthy that SKC had not insisted that one be signed by the claimants in *Electra*. It is not clear why this was omitted, but it may be that SKC felt this was not necessary because they were passing information only to an associated firm, rather than to an 'outsider'. The decision shows that this is not a distinction to be relied upon.

Where the auditor appreciates at the time the audit is performed that access to the working papers will be granted to a third party (or that there is a real prospect of this), it is worth taking extra care with the working papers. This is particularly so if for some reason a release letter is not to be put in place or there is thought to be a risk that the release agreement will be challenged. In such cases the audit team should be clearly briefed as to the possible legal consequences of granting access to the working papers and cooperation with the investigating accountant. Care needs to be taken by both staff and partners to ensure that the audit files do not include statements which would support an allegation that the auditor regarded himself as carrying out the audit for the purposes of the third party as well as for the company, or which damage the auditor's position in other ways. In *Electra*, for example, the judgments suggest that aspects

---

[21]On the question of ownership, see 4.2 above. Where the papers are not audit working papers, the accountant should check whether they belong to him or his client. The accountant will have to disclose at his client's request papers belonging to the client.

of SKC's working papers might well have proved unhelpful to them at trial, because of the extent of the liaison with KPMG that they revealed. SKC's audit planning memorandum referred to their agreement to remain 'in close contact with [KPMG] throughout the due diligence/ audit process'. A letter from SKC to KPMG referred to the importance of 'a clear and consistent position from us on the due diligence and on the audit'. In other words, the audit papers suggested a joint endeavour and this would have reduced SKC's chances of persuading the Court that they were not providing information which they expected KPMG to use in their report and which would thus have been relied upon by the claimants.

3.5.2   The drafting of release and authorisation letters

The careful drafting of the release and authorisation letters is crucial to ensuring that they provide the protection sought. The letters should, of course, be tailored to fit the particular transaction to which they relate and it may be necessary to seek legal advice as to what is required on a particular occasion. Below, we have identified the points which should always be covered and in addition detailed guidance is provided by the ICAEW Statement 'Access to working papers by investigating accountants',[22] the appendices to which contain both specimen authorisation and release letters.

The authorisation letter

This protects the accountant from any complaint of breach of client confidentiality by formally recording the client's consent to the disclosure. The following points should be covered:

- that whilst the accountant agrees to the third party having access, this will only be given on certain conditions;

- that the working papers were prepared for the purpose of the audit (or in the case of disclosure of other working papers, the engagement to which they relate) and not for the purpose to which they are now being put;

- that the client accepts the risk that their disclosure or any explanations provided to the third party may result in the failure of the proposed deal or to changes in its terms and will not seek to hold the auditor responsible for this;

- that the client will not hold the auditor responsible for any misuse by the third party (or any other party to the transaction) of confidential

---

[22] Audit 3/95, issued in October 1995.

information obtained from the papers which are disclosed or from any explanations provided by the auditor;

- that where the auditor's work is incomplete, it should be agreed that he will not accept any responsibility for informing the third party of any developments or changes in his work and/or conclusions subsequent to the disclosure.

A copy of the letter should be countersigned by the client (or where the client is a company, by someone with appropriate authority on its behalf) to indicate an acceptance of the terms.

The release letter

The release (or hold harmless letter) is addressed both to the third party (or parties) and to any investigating accountant (or other professional) instructed to inspect the working papers on their behalf. As mentioned, the client should also be sent a copy to put him on notice of its contents.

Naturally, there is a good deal of overlap with the contents of the authorisation letter. The main elements are a disclaimer of responsibility to the recipients of the letter and a statement that the third party and his advisers will indemnify the accountant against any claims that arise from the giving of access or the provision of information. The following should also be covered:

- that the requested access will be granted but only subject to certain conditions;

- that the working papers were generated solely for the purpose of the engagement to which they relate. The purpose of the engagement should be clearly explained and any limitations which might restrict the usefulness of the working papers to the third party should be clearly identified. In the case of an audit, it would be made clear that the work was performed for the purpose of reaching the statutory opinion, that it related to a particular period and that there may well have been significant events after the end of the audit period. Where possible, it is worth including that the engagement was performed without notice of the transaction now proposed;

- that no representation is being made by the auditor that the working papers are sufficient or appropriate for the third party's purposes or investigations;

- that any explanations which the auditor chooses to make are voluntary and only for the purpose of explaining the working papers.

It should be made clear that the onus is on the third party to verify any statement relating to the client before relying upon it;

- that the terms in the release letter cannot and will not be varied by subsequent agreement (whether in writing or orally). Otherwise it is possible for the conditions which have been carefully set out in the release letter to be overridden by a subsequent conversation or letter, the legal consequences of which may not be intended. Where a greater degree of flexibility is desirable, the letter should provide that no variation will have legal effect unless an amended release letter is issued;

- that the third party and his adviser accept that the auditor owes them no duty of care arising from their reliance upon the papers disclosed and from any explanation or comment made by the accountant. It should be stated that any such reliance is at their risk;

- that the third party is obliged to indemnify the accountant against any proceedings or liabilities in any way connected to the access to the working papers;

- that the working papers shall only be used by the third party and his advisers for the purpose for which it has been granted (i.e., in relation to the proposed transaction);

- that neither the third party nor the adviser are permitted to pass on any information received from the auditor or contained in the working papers, subject to the fact that the information may be passed within the third party's team (including his advisers) solely for the purposes of the proposed transaction.

Again, care needs to be taken to ensure that the individual signing the letter on behalf of a company or other organisation will bind it by so doing. No papers should be released until a copy of both the authorisation and the release letters have been returned duly signed by the client, the third party and (where appropriate) the third party's adviser.

3.5.3 Restrictions on limiting liability

The legal uncertainties that were discussed in the context of disclaimers at **3.4.5** apply equally to the disclaimers that are included in authorisation and release letters. The auditor's disclaimer of liability will only be upheld by the courts if the auditor can establish that it satisfies the 'reasonableness test' laid down in the Unfair Contract Terms Act 1977.[23] This test will be far more easily satisfied if the auditor has not charged the

---

[23]For further details on the steps to be taken in drafting such clauses, see 2.4 above.

third party either for access or for any additional work or information provided.[24] As a result, it is usual for access to the working papers to be provided either free of charge, or on an expenses only basis (the expenses usually being limited to reasonable photocopying charges). Any charges above and beyond this may change the accountant's legal position, whether the fees are paid by the client or by the third party.

3.5.4 Requests for access to documents other than audit working papers

In dealing with requests by investigating accountants for access we have concentrated exclusively on the disclosure of audit working papers, which is the most common form that such requests take. There will be occasions when the request is not connected with an audit or where additional documents are sought. For example, investigating accountants frequently ask for access to tax computations in addition to audit working papers. The considerations already outlined apply equally to non-audit working papers. Of course, the authorisation and release letters used must be amended appropriately to reflect the nature of the request.

One point to bear in mind where the request is not for disclosure of audit working papers is that other documents will not always belong to the accountant.[25] For example, tax computations and the accompanying correspondence with the Inland Revenue are prepared by the accountant as agent for his client and belong not to the accountant (as his audit working papers do) but to the client. The difference that this makes is that the client (as the owner of the documents) has the power to insist on their disclosure. Thus, whilst the accountant should seek agreement to a release letter in the usual way, he is not in such circumstances able to insist on one in the face of any objection from his client. Where the client is very keen to proceed with the transaction and therefore strongly favours disclosure, the accountant may come under pressure to cooperate without the protection of a release letter.

If he is fortunate, the accountant will find that, even where access is requested to documents that belong to the client, a release letter may be

---

[24] There is also a possibility that any disclaimer in connection with the disclosure of audit working papers might fall foul of Companies Act 1985, s310, which renders void any limitation of liability for negligence on the part of the auditor. Whilst the likelihood is that this restriction refers only to the performance of the statutory audit and does not apply to any connected work or to disclosure of the working papers, the position has not been confirmed by case law.

[25] See 4.2 above on the ownership of documents.

agreed to, without the point ever being made that the accountant is not entitled to insist on one. This is particularly likely to be so where access is sought to a mixture of client- and accountant-owned papers. In such a case, a release letter covering all the documents is likely to be agreed and the difference between client-owned and accountant-owned papers need not be referred to in the authorisation and release letters.

3.5.5   The danger of seeking unnecessary information

Where the auditor is being asked to give access to working papers it may be tempting to seek as much information as possible about the proposed transaction before responding to any enquiries. For example, as a condition for giving access to the audit working papers auditors sometimes require investigating accountants to agree to disclose any comments which the investigating accountant intends to make to his client as a result of his review of the auditor's papers. Presumably this is done to provide the auditor with the comfort of knowing what has been said about his opinion and the work underlying it. The risks of this approach outweigh the benefits however. The knowledge acquired offers no protection against a claim and it may be suggested that the auditor has assumed some responsibility in relation to the information he receives. If the auditor receives the information and makes no comment, it may later be alleged that he in some way endorsed it. The situation is particularly difficult if, because of his superior knowledge of the client or the work performed, the auditor forms the view that the investigating accountant's conclusions are inaccurate or misleading. If the auditor expresses his view, he will have been drawn into advising the third party. If he says nothing and is later found to have assumed a duty of care, he will not have fulfilled it. Thus, the auditor is much safer without this sort of information.

3.5.6   Editing the files

In the light of all that has been said about the risks of disclosing the working papers, it would not be surprising if there was occasionally some temptation to edit them before release or to release some whilst holding back others. Both these temptations are best resisted, since unless it is made clear to the client and third party what has been removed/changed, there is a danger that what is released will give a misleading impression. It is unlikely that any explanation could be given about the decision to edit the files without raising concerns and suspicions in the minds of the third party and client.

3.6 The accountant's liability to third parties for reports

So far the focus of this Chapter has been mostly on the auditor. We now turn to the potential liability of the reporting accountant, who is also at risk from third parties who rely on his report alleging that the accountant owed them a legal responsibility.

In summary, although the third party is not a party to the contract between the accountant and his client, the extent of the accountant's duty to the third party may be limited by giving him notice of the scope of the engagement. Where possible, the best option is to provide the third party with a copy of the engagement letter and/or include full details of the engagement in the report. Provided the engagement letter and report are carefully drafted, this should ensure that a third party is not under a misapprehension about the scope of the work performed.

In addition, the accountant will often state in his report that it is intended only for his client (and any other persons to whom a responsibility is accepted) and that the accountant disclaims any liability towards other parties who choose to rely on it. Such a statement will be effective against a third party with notice of the disclaimer, subject to the caveat that the exclusion or limitation of liability will only be valid if the accountant can demonstrate that it satisfies the reasonableness test laid down by the Unfair Contract Terms Act 1977.

3.6.1 The accountant's liability for published information relating to securities

We now turn to a particular area of potential liability for the reporting accountant: his responsibility for the information contained in published documents relating to securities. The accountant may owe investors who rely on that information a legal duty under the general principles of the common law and/or as a result of the statutory framework that regulates the type of investment in question. It is open to a claimant to rely on the common law or a breach of statutory duty or both. Where the accountant owes a responsibility imposed by statute, he will not be able to restrict or remove this by the use of a disclaimer unless the statute allows it. Nor, where a common law duty is owed to investors for the content of published information, would a disclaimer be likely to satisfy the reasonableness test.

3.6.2 The common law

As in other areas, the ability of a third party to hold the accountant responsible for investment losses depends on the relationship between accountant and investor being sufficiently 'proximate', as required by *Caparo*. This area was explored within a year of the House of Lords' decision in that case, in a claim brought by Morgan Crucible Co. plc arising out of its acquisition of another company, First Castle Electronics ('FCE').

Morgan Crucible plc v Hill Samuel & Co. Ltd[26]

Morgan Crucible had acquired FCE after a contested takeover bid. After the acquisition, Morgan Crucible issued proceedings against the former directors of FCE and the company's auditors (amongst others), complaining that pre-bid financial statements and a profit forecast had been negligently prepared and were misleading.[27] The contentious information was contained in a number of defence documents circulated to shareholders, which were also published as press releases and copied to Morgan Crucible.

Morgan Crucible recognised – following the House of Lords' decision in *Caparo* – that in general terms the directors and financial advisers of a target company owed no duty of care to safeguard the interests of a potential bidder in a contested takeover. Thus, they applied for permission to amend their claim to contend that once they had emerged as an identified bidder, the directors of FCE and their financial advisers owed a duty not to be negligent in making representations that might mislead them. The Court of Appeal agreed that this was an arguable claim, which should be permitted to go forward to trial.[28]

For investors who rely on published information for the particular purpose for which it was generated, the hurdle of establishing a sufficiently close relationship with the accountant will not usually create difficulty. The accountant will have to concede that the investor was part of a class of persons whom he expected to rely on the published information.

Al-Nakib Investments (Jersey) Ltd & Another v Longcroft & Others[29]

The third party is in a less favourable position where he relies on the published information for a purpose other than that for which it

---

[26][1991] BCC 82.

[27]In this instance the auditor was also acting as financial adviser to FCE in relation to the contested bid.

[28]The case subsequently settled, and thus the issue was never decided at a full trial.

[29][1990] 1 WLR 1390.

was generated. Thus, investors in the 'after market' are likely to experience greater difficulty in pursuing a successful claim. This issue was addressed in the case of *Al-Nakib Investments (Jersey) Ltd. & Another* v *Longcroft & Others*, where a claim was brought by a subscriber and purchasers of shares against the directors of the company in which they had invested.

The claimant was a shareholder in Combined Technologies Corp. PLC ('CT PLC'). CT PLC incorporated a subsidiary, Mnemos Ltd ('M Ltd'), which it proposed to float on the unlisted securities market. A prospectus was issued, inviting CT PLC shareholders to subscribe for shares in both companies. The claimant subscribed in reliance on the prospectus and made subsequent purchases of further shares, allegedly relying on the prospectus and/or on two interim financial reports.

The claimant subsequently started proceedings against CT PLC and the directors of M Ltd complaining that all three documents contained misrepresentations. The defendants successfully applied to strike out that part of the claim relating to the after market purchases on the basis that it disclosed no reasonable cause of action. The Court agreed that the prospectus had been issued to invite subscription, but not for the purpose of assisting the claimants to decide about subsequent purchases in the market. Similarly, the interim reports were issued for the purpose of informing the shareholders of M Ltd of the activities of the company, and not for investment purposes. A duty of care was therefore owed only in relation to the original subscription.

Possfund Custodian Trustee Ltd v *Diamond*[30]

However, the door is not entirely closed to claims by after market investors. The issue was considered again in the case of *Possfund Custodian Trustee Ltd* v *Diamond*, where the claim related to a prospectus issued by 'D plc' in relation to a flotation on the unlisted securities market. A claim was brought by various investors (including after market investors) against D plc (in receivership), its directors at the time of the placing and its accountants. Some of the defendants applied to strike out the claim in relation to the after market purchases on the basis that those responsible for the prospectus owed the investors no duty of care in relation to these transactions. The application was unsuccessful.

The investors had alleged that the prospectus had not only been aimed at encouraging investment in the flotation, but had also been intended to induce and encourage investors to purchase shares in the after market.

---

[30][1996] 2 All ER 774.

Whilst the Court conceded that the starting point for determining the ambit of the common law duty of care was the statutory purpose of the prospectus, this would not necessarily preclude a wider duty of care if a 'super-added' purpose was shown to exist. The burden of showing its existence might be 'heavy or indeed overwhelming', but was a matter to be determined at a full trial.

Thus, there remains some prospect of a successful claim under the common law in relation to after market investments. *Possfund* reflects the general trend towards increased protection to members of the public and the Court acknowledged that the decision reflected changing market practice in relation to share prospectuses. Certainly, care should be taken to word the Particulars so as to avoid unintended liability to members of the public who purchase shares in the market.

3.6.3 Liability for advice provided to directors

Where the company which issued the published information has subsequently collapsed, the accountant is particularly likely to be sued, since the investors will often have no other viable target from whom to seek to recover their losses. One difficulty for such claimants is that there may be nothing in the published information to which the accountant has given his name that can be attacked.

This was the position in *Abbott & Others* v *Strong & Others*,[31] where investors had purchased shares in a rights issue offered by Resort Hotels Ltd ('Resort') in reliance on a circular to shareholders. This contained a profit forecast from Resort's directors together with a letter from Resort's accountants setting out the basis on which the forecast had been put together, and confirming that it was properly compiled and presented on a basis consistent with Resort's usual accounting policies. The claimants alleged that the circular was grossly misleading as a result of fraudulent misrepresentations that had been made by the then managing director of Resort to the accountants. The issue considered by the Court was whether it was possible that the accountants owed any duty of care to the investors for the accuracy of the figures in the circular beyond that which they owed as a result of their published letter. In other words, did the accountants owe the same duty of care to the investors as they did to Resort by reason of the fact that the accountants knew that their advice to Resort was being used for the circular to investors? The Court held that they did not. In choosing to invest, the claimants had relied on the statements made by Resort's directors in the circular. Whilst advice had

---

[31][1998] 2 B.C.L.C. 420.

been provided by the accountants to Resort for the purpose of enabling the directors to make those statements, the participation of the accountants had not been known to the claimants and it could not therefore be said that they had relied on them.

The duty owed by the accountants might of course have been greater had the extent of their role been made known to the investors. In the context of reliance on published information, however, some protection for the accountant is provided by the fact that the maker of any statement is required to confirm that consent has been given to its inclusion (see below). This would seem to limit the extent to which investors will be able successfully to assert reliance on someone other than the maker of a statement. It should, however, be borne in mind that where investors do not have a direct claim against the company's accountants, they may be able to benefit from a claim brought by the liquidator in the company's name.

3.6.4 Statutory responsibility for published information

Where investors have a complaint about the material contained in published information, they may make a claim for breach of statutory duty rather than for breach of a common law duty of care. A separate statutory regime covers responsibility for information published in relation to securities listed on the stock exchange and unlisted securities, and a brief summary of these is set out below.

Securities listed on the stock exchange: the regime under FSA 1986, Pt IV

Where the accountant is engaged to provide information to be included in listing particulars or a prospectus (the 'Particulars') in relation to securities to be listed on the London Stock Exchange,[32] his work is performed within the framework set out in the Financial Services Act 1986 ('FSA 1986').[33] This is supplemented by more detailed requirements in the 'Listing Rules' (the 'Purple Book') published by the Financial Services Authority (now the UK Listing Authority).[34] Under

---

[32]The regime may also apply to where there is no application for listing: see FSA 1986, s156A.

[33]The Financial Services and Markets Act 2000 replaces the FSA, but at the time of writing is not yet in force.

[34]The role of the UK Listing Authority transferred from the London Stock Exchange to the Financial Services Authority on 1 May 2000.

this regime a reporting accountant is potentially liable to investors who rely on inaccurate published information.

FSA 1986 requires that the Particulars should include 'all such information as investors and their professional advisers would reasonably require, and reasonably expect to find there, for the purpose of making an informed assessment of ... the assets and liabilities, financial position, profits and losses, and prospects of the issuer of the securities; and ... the rights attaching to those securities'.[35]

The FSA 1986 identifies the 'persons responsible' for the Particulars, who can be held accountable for their content.[36] The definition is sufficiently broad to encompass the reporting accountant, although his liability is limited to those parts of the Particulars for which he has accepted responsibility and which appear in (substantially) the form and context to which he has agreed.

FSA 1986, s150 defines the circumstances in which a 'person responsible' for the Particulars will be liable to compensate an investor. Liability may arise where someone acquires securities and suffers loss as a result of 'any untrue or misleading statement' in the Particulars or the omission of any required information. There are, however, a number of possible defences.[37]

After market claims

In contrast to the common law position there is nothing to prohibit an investor in the after market from seeking to pursue a claim under FSA 1986, s150, provided he can satisfy the necessary criteria described above. The more outdated the Particulars, however, the more difficult the investor is likely to find it in order to succeed in a claim. Provided the 'person responsible' held a reasonable belief in the statement (or omission) about which complaint is made when dealing in the securities started, the Court may excuse him if the claimant acquired the securities after such a lapse of time that this is reasonable in the circumstances.

Reliance on experts

The opinions expressed by the reporting accountant in the Particulars will sometimes be based on facts and/or conclusions that he is not in a

---

[35]FSA 1986, s146.

[36]FSA 1986, s152.

[37]FSA 1986, s151.

position to verify. Where the accountant reports on the basis of information provided by an expert (such as an actuary or engineer), he will not generally be liable for matters within their expertise upon which it was reasonable for him to rely.[38]

Advice on the contents of Particulars

The FSA draws a distinction between the liability of a professional who consents to material being published in the Particulars and that of a professional who does no more than advise on their content. Such advice cannot give rise to a liability to investors under FSA 1986, s150.[39] Thus, whilst the reporting accountant may be liable under this section for misleading statements or omissions in any report or letter of comfort included in the Particulars, this liability would not extend to advice about their contents. This is in line with the position that was taken at common law in *Abbott* v *Strong* (see above).

Unlisted securities: the POS Regulations 1995

A very similar regime is in place with regard to any offer to the public of unlisted securities, including the Alternative Investment Market ('AIM'), under the Public Offers of Securities Regulations 1995 ('POS Regulations').[40] Any such public offer must be accompanied by a prospectus (together with a supplementary prospectus in the case of any significant change during the offer period) and, as with listed securities, those responsible for the prospectus(es) may find themselves liable to investors for misleading or untrue statements (or omissions) that have caused loss.

Claims by after market investors

Under the POS Regulations, liability is restricted to investors who have acquired securities 'to which the prospectus' relates and who suffer loss in respect of those securities. The wording suggests that no statutory liability will be owed to investors who purchase securities in the after market. Indeed, this was the view of the Court in *Possfund* (**see above**), although the point was not central to the issue being decided, which related to liability under the common law, rather than to statute.

---

[38]FSA 1986, s151(2).

[39]FSA 1986, s151(8).

[40]SI 1995/1537.

4 Working papers and other documents

4.1 Introduction

This Chapter looks at some of the issues connected with documents:

- Who owns the documents in a firm's possession?

- When does the accountant have a right to retain documents belonging to the client to enforce payment of fees (known as 'exercising a lien')?

- How can the risk that disclosure of working papers may damage the firm be minimised?

- What are the pros and cons of retaining or disposing of working papers?

Throughout this Chapter 'documents' and 'working papers' include not only paper records but also material stored by other means, for example on microfiche or on disk.

4.2 Ownership

The accountant's files will usually contain documents that he has generated and documents received either from the client or from third parties. The question of who owns these documents is something to which little thought usually needs to be given. Ownership is, however, important in three distinct sets of circumstances: first, where fees remain outstanding and the accountant wishes to exert pressure to pay by relying on a lien; second, where there is a request for access to the documents in the accountant's possession; and third, where consideration is being given to disposal of documents.

Although technically it is possible to deal with questions of ownership of documents in the letter of engagement, this is rarely done. Nor, in most instances, is it necessary to do so. The position as regards ownership will therefore usually depend upon two issues:

(i) At the overall engagement level, was the accountant acting as principal or as agent?

(ii) At the individual document level, what is the nature of the particular documents and for what purpose were they passed to or created by the accountant?

We shall deal with each of these issues in turn.[1]

4.2.1 Principal or agent?

An accountant is acting as principal if he is retained to give his independent professional opinion upon something. Examples include acting as auditor, reporting accountant or tax adviser: in each case, the product of the work is the presentation of the accountant's independent view, generally (but not necessarily) in the form of a written report. In these situations the papers the accountant creates for his own purposes in the course of engagement belong to him.

An accountant is acting as agent if the primary end product of his work is not the giving of an independent professional opinion but the furtherance of his client's dealings with another party. Examples include the preparation and submission of a client's tax returns to the Inland Revenue and similar tax compliance work, and situations where the accountant performs one-off commissions for a client such as seeking a buyer for a business. Here the position is that, with some exceptions, documents created by the accountant in the course of his work belong to the client.

The main authority for the propositions just stated is *Chantrey Martin & Co v Martin.*[2] The case concerned a dispute between a firm of accountants and a former employee, the defendant. The firm were seeking damages from the defendant for breaching his contract of service: they said he had walked out on them without giving notice. The defendant, on the other hand, claimed that he had been wrongfully dismissed: he said that this had happened because he had discovered irregularities in the books of an audit client which the audit partner refused to have corrected. The question for the Court of Appeal was the extent to which the firm was required to disclose to the defendant in the litigation the contents of its files relating to that client. This depended upon who owned the relevant documents.

The Court of Appeal held that the firm owned the audit working papers and certain draft accounts and tax computations. These had to be disclosed therefore to the defendant in the litigation. However, correspondence between the firm and the Inland Revenue regarding

---

[1]See also paras 4–18 of ICAEW Statement 1.3.2 ('Documents and Records: Ownership, Lien and Rights of Access') issued in November 1996.

[2][1953] 2 QB 286.

the client's tax affairs belonged to the client and hence was not disclosable.

The distinction between acting as principal and acting as agent will inevitably become blurred at times. This can occur particularly where the accountant is giving tax advice in addition to performing tax compliance work. This type of situation can, however, generally be unravelled by looking more closely at individual documents in order to establish whether they were prepared in connection with the advice or compliance aspects of the work.

Where the accountant has acted as principal, the initial assumption will be that the whole of the contents of his files belong to him. This assumption needs to be tested however. The files may contain documents which it is clear the client only provided on loan and expected would be returned. Issues may also arise, particularly where the work involves pure accountancy, as to the extent of the product the client was entitled to receive. The letter of engagement may also occasionally impact upon the matter. Subject to points of this sort, however, any disputed questions of ownership are likely to be resolved in favour of the accountant.

Where the accountant has been acting as agent the position is more complex and it will generally be necessary to resolve questions of ownership (assuming it is worthwhile to do so) on a document by document basis.

4.2.2 The nature and purpose of the documents

Letters, reports and other documents specifically prepared for the client will belong to the client. Copies of such documents which the accountant keeps as his file record will normally belong to him, regardless of whether he is acting as principal or agent.

Ownership of the accountant's copies of correspondence and other documents passing between him and parties other than the client will depend upon whether he was acting as principal or agent. If he was acting as principal, the documents are likely to belong to him, but if he was acting as agent they will belong to the client.

Ownership of notes of meetings, telephone calls and internal discussions will also depend upon whether the accountant was acting as principal or agent: the rule just stated applies.

Ownership of draft documents and of schedules and other similar working papers will also usually depend upon whether the accountant acted as principal or agent. Here, however, the purpose for which the documents were prepared will on occasion be important. In particular, if the engagement was to provide accountancy assistance, care will need to be taken to assess the extent of the product the client was entitled to expect: was it only to provide completed records or financial statements, or to provide the supporting workings and drafts? In principle, whatever the client was entitled to expect as product will belong to the client.

Also relevant in the accountancy context are the provisions of Companies Act 1985, s221, setting out what accounting records a company is required to keep. Where the accountant is producing documents falling within s221's definition of accounting records,[3] it will be assumed that he is doing so for the company's benefit, and the company will therefore be the owner of them.

Special rules apply where accountants accept appointments regulated by the Insolvency Act 1986.[4]

4.3   Lien

Ordinarily, in so far as documents belong to the client, he has a right to their return. Where, however, the client owes fees, the accountant may sometimes have the benefit of a lien – a right to retain documents which belong to the client until the fees are paid.[5] There are a number of restrictions which may mean that a lien does not exist or cannot be enforced, and these need to be considered carefully before any attempt is made to enforce a lien.

4.3.1   Restrictions on liens

- No lien arises unless the documents are in the accountant's possession for the purposes of the work for which the fees are unpaid. If, for example, a client sought delivery of correspondence with the Inland Revenue relating to his tax affairs and the only bills outstanding related to some other work (for example, assistance with an acquisition), a lien could not be enforced over the tax correspondence.
- A lien may not be exercised over documents which belong to a third party, rather than to the client. For these purposes, 'client' is defined

---

[3]As to which see 4.3.2 below.

[4]These are outside the scope of this book.

[5]See generally paras 19–35 of ICAEW Statement 1.3.2.

narrowly: as the person or entity from whom the fees are legally due. Documents belonging to someone else, however closely related to the client, cannot be made subject to a lien. So, for example, a lien will not arise over documents owned by a client's husband or wife, or by the parent or subsidiary company of a corporate client.

- In the case of corporate clients, no lien can exist over documents which are by law required to be kept at the company's registered office or at some other location, or to be available for inspection. Thus, a lien cannot normally be exercised over a client's register of shareholders or directors' minute books, or over accounting records required to be kept by Companies Act 1985, s221. This was confirmed by the case of *DTC (CNC) Ltd* v *Gary Sargeant & Co.*[6] There, a firm of accountants, which was owed fees of some £4,715, sought to exercise a lien over various accounting documents in its possession. The Court held that these all amounted to 'accounting records' within the meaning of s221 and that as the section prescribed that such records had to be open to inspection by the company's officers no lien could be exercised over them.

- A lien will be overridden where an administrator, liquidator or provisional liquidator has been appointed and they require the handing over of documents pursuant to their statutory powers.[7] There is a limited exception for 'documents which give a title to property and are held as such',[8] but this is seldom likely to be of practical relevance to the accountancy profession.

- The rules just noted in relation to administrators, liquidators and provisional liquidators apply equally in the event of the client's bankruptcy. Hence a lien cannot normally be relied upon as against the Official Receiver or trustee in bankruptcy.[9]

4.3.2 The lien and corporate clients

The effectiveness of the lien as regards corporate clients has been weakened by the decision in the *DTC (CNC)* case.[10] There, the documents

---

[6][1996] 1 BCLC 529.

[7]Insolvency Act 1986, s246(2). As to the statutory powers of administrators, liquidators and provisional liquidators to obtain documents and other assistance, see 5E below.

[8]Section 246(3).

[9]Insolvency Act 1986, s349.

[10]See above.

in issue included sales and purchase invoices, cheque books, paying-in books and bank statements, all of which were held to be 'accounting records' within the meaning of Companies Act 1985, s221. Whether this interpretation of the section was correct is open to debate. Section 221(1) provides as follows:

> 'Every company shall keep accounting records which are sufficient to show and explain the company's transactions and are such as to:
>
> (a) disclose with reasonable accuracy, at any time, the financial position of the company at that time, and
>
> (b) enable the directors to ensure that any balance sheet and profit and loss account prepared under this Part complies with the requirements of this Act.'

Sections 221(2) and 221(3) go on to provide what the accounting records should 'contain', which rather implies that the records in question are something that the company should itself create with a view to recording information appearing in source documentation such as invoices, cheque books or bank statements. However, given the decision in the *DTC (CNC)* case and the view of the judge in that case that 'the potential ambit of accounting records falling within the meaning of s221 of the 1985 Act is very wide indeed', accountants are unlikely now to want to try to exercise a lien as regards documents of this nature unless they have a very significant appetite for litigation.[11]

4.3.3 Other practicalities

While in theory a lien provides an accountant with a significant weapon with which to persuade clients to settle outstanding bills, its availability in practice is, as we have seen, hedged about with restrictions. For this reason the ICAEW suggests that legal advice should be sought before exercising a lien in all but the most straightforward of cases.[12] It also wisely warns that the nuisance value of a lien 'is likely to promote ill-will not only between the parties, but also towards the profession as a whole'.[13]

---

[11] ICAEW Statement 1.3.2, para 25 also refers to the restrictions imposed on the ambit of 'accounting records' by the qualifying words which appear in s221(1) itself. In most instances, however, it will be impossible to give practical application to those qualifying words, and no attempt was made to do so in the *DTC (CNC)* case.

[12] Ibid., para 35.

[13] Ibid., para 33.

For these various reasons, any attempt to exercise a lien needs to be approached with caution. Attempts should always be made to ascertain what lies behind the client's failure to pay and, if there is a genuine dispute, to try to resolve it.[14] Various mechanisms are available for this purpose, such as the ICAEW's fee arbitration service. In cases where the client has a real and immediate need for the documents, it may be possible to take the temperature out of the situation (and perhaps in the long run retain the client) if agreement is reached that the documents will be handed over if the client pays the amount of the disputed fee to a neutral third party to hold on suitable terms pending resolution of the dispute.

4.4 Minimising the risks arising from disclosure of working papers

Working papers, even those owned by the firm, may in certain circumstances have to be disclosed either to the client or to a third party. This is most likely to occur when:

(i) the client wishes access to be given to a third party for the purpose of performing due diligence in relation to a potential transaction;[15]

(ii) disclosure is required by an investigator with statutory powers;[16] or

(iii) disclosure is required for the purposes of actual or threatened litigation, including criminal or disciplinary proceedings.[17]

Disclosure, particularly in the second and third of these situations, inevitably risks opening up the work recorded to critical scrutiny. Most will be at stake when disclosure is given in connection with a negligence claim, but in all cases the firm's work is on show and the information revealed can be central to the outcome of the transaction, claim or investigation in connection with which access is given. The possibility of adverse publicity may also arise.

In a negligence claim the importance of the working papers lies in the fact that they provide (or should provide) a contemporaneous written record of the information available to the accountant, the work performed and the assumptions on which that work was based. If a

---

[14]So far as ICAEW members are concerned, this is required by para 3.2 of Statement 1.210 ('fees').

[15]This is discussed more fully in Chapter 3.

[16]See Chapter 5.

[17]See Chapters 5G, 9 and 10.

claim reaches Court, the account of events revealed by the documents is likely to carry considerable weight with the trial judge, particularly if he is faced with conflicting versions of events from the accountant and the claimant. From this perspective a well-compiled set of working papers can be helpful. However, if overall the underlying work was defective then the working papers, whether well compiled or not, are likely to reveal that. Worse, they may contain loose ends or unhelpful material, which, while not necessarily indicative of any fundamental failings in the work, can be interpreted that way by a claimant and his advisers.

Three questions arise therefore. First, to what extent does it make sense to create working papers at all? Second, on the basis that at least some working papers will be created, what rules should be followed in the preparation? Third, to what extent does it make sense to keep working papers once the engagement for which they are created is concluded?

The first question is, in most professional contexts, only capable of one answer. The reality is that it is impossible to avoid creating documents and files: no engagement lasting any period of time, be it tax, audit or general business advice, could be conducted without them. They are needed as records of what the client wants and expects, of the information the accountant has obtained, and of professional views and judgements as they develop. An ongoing client relationship could not function unless such matters were recorded.

From a risk management perspective, therefore, attention has to focus on the preparation of working papers and on determining which of them should ultimately be kept and for how long. It is to these issues that we now turn.

4.4.1 Creating working papers

As it is in the audit context that issues regarding the content of working papers most frequently arise, what follows has an inevitable focus on that area. Much of what is said is, however, equally applicable to other areas of work. SAS 230 ('Working Papers') requires auditors to:

- document matters which are important in supporting their report (SAS 230.1);

- record their planning, the nature, timing and extent of the procedures performed, and the conclusions drawn from the audit evidence obtained (SAS 230.2); and

- record their reasoning on all significant matters which require the exercise of judgement, and their conclusions on them (SAS 230.3).

As to how much to record, SAS 230, para 7 states:

> 'The extent of working papers is a matter of professional judgment since it is neither necessary nor practical to document every matter auditors consider. Auditors base their judgment as to the extent of working papers upon what would be necessary to provide an experienced auditor, with no previous connection with the audit, with an understanding of the work performed and the basis of the decisions taken. However, even then, that experienced auditor may only be able to obtain a comprehensive understanding of all aspects of the audit by discussing them with the auditors who prepared them.'

A balance has to be struck. Recording too little risks breaching SAS 230 and means that valuable evidence of what was done and why may not be available if it is needed; but recording too much risks inefficiency and the creation of so much paper that the auditor, almost literally, cannot see the wood for the trees. From a risk management viewpoint both these extremes are to be avoided. In cases of doubt, however, it is probably better to record more rather than less. SAS 230, para 8 wisely reinforces this message where difficult questions of principle or judgement arise, for it is in these areas that the auditor's work may be particularly susceptible to later challenge.

Turning to specifics, the 'rules' outlined below will all help towards minimising the risks associated with any future disclosure of working papers. Training and procedures are required to ensure that these rules are implemented as a matter of routine since it can never be possible to predict with any certainty the files which may have to be disclosed in the future. Moreover, if a high standard of record keeping is adopted generally it becomes a habit. The result is that the standard is more likely to be maintained when staff are under time or other pressures, for it is at these times that the risks may be highest.

Rule 1: Document the scope of the engagement

It is vital that the scope of the work to be performed, the respective duties of client and accountant, and the assumptions and information upon which the work is being based are all recorded. The most appropriate and usual way of recording this information is by means of an engagement letter, which will usually be prepared at an early stage.[18]

It is important to record any changes or developments during the course of the engagement which will affect the scope of the work performed. While best practice is to record such changes in a further engagement

---

[18]See Chapter 2.

letter (since in this way it is easy to confirm client acceptance of the changes), this is not always practical or appropriate, particularly if the changes are relatively minor. However, it is essential that the changes and the client's agreement to them are recorded clearly somewhere. This will minimise the risk of the accountant being wrongly criticised later over, for example, something which it was at first agreed would be done but was then agreed would not be done.

Rule 2: Identify who did what and when

All members of the engagement team should understand that when they create a working paper they should date and initial it. It may seem obvious at the time of an engagement who is involved, what their handwriting looks like and roughly when they performed a particular task; but if the working papers have to be revisited several years later none of this will necessarily any longer be obvious. Without the information, it may be difficult to obtain full benefit from the papers that are available.

It also helps to indicate (assuming it is not otherwise obvious) the source and date of receipt of documents provided by clients or other parties. All members of the engagement team annotating these documents, or adding material to previously created working papers, should also initial and date their additions.

Rule 3: Record all client and third party discussions

It is not easy after an interval of months or years to recall what was said by specific individuals on particular dates. In an engagement involving considerable discussion with the same individuals over a number of days or weeks this problem is compounded. Moreover, a person's memory may not only be clouded by the passage of time, it may also be affected by the exigencies of the situation in which he later finds himself. It is not surprising therefore that witnesses on opposing sides in litigation, or with different interests to serve in an investigation, may have different recollections of the same important events and conversations.

For this reason, the importance of keeping notes of meetings and telephone conversations with clients and other parties cannot be over-stressed. There is no need, save perhaps in the most formal or difficult of circumstances, for anything approaching a verbatim record of the discussion, but all matters of substance dealt with should be summarised. In particular, all significant information received during the discussion, and the source of it, should be recorded together with all advice given by the accountant. The note should record the date of the discussion, the parties to it (or attendees at the meeting), and the identity of the maker of the note. Notes taken by a junior member of staff should be reviewed by someone of sufficient seniority to assess whether all the relevant issues have been covered clearly.

At times the client also takes a note of a meeting. If a copy of this is provided at the time, it is sensible to check that it accurately reflects what took place. If there are differences which could lead to misunderstandings, these should be cleared up with the client (and a further note made reflecting this) sooner rather than later.

Rule 4: Take care over the content

It is self-evident that working papers should accurately reflect the information considered by the engagement team and the various issues arising. What is not always so evident is the need to exclude the irrelevant and the frivolous. Examples of this which we have seen include:

- gratuitously derogatory remarks about the client and its employees, including unprovable speculation about individuals' honesty, parentage or competence;[19]

- gratuitously derogatory remarks about other members of the engagement team or the firm;[20]

- doodles of hedgehogs, naked anatomy and (most alarmingly) a smoking gun.

All of the above are best avoided.

Rule 5: Document conclusions and the resolution of loose ends

It is important that where issues and concerns have been raised in working papers there is evidence of them being considered and resolved at the appropriate level. If, for example, the papers raise a concern but there is no record of any response, the impression will be given that the issue was overlooked, when in fact there may have been a good reason why no further action was taken. Similarly, where a problem is resolved through additional work or as a result of discussions with the client, a note should be made. This will avoid the risk that years later the accountant simply cannot recall how a particular matter was sorted out.

---

[19]So, for example, it was recorded of the clients' directors attending a tricky audit clearance meeting: 'Mr X was perfectly helpful and charming, as I had been led to expect. Mr Y sat and grinned like an imbecile throughout'.

[20]As when one individual recorded in writing of a colleague: 'This guy talks a load of horse **** '.

A bare recollection that ultimately something was not a problem, without being able to remember why, is unlikely to prove helpful.

Care should particularly be taken to record the resolution of difficult issues of principle or judgement, including the important steps in the reasoning process. This applies especially where a decision is taken which is for some reason unusual, such as a departure from auditing standards or guidance or the firm's internal manual.

Rule 6: Exercise care over the release of drafts

All draft reports and other documents sent to the client for consideration should be clearly marked as such. In appropriate cases it may be desirable to indicate that the client should not rely in any way on what has been released until there has been further discussion or consideration of the issues involved.

Rule 7: Check the files are in good order at the end of the engagement

A messy, disordered file is likely to leave a poor impression if it has to be examined at a later date. It is obviously best to build files logically from the outset, but at the end of the engagement a check should be made to ensure that this has occurred. A review of this sort also provides the opportunity to remove extraneous material from the file and to ensure that major issues are properly recorded as having been resolved. If loose ends are identified a note can be made to record how they were dealt with, but the note should be dated so as to avoid creating the misleading impression that it was prepared at an earlier stage. (If by the end of the engagement it is clear that something has gone wrong and that a negligence claim or other investigation may ensue, special rules apply: these are dealt with in **Chapter 8**.

Thereafter, the files should be kept intact for so long as the firm's document retention policy requires. The temptation to raid files later for material that may be relevant to another engagement should be resisted. Information of this sort should be copied, and the original papers left in place. To act otherwise risks the suggestion being made later, when memories of the removal of papers have faded, that particular issues were never covered or particular steps were not completed when the work was originally done.

4.4.2 Documents other than working papers

Many firms provide manuals or other internal guidance for staff with a view to trying to ensure that work is done to a high standard and in a uniform manner. It is also common pᵣ̶   ̶ ̶ ̶ ̶ ̶ ̶ ̶ ̶ ̶nal meetings or circulate internal publications or newsletters with a view to keeping staff up to date. Initiatives of this sort are themselves valuable risk management tools, but it should be borne in mind that where such internal material is relevant to a negligence claim or other investigation, their disclosure may be sought.

In the light of this some care is needed in the preparation of such material. Preparers of manuals and other guidance need to have an eye on what is realistic and workable. If a manual is pitched at the level of best (but not always attainable) practice, that fact should be made clear. It can equally be made clear that staff should be trying to implement this best practice where possible. Similarly, care is needed in the use of words such as 'must' or 'ought': they are best used only in relation to the major steps or procedures which the firm absolutely requires to be performed. Where there is an element of discretion, it is preferable to make this clear.

One further area in which a degree of caution needs to be exercised is in staff appraisal and similar records. These too are sometimes requested in the context of negligence claims or other investigations. While assessments of individuals' strengths and weaknesses need to be made frankly, there is a risk in recording weaknesses in a way which is linked too specifically to the conduct of particular engagements.

4.4.3   The role of training and procedures

Training and procedures are required to ensure that staff are aware of and implement rules of the nature outlined above. This should form part of the firm's overall training and procedures in relation to quality control.

At the engagement level, staff (and particularly junior staff) may benefit from further guidance on what type of information needs to be recorded for a particular job. If care is taken at the planning stage to define and explain the issues, a thinner, higher quality file may result. Without adequate training, supplemented by guidance of this sort, staff may fall into the trap of believing that the best and safest course is to record everything. This is liable to be both more risky and less cost-efficient.

Many firms are now actively taking steps to reduce the number of working papers which are created. Policies are specified detailing the documentation that should be created, and staff are discouraged from generating papers that go beyond this. Some issues may be discussed with senior staff but not (at least initially) recorded in writing. One advantage of this is that the increase in face to face communication between junior and senior staff may reduce the number of claims which result from lack of effective communication within the team. That said, the resolution of important issues always needs to be recorded.

4.5 Retention of working papers

While it is clear from **4.4** that a good set of working papers can sometimes be helpful in clarifying or confirming particular points, it is also clear that if something really has gone wrong the working papers are likely to reveal that all too clearly. Not surprisingly therefore, firms start to wonder whether retaining papers is a good idea. Why should they pay the storage costs involved if documents may ultimately prove as likely to damage as to help them?

A number of factors are relevant in an enquiry of this sort. First, it plainly does not make sense to dispose of documents for which there may in the future be a real and practical need. It is assumed for these purposes that what is being discussed are files for which no obvious future need can be identified. Prime candidates in this respect are old audit files from which any material likely to be relevant in the future has been copied forward.

Second, there may be legal or professional reasons why papers have to be retained whether it seems likely that they will be needed or not. We begin by looking at the legal position.

4.5.1 Legal factors

An accountant should not destroy papers belonging to a client or third party unless authorised to do so. To do otherwise would amount to the tort of conversion. As a practical matter, where documents are of no intrinsic importance and have been held for many years, it may be arguable that the consent of the owner to their destruction can be implied. However, the safer course, particularly if the conditions just mentioned are not fulfilled, is either to seek consent to the destruction of the papers or simply to return the documents to their owner.

Examples of documents owned by the client will include correspondence with the Inland Revenue in relation to tax compliance,[21] and the 'accounting records' which a corporate client is obliged to keep by virtue

---

[21] Accountants Digest 205 ('Business Documents–Management and Retention') recommends that tax papers, including correspondence, be returned to the client after a period of seven years. This period was no doubt selected with an eye on the applicable limitation periods for negligence claims, as to which see Chapter 11.

of Companies Act 1985, s221. In this latter connection it should be noted that s222(5) requires that the 'accounting records' of a private company be preserved for a minimum period of three years and those of a public company for six years. By s222(6) any officer of the company failing to take all reasonable steps to secure compliance with this requirement or intentionally causing the destruction of records within the minimum periods specified is guilty of an offence. An auditor is likely to be regarded as an officer of the company for these purposes.

As to documents owned by the accountant, there is no general legal obligation that professional working papers should be preserved. Specific obligations of preservation will, however, arise if the documents may be relevant to civil litigation or are required in connection with various forms of pending investigation. These obligations are explained in **Chapters 5, 9** and **10**. Failure to comply with them can attract potentially severe sanctions. The accountant's professional obligations must also be considered.

4.5.2 Professional obligations

In the audit sphere, SAS 230.4 states that auditors 'should adopt appropriate procedures for maintaining the confidentiality and safe custody of working papers'. SAS 230, para 17 continues:

'There are no specific statutory requirements regarding the period of retention of audit working papers. Auditors exercise judgment to determine the appropriate period of retention bearing in mind possible needs of their client, for example that audited information may need to be included in a prospectus at some future date, and their own needs, including any regulatory requirements. Prior to their destruction, auditors consider whether there is likely to be a need to refer to them again.'

The key point to be drawn from this is that a blanket policy of destroying audit working papers after a relatively short period without consideration of the potential needs of particular clients would be likely to fall foul of SAS 230. Moreover, the SAS suggests that judgement needs to be exercised prior to final destruction even if the firm's policy involves destruction after a relatively lengthy period.

Although not mandatory, the provisions of SAS 230 will provide a benchmark for determining document retention policies in other practice areas. In particular, procedures need to be devised which ensure that documents due for destruction genuinely are no longer likely to be needed for any reason.

4.5.3 Determining a retention policy

It will be apparent from what has been said so far that while SAS 230 can perhaps be regarded as setting a minimum threshold for document retention across all practice areas, different considerations will apply to different areas. For tax compliance work, for example, the determining factor will be the client's ownership of the documents. There, a practical policy, as recommended by Accountants Digest 205,[22] is to return the papers to the client after seven years (when applicable limitation periods are likely to have expired). In the case of audit work, however, considerations of this sort do not apply. Would it therefore make sense to retain audit working papers for only two or three years provided always that the specific requirements of SAS 230 were observed?

The principal reason for keeping audit working papers for many years where there is no other obvious need to do so is to have them available in the event that a negligence claim should arise. Typically, therefore, document retention policies are linked to the primary limitation periods within which such claims can be brought. Given that disclosure of working papers to those pursuing negligence claims is seldom likely to be other than a mixed blessing so far as the accountant is concerned, there is an argument that it is beneficial to destroy working papers as early as possible so that if a claim does later materialise there will no longer be anything to disclose.[23]

While this is an area in which judgements may reasonably differ, our view is that such a policy would be unattractive. Two factors in particular are relevant. First, save in the most speculative type of case, a claimant is unlikely to be deflected from pursuing its claim by the fact that working papers no longer exist. Indeed, the absence of working papers is likely to give the claimant and its advisers considerably greater scope for creativity in framing allegations of negligence. These in turn will be that much harder to meet because the basic information as to what was done and known about at the time of the audit will simply not be recorded.

Second, explaining and justifying such a document disposal policy to a court would not be easy. The obligations to give disclosure of documents in civil litigation require litigants to state what has become of relevant documents which they no longer have in their possession.

---

[22]See previous footnote.

[23]Clearly this could only be done subject to the legal and other restrictions already mentioned.

It should also be borne in mind that being able to demonstrate who did or did not see or know about particular issues or documents can be of crucial importance to individuals caught up in disciplinary proceedings, where liability is personal to the accountant concerned. Working papers may also provide useful mitigation, by setting a context in which a particular failing becomes more readily explainable.

In some instances, firms have a policy of selective destruction of papers at the end of an audit engagement. The usual example is review notes prepared by the supervisor, manager and others. The reason normally given for this is that review notes might be misread or misinterpreted at a later date, and that if review points give rise to a need for more work to be performed, it is better for that work to be recorded separately in the working papers.

SAS 230, para 14 includes the following:

'A written record of points raised during the review of working papers need not be retained providing the working papers demonstrate evidence of the extent of the review process and are updated to record the resolution of any significant matters noted.'

The provisos in the passage just quoted are important, and the first of them is not free from difficulty. There is no doubt that the review notes themselves will provide the best evidence of 'the extent of the review process', and it is not clear what other evidence might exist in the working papers to demonstrate this. That said, a policy of destroying only review notes does not suffer from the two main difficulties identified above in relation to a blanket destruction policy.

Another approach being increasingly adopted is for firms to identify standard documents which will provide evidence of the essentials of the audit work performed. These will be retained at the end of the audit whilst other more peripheral documents are destroyed. Documents to be retained would be designed to meet the following minimum requirements:

- to show that the work has been properly planned and that the plan has been carried through;

- to demonstrate that relevant professional standards and statutory requirements have been fulfilled; and

- to give support for the conclusions reached by providing evidence both of the significant judgements that have been made and of the proper review by senior staff of the work of juniors.

Introduction of such a policy is only likely to be practical where staff are using standardised or computerised record keeping. It is also subject to a number of potential dangers, including in particular the risk that the right information (and in particular the information needed to help defend a negligence claim) is not available when required. Considerable care is needed when designing and implementing systems of this sort. They are only likely to be workable in a large-firm environment.

Subject to the implementation of specific policies limiting the number or type of documents to be kept, a document retention policy in relation to audit working papers is in our view best linked to the primary limitation periods within which negligence claims may be brought. Although there are exceptions, for most practical purposes a negligence claim in relation to audit work will need to be brought within six years of completion of the audit in question. It should be borne in mind, though, that claims issued on the last day of the limitation period do not have to be served for another four months (and may in limited circumstances be renewed for a further period before service). A minimum retention period for audit working papers is thus at least six years and four months after completion of the engagement, but for reasons of practicality and simplicity seven years is perhaps the most realistic period.[24]

Seven years is also likely to be a realistic retention period in relation to many other practice areas. In all cases, however, an eye needs to be kept on the issues of likely future needs for the documents and other considerations such as client or third party ownership. Further specific guidance in particular practice areas such as taxation, trusts and company registrarship can be found in Accountants Digest 205.

4.5.4   Transfer of paper records to other storage media

It is not uncommon for documents to be transferred from paper to microfilm or CD ROM for storage, perhaps after the paper records have been retained for a limited period. This enables the records to be kept for a long number of years at relatively low cost. Before implementing such a process, however, it needs to be borne in mind that if the contents of the papers later need to be used as evidence in Court, it will be necessary to show that the non-paper records are a true copy of the original. With this in mind:

(1) Details should be kept of who performed the transfer and when, together with their confirmation that the contents were fully and accurately transferred.

---

[24]Accountants Digest 205 recommends six years, but this overlooks the ability to hold off serving a claim issued right at the end of the limitation period. Such a practice was surprisingly common in the past, and while the new Civil Procedure Rules may reduce the scope for it to happen in the future it is unlikely to cease entirely.

(2) Care is needed to ensure both that the medium to which the records are transferred is for practical purposes not capable of being tampered with and that access to the stored data is safeguarded. If future access to the data may well be required (for example, because the files contain relatively recent information which may be relevant to future engagements) it may be desirable in the case of storage media such as CD ROM to create two copies, one for secure storage and the other to be available for staff access.

(3) It perhaps hardly need be added that the hardware necessary to obtain access to the stored data should be retained for as long as the data itself is retained.

4.5.5   Access to stored files

The points just made in relation to access to data held on other storage media apply equally in the case of paper records. Care is needed to ensure that access is sensibly controlled and that a record is always made of anyone borrowing a file for any reason. That way, the chances of the files being available if they are needed later are much improved.

5 Powers of third party access

The accountant is likely to be a first port of call for important and reliable financial information in any investigation into a client's affairs. We have already seen the basic rule that information which is confidential to a client should not be disclosed without the client's prior consent.[1] In the situations that are envisaged in this Chapter, such as suspected fraud, insolvency and civil litigation, the client may well not consent. The risk to the accountant of volunteering assistance to a third party is thus potentially great. However, in these instances, particular duties and obligations may be imposed on the accountant by statute or by the court which compel disclosure of information and therefore override the basic rule, provided they are properly discharged.

The relevant statutes confer wide-ranging powers on various government bodies and on liquidators to assist them in carrying out investigations into the affairs of a company or individuals and other office holders. These include, for example, powers to requisition documents. 'Document' is often specifically defined in the relevant statutes. The definitions are not identical. However, the term generally includes information in any form. For example, e-mails, microfilm and material stored on disk will all be caught. In some cases, there is power to require electronic information to be provided in legible form where it is not currently in such form. This could potentially be very costly, for example if it required retrieval of data from outdated systems.

In some instances, there are also express powers to require the accountant to attend and answer questions, possibly on oath. Often the answers will be transcribed.

The auditor is usually regarded as an officer of the company for the purposes of these powers. In some instances, there are express additional duties imposed on the auditor as a result. It is important also to note that these provisions may sometimes apply to past as well as present auditors of the company.

---

[1] See Chapter 1.

The powers of different third parties vary in their scope and in the specific mechanics for exercising them, depending on the particular statutory framework in each case. For example, in some instances a Court Order is required and in others not. Usually, reasonable notice of exercise of these powers will be given to the accountant as a professional advisor. However, the possibility of a dawn raid cannot be ruled out.

This Chapter covers access by the following:

A.   The Serious Fraud Office.

B.   The police.

C.   The Inland Revenue.

D.   HM Customs and Excise.

E.   Insolvency Act office-holders.

F.   Regulators.

It also covers:

G.   Witness summons and non-party discovery.

5A   Serious Fraud Office ('SFO')

5A.1   Background

In 1986 the Roskill Report was published following consideration by the Roskill enquiry as to the ways in which the system for prosecution of complex and serious fraud cases could be improved. One of the report's main recommendations was that the investigation and prosecution of serious fraud should be undertaken by one body. The Criminal Justice Act 1987 therefore made provision for the establishment of the Serious Fraud Office for England, Wales and Northern Ireland, and this came about in April 1988. The stated aim of the SFO is 'to investigate and prosecute serious fraud and so deter fraud and maintain confidence in the probity of business and financial services in the United Kingdom'.

The objective of the SFO is to investigate any suspected offence which appears to the Director of the SFO on reasonable grounds to involve serious or complex fraud (CJA 1987, s1(3)). Prosecution may follow, also conducted by the SFO. These powers are vested in the Director of the SFO, but may be exercised in conjunction with any 'proper person'. In practice, the powers that we are most concerned with in this Chapter will be exercised by a lawyer or accountant or, less frequently, by a police officer working for the SFO. These powers are not, however, exercisable by the police working alone.[2]

As we will see, these are powers of compulsion. As such, they override the duty of confidentiality which ordinarily prohibits the accountant from disclosing matters relating to a client's affairs without the client's prior consent.

Somewhat surprisingly perhaps, 'fraud' is not a term defined in English criminal law. There are, however, a large number of offences (e.g., false accounting, fraudulent trading, conspiracy to defraud and theft), which may form the basis for a charge of fraud.

In addition, there is no definition of 'serious and complex fraud' in CJA 1987. However, in deciding whether to take on a case, the SFO will have regard to certain factors, for example the size of the case (normally at least £1 million in value) and whether legal and accounting skills are needed as well as investigative skills.

---

[2]For a description of the separate powers of the police, see 6B below.

5A.2   SFO powers

The key powers of the SFO that might affect the accountant are contained in CJA 1987, s2. These are exercisable whenever the Director believes that there is good reason to do so for the purposes of investigating the affairs of any person (including a company). As that would suggest, the Director has a very broad discretion in choosing whether – and if so when – to exercise these powers, which in practice makes any decision extremely difficult to challenge.

The powers are formally exercised by notice in writing. This is generally referred to as a 'Section 2 notice'. The form and content of the notice is looked at in detail below, where an example is also set out.[3]

The relevant powers are as follows:

- **The power to require production of information** (CJA 1987, s2(2)): Any person whom the Director has reason to believe has information relevant to any aspect of the investigation may be required to answer questions or 'otherwise furnish information'. They can be required to do so either immediately ('forthwith') or at a specified time and place.

- **The power to require production of documents** (CJA 1987, s2(3)): Any person may be required to produce specified documents, or documents of a specified description, which appear to the Director to relate to any matter relevant to the investigation. Again, they can be required to do so immediately or at a specified time and place. Where documents are no longer held, there is also the power to require the person to state where the documents are, to the best of his knowledge and belief (s2(3)(b)). The Director then has the power to take copies of (but not to take away originals), or extracts from, any documents that are produced, and to require the producer to provide an explanation of any of them (s2(3)(a)). 'Document' is widely defined to include information recorded in any form.

- **The power to obtain a search warrant** (CJA 1987, s2(4) and (5)): In limited circumstances, a warrant may be obtained by the SFO from the Court. This applies where there is failure to comply with a Section 2 notice, where it is not practicable to serve a Section 2 notice, or where to do so might seriously prejudice the investigation (e.g., because there is reason to believe that the documents would be destroyed). The warrant will be exercised by a constable, wherever practicable accompanied by an appropriate person – usually a member

---

[3]See p 108.

of the SFO. The premises specified in the notice may be entered using reasonable force and searched. The warrant authorises the constable to take possession of the documents specified, or to take steps necessary for their preservation. In practice, it is unlikely that these powers will be exercised against an accountancy firm in the ordinary course of events. It should be borne in mind, however, that they are specifically exercisable in instances where there is a failure to comply with a Section 2 notice.

5A.3 Risks to the firm

It is important to be aware of the risks to the firm which potentially arise whenever Section 2 powers are exercised against an accountant. These include:

- First, although the SFO are likely to be investigating the accountant's client and not the accountant, the reality is that in many fraud trials the defendant will argue that he placed reliance upon the work of his professional adviser as a key plank in the defence. The accountant's work will therefore be examined in detail by the Court at trial in considering this defence. An accountant whose work is at the centre of the proceedings may well feel 'on trial' as that work is put under the microscope and there is inevitably a corresponding risk that a civil claim against the firm will follow. Any claim would most likely be in negligence or in contract with a view to recovering loss suffered as a result of the fraud.

- Second, although, as we have seen, these are powers of compulsion, care must still be taken to ensure that information confidential to a client is not wrongfully disclosed. Examples include mistaking the scope of the notice or handing over documents/information belonging to another client (not covered by the notice), which have been placed on the wrong files. This, too, could potentially lead to claims against the firm.

These key factors are always to be borne in mind when dealing with the SFO. Cooperation tempered with circumspection is to be advised therefore.

5A.4 Service of the notice

CJA 1987 makes no provision for the mechanics of serving the Section 2 notice. It does not specify, for example, that the Section 2 notice has to be served and exercised during normal business hours, or upon whom it may validly be served. If the power is intended to be exercised 'forthwith', then the possibility of the SFO arriving at the accountant's office without warning cannot be ruled out. It is unlikely, however, that a Section 2 notice will be served 'cold' on a professional adviser. An initial approach will be made by the SFO, for example, to the partner in charge of the matter or client, with a request for assistance.

In view of the duties of confidentiality owed by the accountant to the client, the risk of volunteering information to the SFO (as with any other regulating authority) is significant. For the accountant's protection it is therefore considered advisable to insist on a Section 2 notice being served, addressed to an individual within the firm (e.g., the engagement partner). This is likely to be done either by post or in person.

In general, the SFO may approach the partner first for a general discussion as to the role undertaken in relation to the client's affairs and to identify what documents may be held. This discussion should take place pursuant to a Section 2 notice. A further Section 2 notice may then be served requiring production of documents. Once the documents have been reviewed, the SFO will move on to seeing individual witnesses who worked on the files and will ask detailed questions. Separate Section 2 notices addressed to each individual should be served requiring attendance for interview – the notice will probably also require production of the files so that reference can be made to their contents as necessary during the interview. There is no limit to the number of Section 2 notices that can be served.

The SFO are prepared to be somewhat flexible. Therefore, the ideal is to set up a dialogue with them from the outset, aiming for cooperation whilst dealing on your own terms as far as possible.

5A.5   Form of the Section 2 notice

A specimen Section 2 notice is set out below.

SPECIMEN SECTION 2 NOTICE

Andrew Partner Esq
Squeaky & Clean
Pristine Buildings
Anytown SF0 4HQ

**Criminal Justice Act 1987
Section 2**

NOTICE REQUIRING ATTENDANCE TO ANSWER QUESTIONS, FURNISH INFORMATION AND PRODUCE DOCUMENTS

PERSONS UNDER INVESTIGATION: HIDE IT PLC; ITS SUBSIDIARIES
AND RELATED COMPANIES; GEOFFREY B HIDDEN

1. The Director of the Serious Fraud Office has decided to investigate suspected offences which appear to her to involve serious or complex fraud.

2. I am a member of the Serious Fraud Office who has been authorised by the Director of the Serious Fraud Office to exercise on her behalf all the powers conferred by Section 2 of the CJA 1987 ('the Act').

3. There appears to me for the purposes of the investigation referred to at 1 above, to be good reason to exercise the powers conferred by Section 2 (2) and (3) of the Act for the purpose of investigating the affairs of the persons under investigation.

I have reason to believe that you have relevant information about the affairs of the persons under investigation, and therefore I require you to answer questions or otherwise furnish information to me with respect to matters relevant to the investigation at 1 Sleuth's Corner, Anytown, SF0 0PQ on Tuesday 3 October 2000 at 9.30 am. I also require you to produce to me at the same place, on the same date and at the same time the following documents which appear to me to relate to matters relevant to the investigation:

All correspondence, financial records, books, papers, files including all audit, corporate finance, tax and other files and the contents thereof including any internal memoranda, records and reports, which have been created by Squeaky & Clean or which have been created by others which are in your custody or under your control from 1 May 1993 to date relating to the affairs of Hide It plc and its subsidiaries and related companies including Hide It Here plc, Hide It There plc and Hide It Under the Carpet Limited; and relating to the affairs of Geoffrey B Hidden from 6 April 1994 to date.

. . . .

Signed: A. Fit-Person
A member of the Serious Fraud Office

Dated: 4 September 2000

NOTE: Failure without reasonable excuse to comply with these requirements is a criminal offence. It is also a criminal offence to destroy or otherwise dispose of, or to cause or permit the falsification, concealment, destruction or disposal of documents which you know or suspect are or would be relevant to the investigation.

We will now look at the form of that notice in detail and highlight points to look for when faced with this in practice.

5A.5.1 Addressee

Andrew Partner Esq
Squeaky & Clean
Pristine Buildings
Anytown SF0 4HQ

The notice will generally be served on a specified person at the firm–most probably the client partner in the first instance. Separate notices will be served on members of the engagement team who are to be interviewed.

5A.5.2. Heading

Criminal Justice Act 1987
Section 2

NOTICE REQUIRING ATTENDANCE TO ANSWER QUESTIONS, FURNISH INFORMATION AND PRODUCE DOCUMENTS

This is self explanatory and makes clear the purpose of the document. Also, whilst the Section 2 powers available to the SFO may be exercised individually, in practice they will often be exercised concurrently (as in the example) and a single notice is sufficient for this.

Caution should be exercised before contacting the client. The situation may be very sensitive. The accountant would be ill advised to alert the client to the fact of the investigation if the SFO requests that this is not done – even though they do not have express powers to require this. Depending on the circumstances it may not be possible or practicable to get instructions anyway – for example, if the company is in disarray due to the appointment of insolvency practitioners.

5A.5.3. Persons under investigation

PERSONS UNDER INVESTIGATION: HIDE IT PLC; ITS SUBSIDIARIES AND RELATED COMPANIES; GEOFFREY B HIDDEN

The named entities are those to whom the investigation relates. Careful attention should be paid to this. For example, the specimen refers to *subsidiaries* of Hide It plc. If it did not, documents relating to the affairs of any subsidiary would fall outside the scope of the investigation and production of these would be a breach of the accountant's duty of confidentiality to that subsidiary. In practice, the description of the persons under investigation is likely to be very widely drawn as in the example. However, if documents relating to a subsidiary not named in the notice are sought, then it would be advisable to clarify this with the SFO prior to handing them over. If appropriate, ask the SFO to amend the notice accordingly so that the firm's position is protected.

5A.5.4. Preamble

> 1. The Director of the Serious Fraud Office has decided to investigate suspected offences which appear to her to involve serious or complex fraud.

This is a wide discretion which will not in practice be open to challenge by the recipient of the Section 2 notice. The important thing is that this forms the basis of the SFO's right to exercise the Section 2 powers. The wording should therefore simply be checked to ensure that the powers are purportedly being exercised on the correct basis. If the wording were omitted, for example, it would be appropriate to ask for an explanation as to the basis of the notice.

> 2. I am a member of the Serious Fraud Office who has been authorised by the Director of the Serious Fraud Office to exercise on her behalf all the powers conferred by Section 2 of the CJA 1987 ('the Act').

The Director may exercise the SFO's powers in conjunction with any 'proper person'. Again, this is a discretion and the suitability of the person is very unlikely to be open to challenge. However, it is advisable for the accountant to ask for some identification and check that the person serving the Section 2 notice is who he says he is. If the person is not a member of the SFO, he must have specific authority from the Director (usually in the form of a letter signed by the Director). It is sensible to ask to see the signed authority to verify this and to check that it gives authorisation in respect of the relevant investigation. The name of the Director at any given time will be printed on the SFO's stationery.

> 3. There appears to me for the purposes of the investigation referred to at 1 above, to be good reason to exercise the powers conferred by Section 2 (2) and (3) of the Act for the purpose of investigating the affairs of the persons under investigation.

Again, the question whether there is 'good reason' to exercise these powers is a part of the Director's discretion (exercised by the member of the SFO signing the notice) and is unlikely to be open to challenge by the recipient of the Section 2 notice. The key point to consider is whether the Section 2 notice is seeking disclosure of documents and information which are relevant *for the stated purpose* (i.e., an investigation into the affairs of the companies/persons named in the section of the notice headed 'Persons under Investigation'). If this appears not to be the case, it is advisable to seek clarification from the SFO. An open dialogue with the SFO can again generally assist here in establishing as much information as possible about the investigation.

5A.5.5. Main body of the notice

> I have reason to believe that you have relevant information about the affairs of the persons under investigation, and therefore I require you to answer questions or otherwise furnish information to me with respect to matters relevant to the investigation at 1 Sleuth's Corner, Anytown, SF0 0PQ on Tuesday 3 October 2000 at 9.30 am.

Detailed guidance on the procedure for and approach to be taken at interviews is given at **5A.6** below.

> I also require you to produce to me at the same place, on the same date and at the same time the following documents which appear to me to relate to matters relevant to the investigation:
>
> All correspondence, financial records, books, papers, files including all audit, corporate finance, tax and other files and the contents thereof including any internal memoranda, records and reports, which have been created by Squeaky & Clean or which have been created by others which are in your custody or under your control from 1 May 1993 to date relating to the affairs of Hide It plc and its subsidiaries and related companies including Hide It Here plc, Hide It There plc and Hide It Under the Carpet Limited; and relating to the affairs of Geoffrey B Hidden from 6 April 1994 to date.

As can be seen, it is not necessary for the Section 2 notice to name individual documents; descriptions of types of files and documents are sufficient. The description given is usually as broad as possible. It should

112

nevertheless be carefully considered. For example, if the Section 2 notice asks for production of 'audit files', disclosure of files other than audit files would be outside the scope of the notice. This would be a breach of confidentiality. Generally, the accountant must check carefully to ensure that only documents and information falling within the scope of the Section 2 notice are being disclosed.

As we have seen, papers in an accountant's files may belong in part to the accountant and in part to the client.[4] However, whereas in other circumstances an accountant may be entitled to remove from the files papers belonging to the firm and retain these, that is not so in the case of disclosure pursuant to a Section 2 notice; if the notice refers to a file, the whole file must be disclosed.

There is one significant exception to this. The SFO expressly has no power to order production of privileged material.[5] For example, a written legal opinion obtained by the accountant as to his firm's position in connection with the engagement may well on the face of it fall within the scope of the Section 2 notice as (in the example) 'papers . . . relating to the affairs of Hide It plc'. However, such documents fall outside the scope of the SFO's powers and need not (and indeed should not) be disclosed. Similarly, in certain limited circumstances the accountant's files may contain documents which are privileged in the hands of the client and these ought not to be disclosed. Such documents remain privileged in the client's hands and such privilege can only be waived by the client.

A further point to highlight is that, whilst they are entitled to inspect the originals, the SFO are only entitled to make copies of the documents. They are not entitled to remove the originals. In practice, this will usually mean that the firm will be obliged to provide copies, the cost of which is unlikely to be recovered.

As we have seen above, the SFO can compel production of documents 'forthwith'. As is more usual, in the example a specified future date and place is given. Hopefully, one might be able to come to a mutually convenient arrangement as to timing. However, on no account should the stipulated time simply be disregarded as inconvenient; ultimately any attempt to rearrange the appointment is against the backdrop of sanctions that exist for failing to comply with the Section 2 notice.

---

[4] See 4.2 above.

[5] Criminal Justice Act 1987, s2(9).

5A.5.6 Signature block and penal notice

> . . . .
>
> Signed: A. Fit-Person
> A member of the Serious Fraud Office
>
> Dated: 4 September 2000

As mentioned above, the accountant is entitled to ask for proof of identity or, where the bearer of the notice is not a member of the SFO, to see the letter of authority from the Director authorising them to carry out the powers on her behalf.

> Note: Failure without reasonable excuse to comply with these requirements is a criminal offence. It is also a criminal offence to falsify, destroy or otherwise dispose of, or to cause or permit the falsification, concealment, destruction or disposal of documents which you know or suspect are or would be relevant to the investigation.

This speaks for itself. Although it is perhaps unlikely that an accountant would fall foul of these penalties in the ordinary course, it is important to be aware that they exist and are the ultimate sanction for failure to comply with a Section 2 notice.[6] The message is clear: on no account should material (other than privileged or irrelevant material, e.g., belonging to another client and wrongly filed) be removed from the files and the working papers must not be tampered with in any way. It is strongly advised that legal advice be obtained if at all possible in advance of making any disclosure, and in any event if in any doubt about how to comply. If the documents are to be disclosed 'forthwith', it may still be possible to ask for the firm's solicitor to be permitted to attend the premises to give assistance 'on the hoof'.

5A.6   Practical pointers for interviews

As we have seen, the SFO has the power to require production of information (CJA 1987, s2(2)): any person whom the Director has reason to believe has information relevant to any aspect of the investigation may be required to answer questions or 'otherwise furnish information'. This

---

[6]See 5A.8 below.

power is also exercised by means of a Section 2 notice. It may be exercised 'forthwith', but for the accountant, in practice this is commonly dealt with by appointment.

We have already mentioned the benefit of building a cooperative dialogue with the SFO. This can also be of assistance in the context of interviews. Hopefully, one might be able to agree, for example, that the interview be held at the accountant's own offices and on an informal basis. If this cannot be agreed, the interview will be formal and will be tape-recorded; this can be an intimidating experience.

Set out below are some points to highlight with regard to interviews:

- The interviewee is not entitled as of right to prior notice of the questions that will be asked. Even a general idea of the areas to be covered may not be provided if the SFO want to obtain the accountant's unhindered recollection of relevant events. One of the benefits of cooperation may be that a better idea of the questions and the areas that are to be covered will be received. Even then, this may be very broad. The interviewee is, of course, entitled to (and indeed urged to) look at the files prior to the interview to refresh the memory.

- The interviewee is entitled to request that they be legally represented at the interview. Although in practice the lawyer will not be able to intervene significantly, they might, for example, object if the questioning were to stray beyond the scope of the investigation or request further time to consider specific questions and revert with answers if, for instance, the witness were to need to look at other documents to refresh his memory. Interviewees invariably find it beneficial to have a lawyer present with them, however, and the lawyer can fulfil a useful monitoring role. They can also provide helpful general guidance on what to expect at the interview and how best to conduct oneself, which can lend much needed confidence.

- If possible, try to negotiate to hold the interview at the firm's office, or perhaps the office of the firm's lawyer; this is less intimidating for the interviewee in comparison to the windowless room in unfamiliar surroundings that the SFO will most likely arrange at their offices. Bear in mind also that the SFO's own offices have the equipment necessary for taping the interview (see below) and for that reason also a different venue may be attractive.

- The interviews can be long. Ensure in advance that there will be breaks for the interviewee for refreshment and try to agree at what intervals these should occur.

- There is no obligation to take an oath at an interview by the SFO. However, those conducting the interview will explain their powers and the penalties for non-compliance.

- The interview may be taped. It is in the accountant's interests to try to negotiate that taping will not take place – but it may not be possible to achieve this. If the interview is taped, a full transcript will be prepared and will be provided to the interviewee for checking and signing. A copy of the tape will be provided on request to allow the interviewee to check the transcript. Both the tape and the transcript are potentially disclosable in civil proceedings. Given that it may be difficult to give the best or most appropriate answer to questions of which no notice has been received when put on the spot, greater protection is likely to be afforded to the accountant if the answers are not recorded prior to making a full witness statement after the interview (see below), when the areas to be covered are more fully understood and there is the benefit of detailed access to the papers. In any event, detailed notes will be made by the SFO at the interview. These will be disclosed to the defendant in the criminal proceedings. If notes are taken by the interviewee or their lawyer, these are also potentially disclosable in any future civil proceedings against the firm if they are merely a record of the discussion.

- After the interview, the interviewee will usually be asked to put a witness statement together. In order to protect the firm's position, if possible this should only be done in response to a formal witness summons[7] requiring the accountant's attendance at trial. Before signature, the statement will have to be agreed/accepted by the SFO in the light of the answers given at the interview. It will form the basis of the accountant's evidence when called to appear as a witness for the prosecution in court at the fraud trial. Cross-examination on that evidence will then follow. The evidence will be transcribed by Court shorthand writers although a written transcript will only be prepared in response to requests by interested parties. If the accountant has any such transcripts in his possession, they are potentially disclosable in any subsequent litigation against the firm. Further cross-examination may then follow on any differences in the answers given at each trial.

- It is strongly advised that the statement be prepared with the help of the firm's lawyer. There is a risk that an initial draft witness statement prepared for the interviewee by the SFO will be couched in black and white terms and will not be in a form that the interviewee would be prepared to sign. Such a draft could potentially be very damaging

---

[7]See 5G.1 below.

to the firm's position. Nevertheless, that draft may be disclosable to the accused in the subsequent fraud prosecution as 'unused material', i.e., material in the hands of the SFO which, though not relied on by the prosecution, has to be provided to the defendant. Preparation of the draft statement with the assistance of the firm's lawyer allows the interviewee the opportunity to present a more balanced account.

- A further important point is that any drafts passing between the interviewee and/or his lawyers and the SFO do not attract legal professional privilege and will therefore also be potentially disclosable in any subsequent civil litigation. Cross-examination of witnesses on the changes between draft statements at a fraud trial is not unknown and may also be damaging to the credibility of the witness. However, intermediate drafts prepared by the lawyer for discussion with the witness and which are not produced to the SFO will attract legal professional privilege.

- In general, care should be taken in any correspondence with the SFO as this may also be disclosable and may be damaging if ill-considered.

5A.7 Gateways: Disclosure by the SFO to third parties

CJA 1987, s3 sets out the circumstances in which the SFO is permitted to pass information received in the course of an investigation through a 'gateway' to other interested parties. Clearly, such onward disclosure potentially exposes the accountant to further risk.

CJA 1987, s3 expressly permits the SFO to enter into agreement not to disclose material that is passed to them. However, this is unlikely to be practicable given that the SFO will have no interest in protecting a witness unless failure to do so would otherwise damage their investigation or prosecution.

Disclosure is permitted, for example, to any government department and to any 'competent authority'. For the accountant, the most important examples are likely be the Official Receiver and the relevant professional regulatory and/or disciplinary bodies. Permitted gateways also include bodies exercising the equivalent functions of the SFO outside the UK. In that context, it is also worth noting that the SFO is expressly empowered to exercise its powers under section 2 in response to a request from an overseas tribunal or other authority and to pass the information so obtained on to that authority overseas. The rationale behind this is to assist in tackling international fraud.

Significantly, liquidators are not included as a 'competent authority' for this purpose and the courts[8] have held that the SFO has no implied power to disclose to a liquidator documents or information obtained pursuant to its section 2 powers in response to an application by the liquidator for production pursuant to Insolvency Act 1986, s236.[9]

5A.8   Possible penalties for failure to comply

It is unlikely that the penalty provisions in CJA 1987 will be invoked against the accountant save in the most unusual circumstances. However, it is important to be aware that these underpin the SFO's powers.

The following constitute a criminal offence punishable as stated:

- Failure without reasonable excuse to comply with any requirement imposed by section 2: liable for imprisonment for up to six months and/or a fine.

- Knowingly or recklessly making a material false or misleading statement: liable for imprisonment if convicted for more serious contraventions for up to two years and/or a fine; for less serious contraventions for up to six months and/or a fine.

- Knowing or suspecting that there is to be an SFO investigation and falsifying, concealing, destroying, or disposing of relevant documents (or causing or permitting this) with the intention of concealing facts: punishable by imprisonment of up to seven years and/or a fine; or where less serious contravention, for up to six months and/or a fine.

Any individual unfortunate enough to fall foul of these provisions is also likely to find themselves subject to disciplinary action.

Put simply: it just isn't worth it!

---

[8]See *Morris* v *Director of Serious Fraud Office* [1993] Ch 372. The judgment goes on to say that where an office-holder seeks an order under the Insolvency Act to compel a statutory body (e.g., the SFO) to produce documents obtained under that body's own powers, those from whom documents are seized or their true owners are in general entitled to an opportunity to object.

[9]See 5E.2 below for a description of the powers of liquidators in this context.

5B   The police

Unlike the Serious Fraud Office, the police have no inherent powers to require production of documents or to compel potential witnesses to answer questions. The statutory provisions dealing with such powers as they do have are numerous and the procedure varies depending upon the circumstances and the type of evidence sought.

5B.1   Production of documents

The relevant provisions insofar as they relate to confidential material held by an accountant relating to a client's affairs appear in the Police and Criminal Evidence Act 1984. These provisions are distinct from the police's general powers of search and seizure. The key aspects are:

- Documents or records which are held on a confidential basis by a person who has created or acquired them in the course of a profession, such as an accountant, are 'special procedure material' as defined (PACE 1984, s14(2)). The procedure to be followed by the police to gain access to it (PACE 1984, s1) is described below.

- There are, however, certain powers of seizure which may apply where the police are lawfully on the accountant's premises, irrespective of the above provisions (PACE 1984, s19).

- Legally privileged material is specifically exempt from search powers and the court will not issue a search warrant in respect of this (PACE 1984, s9(2)(a)). It is also expressly excluded from the seizure powers referred to above (PACE 1984, s19(6)).

- 'Documents' is widely defined and includes, for example, all material in written and electronic form.

5B.2   Procedure for access to special procedure material

The police may request access to papers in the accountant's possession as evidence of an offence. If access is granted, no Court Order will be required. However, as we have already seen, information which is confidential to the client should not be disclosed without the client's consent.[1]

Such consent is perhaps unlikely to be forthcoming in the circumstances, in which case the police have to apply to a circuit judge for a production

[1]See Chapter 1.

order. (The judge also has power to issue a search warrant, but only in exceptional circumstances.) The conditions that have to be satisfied to obtain the order are onerous. The judge has to be satisfied, for example, that a serious arrestable offence has been committed, that the material is likely to be of substantial value to the investigation, and that its production is in the public interest. The judge must also be satisfied that other methods of obtaining the evidence have been tried without success and the police should therefore first seek the consent of the accountant as holder of the evidence.

Once the application has been made, the accountant will be served with a notice of the application and the accountant is entitled to be heard on the hearing of the application. The notice should contain a description of all the evidence sought and of the nature of the offence under investigation. The effect of the notice is to 'freeze' the accountant's papers which must not be concealed, destroyed, altered or disposed of until the application has been dealt with and any production order complied with. The defendant in or target of the criminal proceedings has no right to be heard at this application. If the defendant or target is the client, there is no obligation to inform him of the application. It would, however, be unwise for the accountant not to seek to correct or bring to the Court's attention any obvious errors made in the application in order to avoid any suggestion that the order might have been made on the basis of false information.

If the order is made at the hearing, the accountant will be required within a specified period either to produce the material specified in the order to a constable for it to be taken away, or to give a constable access to it. No search of the firm's premises by the police will therefore be necessary (or permitted). Care should be taken when granting access to the papers that the order is strictly complied with in terms of what is produced, to avoid breaches of confidentiality to this, or another, client.

The Court has the power to penalise anyone for failure to comply with a production order. In most instances, this will be by way of fine and/or imprisonment for contempt of court.

5B.3 Powers of seizure

In addition to the powers to obtain an order for production, the police have certain general powers to seize material when they are already lawfully on the premises. If they enter premises with the consent of the occupier, they may then seize anything they find where there are reasonable grounds for suspecting (1) that it is evidence in relation to any offence, and (2) that it is necessary to seize it to prevent it being concealed, lost, destroyed or altered (s19(3)). Therefore, if they visit the firm's offices for whatever reason and are invited to enter, they may then seize papers without the need for a production order – provided the conditions mentioned in s19(3) are satisfied. These powers expressly refer to computerised information and the police can require this to be produced in legible form for removal (s20). The police are obliged on request to provide a record of anything that has been seized (s21(1)).

The police are not entitled to enter the premises under a pretext with a view to looking for such material – to do so would amount to trespass.

It is perhaps unlikely that the conditions required for seizure will be satisfied in the case of papers held by an accountant. If they are, the police are not entitled to remove large numbers of papers wholesale without having considered whether there is reasonable cause to believe that each file may constitute evidence in relation to the offence.

5B.4   Interviews by the police

As mentioned, the police have no inherent powers to compel the accountant to attend and answer questions, unlike the Serious Fraud Office, for example. To preserve client confidentiality, the accountant should only assist the police in their enquiries with the consent of the client or in response to a witness summons compelling attendance to give evidence at the criminal trial.

5C   Inland Revenue

5C.1   The Revenue's powers to obtain information

The Inland Revenue have a formidable array of powers to assist them in obtaining information about taxpayers' affairs and ensuring that they pay the correct amount of tax. The report of the Keith Committee in March 1983[1] was a catalyst for change: the Finance Act 1989, implementing certain of the Keith Committee's proposals, extended the power of the Inspector to require production of documents by a taxpayer or other persons. The provisions apply to income tax, corporation tax (including advance corporation tax) and capital gains tax. As a result of Finance Act 1990, s125 (implementing European Communities Directive 77/799/EEC), the Inspector's powers extend to information relating to income and capital taxes liabilities in other member states of the EU.

5C.2   The Revenue's approach to the conduct of investigations

The Inspector's normal practice is to seek information direct from the taxpayer concerned on a voluntary basis and only if that is unsuccessful to approach a third party. This is consistent with the statement in the Revenue's manual that the normal way of settling an investigation is by negotiation. It is the Revenue's policy to seek a settlement with the taxpayer by means of a formal contract under which, in consideration of the Board of the Inland Revenue relinquishing the right to take proceedings against the taxpayer, the taxpayer agrees to pay lost tax, interest and penalties.

The Revenue have issued a Statement of Practice[2] which summarises how its powers work in relation to accountants' working papers and how the Revenue will use those powers in practice. The Revenue will not call for an accountant's working papers on a routine basis but will normally only do so where they have been unable to satisfy themselves by other means that the accounts or returns of the accountant's client are complete and correct. The Revenue will continue with its general policy of seeking access on a voluntary basis and will only use its formal powers where this is considered absolutely necessary.

---

[1]Report of the Committee on Enforcement Powers of the Revenue Departments. Volumes I (Chapters 1–15) and II (Chapters 16–28) Cmnd Paper 8822.

[2]SP5/90.

5C.3   Voluntary cooperation: points to watch out for

The accountant will generally owe an express or implied duty of confidentiality to the client.[3] The accountant must therefore take care not to respond to the Inspector's enquiries without first obtaining the client's instructions and authority to do so. In addition, where the Inspector requires delivery or production or inspection of documents, the accountant must consider the question of ownership of the documents before complying with the Inspector's request.[4] Apart from taking the client's instructions and considering to whom documents belong, the accountant should consider whether the Inspector is actually entitled to sight of the documents requested or has inadvertently or deliberately framed the request too widely, with the result that other matters not within the scope of the present investigation may come under scrutiny. The accountant should take care to avoid setting unhelpful precedents over the type of documents he is prepared to present to the Inspector.

The Revenue recognise that third parties who are under a duty of confidentiality cannot be expected to comply with anything short of a formal notice. However, provided the accountant offers cooperation, but remains vigilant to keep the investigation within limits, it will not automatically follow that the Inspector will resort to powers of compulsion. The accountant should check to see whether the scope of the Inspector's request can be restricted to information explaining particular entries.

5C.4   The Revenue's powers of compulsion

The various powers of compulsion that can be employed by The Revenue are set out in Taxes Management Act 1970, s20. In summary, those powers are:

- to require any person by notice in writing to deliver up documents containing information relevant to any tax liability of the taxpayer;[5]

- to apply to the Court for an order for production of documents required as evidence, where there are reasonable grounds for suspecting the commission of an offence involving serious fraud in connection with tax;[6]

- to apply to the Court for a warrant to enter and search premises and to seize and remove evidence, where there are reasonable grounds

---

[3]See Chapter 1.

[4]Guidance regarding ownership of documents appears at 4.2 above.

[5]TMA 1970, s20(3).

[6]TMA 1970, s20BA (as inserted by the Finance Act 2000).

for suspecting the commission of an offence involving serious fraud in connection with tax and that evidence of it is to be found on those premises.[7]

5C.5   Protected documents

Three classes of document are excluded from the documents which third parties (including accountants) can be required to produce pursuant to the various powers in TMA 1970, s20:

- documents brought into existence specifically to support the conduct of a pending appeal;[8]

- audit papers;[9]

- relevant communications relating to the giving or obtaining of tax advice;[10]

- where a search warrant is obtained, items subject to legal privilege, as defined.[11]

Two of these classes require further consideration.

'Audit papers' are defined as papers which are the property of an auditor appointed under a statutory provision (e.g., the Companies Act) and which have been prepared by or for the auditor to enable him to perform his duties as auditor. The protection is extended to papers which are the property of an accountant appointed to carry out a non-statutory third party independent audit (e.g., under the terms of a partnership deed).

'Relevant communications' are communications between a tax adviser and his client (or another tax adviser of the client) made for the purposes of giving or obtaining advice about the client's tax affairs. They include not only letters and faxes, but also notes of meetings and telephone conversations.

The protection for both these classes of document can be reduced where the accountant organises accounting, audit and tax compliance work in such a way that it is all recorded in one file. In the case of a company, there may be no clear distinction between pure audit work and work leading to the creation of accounts and tax computations. In certain

---

[7]TMA 1970, s20C.

[8]TMA 1970, s20B(2).

[10]TMA 1970, s20B(9) and (10).

[11]TMA 1970, s20C (4) as substituted by the Finance Act 2000.

cases, business records may be deficient and it could be argued that the accountant's working papers seek to repair those deficiencies and are therefore in effect part of the records of the business.

The Revenue may seek access to information showing how an entry in accounts, returns or other information submitted to the Revenue was arrived at; however, information showing why the entry was arrived at in that way remains protected. The auditor or tax adviser can provide copy documents, with the protected parts blanked out, but the Revenue can request inspection of the originals, when the protected parts can be kept covered up if desired.

'Items subject to legal privilege' are specifically excluded from the Revenue's search and seizure powers.[12] This expression includes communications between a legal adviser and the client made in connection with the giving of legal advice to the client or in contemplation of legal proceedings, in each case where the document is 'in the possession of a person entitled to possession of them'.[13] Where the tax adviser is also a lawyer, therefore, it may be possible to claim legal privilege to protect documents from disclosure in relation to a client's tax affairs where the documents are in the hands of the client. In addition, communications between a legal adviser and an accountant representing his client made in the same specified circumstances are also covered and should not be disclosed.

5C.6   Enquiry into a taxpayer's liability

To enable him to enquire into a taxpayer's tax liability, an Inspector may by notice require persons other than the taxpayer to deliver to him documents which, in his reasonable opinion, contain or may contain information relevant to any tax liability to which the taxpayer is, or may be, or may have been, subject, or to the amount of such liability.[14] These powers are restricted to the production of documents and do not extend to the provision of other particulars or information regarding the taxpayer.

'Taxpayer' includes a company which has ceased to exist or an individual who has died not more than six years prior to the date of the notice.[15]

---

[12]See s20C(4) as substituted by the Finance Act 2000.

[13]Section 20C(4A) as inserted by the Finance Act 2000. The substituted provision caused potential confusion by stating that it extended only to privileged documents in the possession of a barrister, advocate or solicitor. There is a procedure to resolve disputes as to legal privilege – see TMA 1970, Sch 1AA, para 6.

[14]TMA 1970, s20(3).

[15]TMA 1970, s20(6) and s20B(7).

'Document' means anything which records information of any description.[16] A document includes not only letters, memoranda and calculations therefore, but maps, plans, graphs, drawings and photographs, in addition to disks, tapes or other devices from which data can be reproduced, films, negatives, tapes or other devices from which a visual image can be reproduced. The Revenue have powers of access to any computer which produced relevant documents and can require assistance to inspect and check the computer's operation.[17] The accountant should, therefore, take care over electronic communication, which has a tendency to be more informal and less guarded than traditional correspondence.

The conditions governing the issue of a notice requiring delivery of documents are as follows:

- the notice must be authorised by the Board of the Inland Revenue;[18]

- consent must be obtained from a General or Special Commissioner, who must be satisfied that the Inspector is justified in proceeding under these provisions;[19]

- the notice must name the taxpayer with whose liability the Inspector is concerned;[20]

- a copy of the notice must be given to the taxpayer concerned;[21]

- the notice must specify the documents to be supplied;[22]

- the documents must be in the accountant's possession or power;[23]

- the taxpayer must have been given a reasonable opportunity to provide the documents in question;[24]

---

[16]TMA 1970, s20D(3), which refers to Civil Evidence Act 1968, s10, now Civil Evidence Act 1995, s15(1), and also to Finance Act 1988, s127.

[17]FA 1988, s127.

[18]TMA 1970, s20(7).

[19]TMA 1970, s20(7)(a) and (b).

[20]TMA 1970, s20(8); however, a notice may require production of documents relating to a taxpayer or class of taxpayer whose identities are unknown: TMA 1970, s20(8A).

[21]TMA 1970, s20B(1A) however, a copy need not be supplied if the Inspector satisfies a General or Special Commissioner that he has reasonable grounds for suspecting the taxpayer of fraud and the Commissioner so directs.

[22]TMA 1970, s20(8D).

[23]TMA 1970, s20(1)(a).

[24]TMA 1970, s20B(1).

- the notice may not require production of documents or information relating to the conduct of an appeal which is pending;[25]

- the notice must specify a date for compliance, not less than 30 days after the date of the notice;[26]

- the notice may not require documents which are personal records or journalistic material;[27]

- the notice may not be issued more than six years after the date of death of a taxpayer;[28]

- a document need not be delivered if the whole of it originated more than six years before the date of the notice.[29]

Unless the Commissioner directs otherwise, the Inspector is required to provide the accountant with a written summary of his reasons for applying for consent to issue the notice, being satisfied that the assessment or collection of tax would otherwise be prejudiced.

5C.7 Matters to consider in relation to a notice under section 20(3)

The Revenue's manual requires that wherever use of formal procedures is contemplated, the Inspector must first give the accountant a reasonable opportunity to deliver or make available the documents in question (a 'precursor notice').[30] Any subsequent notice under s20(3) should not ask for more than was originally requested informally pursuant to the precursor notice and the accountant should check to ensure that this is so.

On receipt of a notice under s20(3) an accountant should also check that the notice is not invalid because it goes beyond the terms of that provision (for example, in relation to an investigation of an assessment

---

[25]TMA 1970, s20B(2).

[26]TMA 1970, s20(8D)(a).

[27]TMA 1970, s20(8C). Personal records concern an identifiable individual (living or dead) and relate to physical or mental health or spiritual counselling or assistance; journalistic material is material in the possession of a person who acquired or created it for the purpose of journalism.

[28]TMA 1970, s20B(7).

[29]TMA 1970, s20B(5); however, the Commissioner may approve the exclusion of the time limit where there are reasonable grounds for believing that tax has been, or may be lost due to the fraud of the taxpayer.

[30]TMA 1970, s20B(1).

made on a company, because personal information is sought about the directors); any procedural errors should be identified and consideration should also be given to whether the notice is unfair, oppressive or irrational (for example, the accountant is required to search an inordinate quantity of records relating to a lengthy period).

Where a notice relates to an unidentified taxpayer, an accountant can object in writing to the Inspector within 30 days on the grounds that it would be onerous for him to comply with it.[31] In these circumstances, failing an agreement as to how the notice is to be dealt with, the matter must be referred to the Special Commissioners.

The accountant can elect to deliver photocopies rather than originals of documents requested in a notice.[32] Unless return of the copies is requested, it may be assumed that the copies are intended to become the property of the Revenue.

Original documents delivered to the Revenue remain the property of the deliverer. The accountant should request a receipt for documents delivered and is entitled to the return of the documents with the least delay consistent with the Revenue's requirements.

Where an accountant is convicted of any tax offence, or a penalty is imposed on the accountant for assisting in the preparation of a tax return or accounts or delivery of any information to be used for tax purposes which he knows to be incorrect, documents can be demanded irrespective of the protection conferred on working papers of an auditor or tax adviser.[33]

Where a notice is served in respect of an unnamed taxpayer and the accountant's working papers contain details giving the identity or address of any of the unnamed taxpayers or any person who has acted for them, the protection given to audit papers and relevant communications is restricted.

5C.8   New powers relating to the Revenue's investigation of serious fraud

New powers have recently been enacted to assist the Revenue's investigation of suspected tax fraud.[34] As we have remarked, considerations of client confidentiality inhibit the accountant and other professionals from

---

[31]TMA 1970, s20(8B).

[32]However, the Revenue reserve the right to take the original document. If they do so, they must follow a specific procedure–see below.

[33]TMA 1970, s20A.

[34]TMA 1970, s20BA was inserted by the Finance Act 2000.

supplying evidence required in a prosecution on a voluntary basis. To overcome this it has in the past often been necessary for the Revenue to take the step of obtaining a warrant under s20C to search the accountant's premises and seize the evidence.

The new powers are designed to allow the Revenue to obtain this evidence without the need to do so and in that respect represent a widening of the Revenue's powers. Indeed, it is now the case that the Board of the Inland Revenue may not approve an application for a warrant unless they have reasonable grounds for believing that use of the new procedure might seriously prejudice the investigation.[35] This is thought unlikely to be the case in the vast majority of applications relating to accountants.

An order may be made where the Court (a circuit judge) is satisfied that there are reasonable grounds for suspecting that an offence involving serious fraud in connection with, or in relation to, tax has been or is about to be committed, and that documents that may be required as evidence are or may be in the accountant's possession.[36] The order requires the accountant to deliver to the Revenue the documents specified or described in the order within 10 working days – or other shorter or longer period as specified.[37] However, the procedure envisages that a longer period may then be agreed with the Revenue.[38]

We have seen before[39] that 'serious fraud' is not defined; however, in this context it covers an offence of which the actual, likely or intended result would be either a substantial financial gain to any person or serious prejudice to the proper assessment and collection of tax. An offence which would not of itself be likely to constitute serious fraud may still lead to the issue of a notice if there are reasonable grounds for suspecting that it formed part of a course of conduct likely to result in either of the situations referred to above.[40]

Notice of the application must be given in writing to the accountant not less than three working days before the hearing[41] and must contain the following:

---

[35]TMA, s20C(1)(1AA).

[36]TMA, s20BA(1)(a) and (b).

[37]TMA, s20BA(1)(2).

[38]Draft Orders for the Delivery of Documents (Procedure) Regulations 2000, para 6(1)(b). At the time of going to print these were contained in a draft dated 19 June 2000.

[39]See 5A.1 above.

[40]TMA 1970 s 20(C)(1A).

[41]Unless the court is satisfied that this would seriously prejudice the application: see TMA 1970 Sch 1AA, para 3.

- the date, time and place of the hearing;

- the specifications or descriptions of documents which are the subject of the application;

- a general description of the suspected offence to which the application relates; and

- the name of the person suspected of committing that offence.[42]

The accountant can comply with the order either by delivering the documents personally to the officer specified in the order or by sending them to the officer at the address specified in the order.

Where the order applies to a document in electronic or magnetic form, there is a requirement to provide the information in a legible form.[43]

5C.9 Matters to consider in relation to a notice under section 20BA

Once a notice of application under TMA 1970, s20BA has been served, the accountant expressly must not:

- conceal, destroy, alter or dispose of any document to which the application relates, or

- disclose to any other person (i.e., including the client) information or any other matter likely to prejudice the investigation of the offence to which the application relates.[44] It is therefore perhaps inadvisable to inform the client that the notice has been received or to provide any details without first obtaining the written permission of the relevant officer.[45]

The notice should be considered to check that the correct period of notice has been given, that its scope falls within the wording of s20BA and that it contains the required information. Consideration should also be given at this stage as to whether the notice – which will form the basis of any subsequent order – is thought to be unfair, oppressive or irrational.

---

[42]Draft Orders for the Delivery of Documents (Procedure) Regulations 2000 paragraph 4. At the time of going to print these were contained in a draft dated 19 June 2000

[43]TMA 1970, Sch 1AA, para 7(3).

[44]TMA 1970, Sch 1AA, para 4(1). Breach of these obligations is punishable as a contempt of court, i.e., by fine and/or imprisonment. See Sch 1AA, para 4(4)(1).

[45]See TMA 1970, Sch 1AA, para 4(2).

Section 20BA does not apply to items subject to legal privilege and no order may therefore be made in respect of these. The notice should therefore be considered in the light of this.

It is expressly provided that the accountant may attend and be heard at the application (unless the Court is satisfied that this would seriously prejudice the investigation – which seems unlikely in the vast majority of cases).[46] This may well not be necessary if on due consideration there are no issues arising out of the notice. However, where issues do arise it may be advisable to attend and bring these to the Court's attention as failure to do so at this stage will make it difficult subsequently to challenge the order. It is very unlikely that the application could successfully be challenged by the accountant on the basis that the Revenue do not have reasonable grounds to make the application, however.

5C.10 Powers of search and seizure

The most draconian of the Revenue's powers is the ability to obtain a warrant to enter and search premises and to seize documents. As explained above, the Board of the Inland Revenue may not now approve the application for a warrant unless they have reasonable grounds for believing that use of the procedure under s20BA outlined above might seriously prejudice their investigation.[47]

Unlike the other Revenue powers referred to above, the power of search and seizure is exercised without warning. Anyone unsure about precisely what is involved would do well to read Lord Denning's account of the search and seizure operation in the *Rossminster* case:[48]

> 'It was a military style operation. It was carried out by officers of the Inland Revenue in their war against tax frauds. Zero hour was fixed for 7am on Friday, July 13, 1979. Everything was highly secret. The other side must not be forewarned. There was a briefing session beforehand. Each team was to be accompanied by a police officer. Sometimes more than one. The role of the police was presumably to be silent witnesses; or maybe to let it be known that this was all done with the authority of the law: and that the householder had better not resist–or else!

---

[46]TMA 1970, Sch 1AA, para 3(1)(b).

[47]See TMA 1970, s20(C)(1)(1AA).

[48]See *R v Inland Revenue Commissioners and Others, ex parte Rossminster Limited and Others* [1979] 3 All ER 388 (first instance); [1979] 3 All ER 396 (Court of Appeal); [1980] 1 All ER 80 (House of Lords).

'Everything went according to plan...in the early morning of Friday, July 13–the next day–each team started off at first light. Each reached its objective. Some in London. Others in the Home Counties. At 7am there was a knock on each door. One was the home in Kensington of Mr Ronald Anthony Plummer, a chartered accountant...He came downstairs in his dressing-gown...They went to the safe and took building society passbooks, his children's cheque books and passports. They took his daughter's school report. They went to his bedroom, opened a suitcase, and removed a bundle of papers belonging to his mother. They searched the house. They took personal papers of his wife.

'Another house was the home near Maidstone of Mr Roy Clifford Tucker, a fellow of the Institute of Chartered Accountants...They took envelopes addressed to students who were tenants. They went up to the attic and took papers stored there belonging to Mr Tucker's brother. They took Mr Tucker's passport.

'The main attack was reserved for the offices...of the Rossminster group of companies of which Mr Plummer and Mr Tucker were directors...   ... As far as my knowledge of history goes, there has been no search like it–and no seizure like it–in England since that Saturday, April 30, 1763, when the Secretary of State issued a general warrant by which he authorised the King's messengers to arrest John Wilkes and seize all his books and papers...He applied to the Courts. Pratt C J struck down the general warrant

'To enter a man's house by virtue of a nameless warrant, in order to procure evidence, is worse than the Spanish inquisition; a law under which no Englishman would wish to live an hour; it was a most daring public attack made upon the liberty of the subject.'

The litigation centred on the validity of the warrants and the seizure of documents by the Revenue officers executing them. In spite of the criticism of the Revenue's conduct, which is apparent from Lord Denning's words, the eventual outcome of the case was that the House of Lords held that the occupants of premises searched pursuant to warrants issued under s20C had no right to be told at that stage:

- what offences were alleged to have been committed;

- who was alleged to have committed them;

- the 'reasonable grounds' for suspecting that a tax fraud had been committed, which satisfied the circuit judge who issued the warrant.

They also held that the existence of 'reasonable cause to believe' that anything found on the premises might be required as evidence (for the purpose of proceedings in respect of the suspected offences) was a question of fact, to be tried on evidence.

The powers conferred by s20C can be exercised where an officer of the Board of the Inland Revenue gives information on oath to the appropriate judicial authority (a circuit judge in England and Wales; a sheriff in Scotland; a County Court judge in Northern Ireland) that there is reasonable ground for suspecting that an offence involving serious fraud in relation to tax is being, has been, or is about to be, committed, and that evidence of it is to be found on the premises specified in the officer's information.[49] The judicial authority has to be satisfied that the officer is acting with the specific approval of the Board given in relation to the particular case.[50]

A warrant under this provision must be in writing and it may authorise an officer of the Board to enter and search named premises, by force if necessary, at any time within 14 days of its issue.[51] A specimen warrant appears below.

SEARCH WARRANT

To: [name of Searching Officer] and to the persons named in the first schedule annexed to this warrant officers of the Board of Inland Revenue.

Information on oath having been laid this day by [name of Searching Officer] in accordance with the provisions of section 20C of the Taxes Management Act 1970 stating that there is reasonable ground for suspecting that an offence involving fraud in connection with or in relation to tax has been committed and that evidence of it is to be found on the premises described in the second schedule annexed hereto. You are hereby authorised to enter those premises, together with all or any of the officers of the Board of Inland Revenue named in the first schedule hereto and together with such constables as you may require, if necessary by force, at any time within 14 days from the time of issue of this warrant, and search them; and on entering those premises with this warrant you may seize and remove any things whatsoever found there which you have reasonable cause to believe may be required as evidence for the purposes of proceedings in respect of such an offence.

Dated this   day of

[name of Circuit Judge]

Circuit Judge

---

[49]TMA 1970, s20C(1)(a).

[50]TMA 1970, s20C(1)(b).

[51]TMA 1970, s20C(1).

The First Schedule

[names of Officers of the Board of Inland Revenue]

The Second Schedule

Dated [date]

[address of premises to be searched]

[name of Circuit Judge]

Circuit Judge

5C.11 Points to be checked in connection with a warrant under section 20C

- authority: (in England and Wales) that it has been issued by a Circuit Judge;

- date of issue: execution must be within 14 days of the date of issue;

- the premises to be searched must be specified;

- the officers carrying out the search *may* be specified;

- the time of the search *may* be specified;

- the warrant *may* specify that the search is only to take place in the presence of a constable in uniform.

The warrant does *not* have to specify:

- the particular offence that has been committed, or that the Revenue suspects or has grounds to suspect has been committed;

- whom the Revenue suspects of committing the offence, or when it suspects the offence was committed;

- a particular addressee;

- the documents to be seized.

The officer in overall charge of the investigation should be named in the warrant. He may take with him any other person whom he considers necessary; he will often be accompanied by members of the police or SFO. The officer's powers extend to search of any person on the premises whom he has reasonable cause to believe possesses anything which may be required as evidence. While the warrant simply confirms power to

134

entry and search, the officer who enters premises under its authority may seize and remove anything which he has reasonable cause to believe may be required as evidence in proceedings relating to fraud.[52]

In addition to checking the warrant itself for the points referred to above and obtaining proof of identity of the members of the raiding party, an accountant should bear in mind the following:

- the officer must provide a copy of the warrant, endorsed with his name, to the occupier of the premises or anyone apparently in charge of them;

- if anything is seized, a list must be endorsed on or attached to the warrant which will be returned to the Court and retained there where it can be inspected by the occupier;

- a record of items removed must be provided on request within a reasonable time to the occupier or any person who had custody and control of the items removed. If a copy of the item would suffice for use as evidence, the original must be returned without delay;

- if a request is made to the officer in charge before items are seized, supervised access to such items must be allowed; similarly, if a request is made prior to seizure for a copy of the item, then the copy, or supervised access to make a copy, must be given within a reasonable time; however, this may be denied if the officer believes that it would prejudice that or any other investigation or subsequent proceedings.

5C.12 Sanctions

A person who intentionally falsifies, conceals, destroys or otherwise disposes of a document which has been requested by the Revenue, or who causes or permits any of these actions, is – subject to certain extenuating circumstances – guilty of a criminal offence punishable on summary conviction by a fine not exceeding the statutory maximum,[53] or on conviction on indictment, imprisonment for up to two years.[54]

Failure to comply with an order for production of documents under s20BA is punishable as a contempt of court and could lead to a fine and/ or imprisonment.[55]

---

[52]TMA 1970, s20C(3)(b).

[53]Currently £5,000.

[54]TMA 1970, s20BB(5).

[55]TMA 1970, Sch 1AA, para 9.

5C.13 Other Revenue powers

Accountants can also find their premises (including, in some circumstances, private dwellings) subject to entry and search as 'servants or agents' of a wide category of individuals including employers and employees.[56] Under these powers, Inspectors of the Department of Social Security and the Revenue can cooperate in examinations and enquiries of business records or any matters on which they may reasonably require information.

Accountants should be aware of the fact that exchanges of information may take place at local level as a result of reciprocal arrangements between the Revenue and HM Customs & Excise.[57]

---

[56]Social Security Administration Act 1992, s110.

[57]FA 1972, s127.

5D   HM Customs & Excise

5D.1   Customs' powers to obtain information

Customs' powers to obtain information from traders, their tax advisers and others are contained in Value Added Tax Act 1994, Sch 11. These powers oblige the trader to furnish such information as Customs may reasonably specify, including information held by a third party such as a tax adviser. Customs' powers extend only to documents relating to the supply of goods or services or to the importation or acquisition of goods and services. Once again, 'document' in this context is very widely defined and includes material held in electronic forms;[1] it expressly includes any profit and loss account and balance sheet relating to the business relevant to the supply.[2]

Customs' powers are very widely drawn and, except in relation to the exercise of powers of search and seizure, do not require application to the court for implementation. The rationale given for this is that because VAT is a self-assessed tax, suitable powers are needed to enable Customs officers to determine whether or not the trader has accounted properly for the tax.

Customs is also empowered[3] to exchange information with the Revenue, as well as relevant authorities in other member states of the EU. The Revenue are an increasingly fertile source of intelligence.

5D.2   Customs' approach to the conduct of investigations

Customs has issued a Statement of Practice briefly outlining its legal powers and practice concerning access to business records and information.[4] This states that Customs will seek access to information and records selectively and on a voluntary basis and will only use its formal legal powers 'where all else fails'.

It is Customs' stated practice to deal direct with the trader, rather than the tax adviser. However, where the tax adviser becomes involved at the

---

[1]VATA 1994, Sch 11 para 3.

[2]VATA 1994, Sch 11 para 7(4).

[3]See Finance Act 1972, s127.

[4]See HM Customs & Excise Statement of Practice: Confidentiality of VAT Matters, set out in full in VAT leaflet 700/47/93.

client's request, care must be taken, as always, not to breach duties of confidentiality owed to the client by responding to Customs' demands without the client's authority.[5]

5D.3   Matters to consider

Customs' Statement of Practice recognises the duty of confidentiality owed by the tax adviser to the client. Customs will not normally request the tax adviser or client to produce confidential opinions or advice contained in communications between them including, for example, notes of meetings or telephone calls, correspondence and management letters. However, there is no equivalent protection to that which exists in relation to Revenue powers,[6] and where documents are requested, careful consideration needs to be given to whether or not documents are subject to Customs' formal statutory powers to obtain information. It may be argued, for example, that advice on the question of whether or not a supply is taxable can never relate to the supply itself and therefore documents recording such advice cannot be relevant for Customs' purposes. This argument would appear to carry particular weight in circumstances in which the advice was given after the supply in question.

Where documents contain 'mixed' information (i.e., information relating to goods and services and confidential advice), an extract may be accepted by Customs, provided it is supported by a written statement from the tax adviser stating his opinion that Customs does not have power to see the remainder of the documents. For this reason, it may be advisable for the tax adviser to distinguish between information relating to goods or services and confidential advice when creating documents and perhaps even to deal with them in separate documents where practicable.

Customs is entitled to take copies of and extracts from any document produced for inspection. Requests for copies are entirely usual and should be agreed with Customs whenever possible. However, Customs is also empowered to require production of original documents in the possession of the tax adviser and a person authorised by Customs may remove such documents;[7] a receipt must be provided. Any lien that the tax adviser has on the removed papers is expressly unaffected by the exercise of this power.[8]

---

[5]See 1.3 above.

[6]See 5C.5 above.

[7]VATA 1994, Sch 11, para 7(6).

[8]VATA 1994, Sch 11, para 7(3) and (6).

5D.4 Powers of search and seizure

Customs has powers which mirror those available to the Revenue[9] enabling it to compel access to the tax adviser's premises to obtain information.[10] To exercise these powers an application must be made to a Justice of the Peace for a production order, usually on notice. Before granting the order the Court must be satisfied that an offence in connection with VAT is being, or is about to be, committed and that evidence of that offence is to be found at the tax adviser's premises.

Once granted, the order empowers an authorised person to enter and search premises in accordance with the terms of the order. The scope of the Court's order should therefore be scrutinised closely. In particular, the order has to be exercised within seven days or such longer period as may be specified. Compliance with this requirement should be checked. The tax adviser should take care not to breach his duty of confidentiality to the client by ensuring that only documents falling within Customs' powers and within the scope of the order are disclosed. Customs is permitted to take copies of documents to which the order relates and to remove the originals where necessary. It may be possible to agree that copies will be provided while the originals are retained. Where information is recorded on a computer, there is an obligation to produce it in visible and legible form and, if necessary, in a form that can be removed.[11]

Upon executing such an order, Customs must within a reasonable time provide a record of items removed from the premises and must usually allow access to documents removed and permit copies to be taken.[12] It is strongly advised, however, that the tax adviser make an independent record of all documents disclosed, so far as practicable.

5D.5 Sanctions

A person who is knowingly concerned in, or who takes steps with a view to, the fraudulent evasion of VAT by himself or any other person is liable on summary conviction to either or both a penalty of the statutory maximum,[13] or three times the amount of the VAT (whichever is

---

[9]See 5C.10 above.

[10]VATA 1994, Sch 11, para 11.

[11]VATA 1994, Sch 11, para 11(4).

[12]VATA 1994, Sch 11, para 12.

[13]Currently £5,000.

greater), or to imprisonment for a term not exceeding six months or on conviction on indictment to either or both an unlimited penalty or imprisonment for up to seven years. A person who, with intent to deceive, produces, furnishes, sends or otherwise makes use of any document which is false in a material particular, or who intentionally or recklessly makes a statement which he knows to be false in a material particular, shall be liable on summary conviction to either or both a penalty of the statutory maximum (as before), or imprisonment for up to six months, or on conviction or indictment to either or both an unlimited penalty or imprisonment for up to seven years.

5D.6   Witness summonses

Customs has no power to compel the tax adviser to attend for interview and the tax adviser should be wary about volunteering such assistance to Customs. To compel attendance at any trial, a witness summons has to be issued in the usual way.[14]

---

[14]See 5G below.

5E Requests from Insolvency Act Office-holders (liquidators, etc)

5E.1 Introduction

Under the Insolvency Act 1986, administrators, administrative receivers, liquidators and provisional liquidators of insolvent companies (whom the Insolvency Act refers to as 'Office-holders'), and trustees in bankruptcy, are provided with certain powers which may be exercised against third parties to obtain property, documents and information, and may apply to the Court (as may the Official Receiver) for the exercise of additional powers against third parties granted by the Insolvency Act.

These provisions create a powerful tool for Office-holders and trustees in bankruptcy. It is important to appreciate the dangers to the accountant inherent in these powers arising from the fact that the Office-holder or trustee in bankruptcy is not only obliged to investigate the affairs of the insolvent company or person, but also to realise assets including causes of action against professional advisers. As a class of potential litigants against accountants, Office-holders and trustees in bankruptcy are in the privileged position of having an opportunity to obtain accountants' working papers and to put questions to them, in advance of bringing any civil claim against them. This situation was recognised by the House of Lords in *British & Commonwealth* v *Spicer & Oppenheim*.[1] Despite considering the strength of these powers to be a factor in reaching their judgment, the House of Lords nevertheless ordered the audit firm concerned in that case to produce their working papers to the Office-holder, even though they were not the auditors of the insolvent company concerned. The order was made in recognition of the fact that the Office-holders were investigating the affairs of the company that had been the subject of the audits, which had subsequently been acquired by British & Commonwealth and less than two years later entered into administration showing a deficiency of some £279 million.

In view of the very distinct possibility that enquiries from Office-holders and trustees in bankruptcy will lead to litigation against accountants, they need to be handled with particular care. It is generally advisable to obtain legal advice.

Accountants may be subject to statutory powers in a number of different guises:

- As persons having in their possession or control company property[2] or a bankrupt person's property.[3]

---

[1] [1993] AC 426.

[2] Insolvency Act 1986, s234; s236(2)(b) and s237 (possession only).

[3] Insolvency Act, s365; s366(1)(b) and 367 (possession only).

- As a past or present officer of the insolvent company.[4] 'Officers' will include auditors who have been appointed officers in compliance with the Companies Act 1985.[5]

- As a person known or supposed to be indebted to the insolvent company[6] or bankrupt person.[7]

- As a person whom the Court thinks capable of giving certain information concerning the insolvent company[8] or bankrupt person.[9]

However, the powers to which accountants may be subject will vary according to the applicable statutory provision.

This section does not seek to deal with the obligations which may arise where accountants act in a formal capacity in relation to an insolvent company or individual (e.g., as supervisor of a voluntary arrangement, or as a receiver or Office-holder).

5E.2   Insolvent companies

Overview

The various powers provided to Office-holders or to the Court under Insolvency Act, s234–237 apply where:[10]

(a)   an administration order is made;[11] or

(b)   an administrative receiver is appointed;[12] or

---

[4]Section 235; s236(2)(a) (which does not specifically refer to 'past' officers). Section 235 extends to persons who are officers of a company which is itself (or has been within a year of the 'effective date') defined at s235(4) an officer of the insolvent company.

[5]Auditors not so appointed will not be officers. See *Re Western Counties Steam Bakeries & Milling Co.* (CA)[1897] 1 Ch.617 and more recently *Mutual Re* v *Peat Marwick* (CA) [1997] 1 Lloyds Law Reports 253. Auditors should consider whether they have been so appointed in ascertaining whether they have a duty under Insolvency Act 1986, s235.

[6]Section 236(2)(b).

[7]Section 366(1)(b).

[8]Section 236(2)(c).

[9]Section 366(1)(c).

[10]Section 234 and s235(1) and s236(1).

[11]Under Insolvency Act 1986, Pt II.

[12]Ibid., Pt III.

(c) the company goes into liquidation;[13] or

(d) a provisional liquidator is appointed.[14]

It is important to note that the powers will not be triggered by the appointment of receivers over part (as opposed to the whole) of a company's property. Receivers who are not administrative receivers do not have powers under s234–237.

The provisions create two overlapping regimes. On the one hand, s235 imposes certain duties on officers, while s234 and s236–237 create powers for the Court over a much wider class of persons possessing property or information. Accountants who are officers may therefore owe such duties and also be subject to the powers exercisable by the Court. Insolvency Act Office-holders will generally be the moving force behind the exercise of Insolvency Act powers by the Court.

Office-holders tend to put their requests for information and documents in writing before resorting to an application under s236 or s234. On receipt of such a request an accountant will need to consider:

(a) whether s235 applies to him, i.e., is he under a duty to comply with a request made by an Office-holder?

(b) if s235 does not apply, should he voluntarily comply with the request in order to avoid the formal procedures under s234 and 236?

(c) whether any material held by him is subject to a duty of confidentiality to a third party such that he should obtain that party's consent to disclosure in the absence of a Court Order.

Power of the Court under section 234

Section 234(2) empowers the Court to require any person who has in their possession or control any property, books, papers or records to which the company appears to be entitled,[15] to deliver such items to the Office-holder. The section is silent as to who may apply for such an order.[16]

---

[13] Ibid., Part IV. Section 247(2) defines 'goes into liquidation' as occurring when a company makes a resolution for voluntary winding-up under s84 or (in the absence of such a resolution) when a winding-up order is made by the Court under s125.

[14] Under ibid., s135.

[15] Ownership is dealt with at 4.2 above

[16] Since an administration order may have not appointed an administrator, and winding-up may commence prior to appointment of a liquidator, it is possible to conceive of circumstances where an order under s234 could be made for delivery on the making of such an appointment.

Section 234 will not apply therefore to audit working papers, which belong to the auditor, but will apply to accounting records relating to the company held by the accountant as agent for the company such as bank statements, ledgers etc., or to other papers relating to work performed in the course of advising the company.

Section 234 subsections (3) and (4) operate to protect an Office-holder who has seized or disposed of property which he wrongly, but reasonably, believed he was entitled to seize or dispose of, whether under a Court Order or otherwise, except where loss or damage is caused by his own negligence.[17] This highlights the importance of ensuring that any documents and property given up to the Office-holder are not the property of the accountant or of another client.

Duty of officers under section 235

Section 235 is most likely to be of relevance to accountants appointed as auditors appointed under the Companies Act, since they will be officers for the purposes of this section.

Further, under this section (and s236) 'Office-holder' also includes the Official Receiver, whether or not the liquidator, in the case of a company which is the subject of a winding-up order.

Section 235 covers past officers as well as present officers of the insolvent company. Although the section also covers employees of the insolvent company under contracts for services, accountants in private practice will not be employees of a client company simply because they have contracted to perform services.[18]

Any person who is covered by s235 is under a duty to:

- give to the Office-holder such information concerning the company and its promotion, formation, business, dealings, affairs or property as the Office-holder may at any time after the effective date[19] reasonably require;
- attend on the Office-holder at such times as the latter may reasonably require.

In contrast to s234, this provision is not limited to information, etc., which belongs to the company and so will extend to audit working

---

[17] In order to avoid such protection arising, the accountant should explain at the time of seizure or disposal any reasons why the Office-holder is not entitled.

[18] Various factors will determine whether a relationship of employment exists, e.g., degree of control over manner in which tasks are performed, whether services performed for others, and whether paid only by the company.

[19] See Footnote 13.

papers. 'Information' is open to a wide construction so that it may include the provision of documents and extend to giving written or oral statements under examination to the Office-holder.

Certainly, it is generally considered preferable to provide information under this section, where there are no detailed procedures laid down for the provision of information, than to be subjected to a more formal Court examination under s236.

However, regardless of the accountant's own preferred procedure, it is important to recognise that s235 imposes a duty on any person to whom it applies. Default without reasonable excuse is punishable by a fine.

Reasonableness of requests

The scope of the duty under s235 is most obviously limited by the wording that subjects any requests made by the Office-holder to a requirement of reasonableness. In practice, the circumstances in which it is possible to justify a refusal of a request for information under s235 are generally likely to be limited. Depending on the facts, it may nonetheless be possible to show that that the request is unreasonable on its face – for example, because the request imposes an impossibly short timescale for the production of voluminous documentation languishing in the archives. It would also be unreasonable for the Office-holder to refuse to allow the accountant's lawyers to attend questioning. If the Office-holder decides to instruct a lawyer to conduct the questioning, it would be reasonable to expect the Office-holder to forewarn the accountant who is to attend the examination.[20]

It appears (by analogy with the decision relating to a s236 application in *British & Commonwealth* v *Spicer & Oppenheim*[21]) that the volume of documentation involved is unlikely to be a justification in itself for the refusal of a request, although it will be a factor.

Alternatively, it may be possible to demonstrate that the request is unreasonable by reference to the Office-holder's requirements for the performance of his functions. However, since these functions include the investigation of a company's affairs, and may involve the consideration of bringing litigation, the parameters of the Office-holder's purposes are rather loosely defined and this may present difficulties in contesting any request on this ground.

---

[20]See 5E.4 below for further commentary on 'Preparing for the examination'.

[21][1993] AC 426.

In certain circumstances, it may be possible to demonstrate that the particular purpose behind the request is restricted (e.g., to obtaining information to enable the Office-holder to assist in tracing company assets) in such a way that information about the way in which the accountant performed an engagement is irrelevant. For this reason it is always sensible to ask the Office-holder to clarify the purpose of the request being made (although there is no positive obligation on the Office-holder to comply with such a request). In cases where the Office-holder's purpose is limited and does not justify access to the whole body of the accountant's working papers, it may be prudent to ask that a request for access to working papers is broken down into requests for specific documents within those papers that may relate to that particular investigation.

Duty of confidentiality

An important issue which commonly arises for the accountant faced with a request which falls under s235 is whether any duty of confidentiality to a third party arises in relation to information or documents. Such a duty is often owed where the accountant has, for example, acted for other companies within the same group, or has performed reporting engagements at the company's request for a third party (such as a source of external finance or a regulator). However, the mere fact that documents relate to a third party does not necessarily mean that the accountant owes that party a duty of confidentiality.

A duty of confidentiality owed to third parties is subject to an implied qualification where disclosure is made under compulsion of law.[22] Notwithstanding this principle, accountants who are subject to requests under s235 and are in possession of information or documents which are confidential to third parties commonly ask for those parties' consent to disclosure before providing material to the Office-holder. Whether the resulting delay or any refusal of consent would provide a reasonable excuse for withholding the documents is likely to depend on the circumstances, although there is no judicial guidance on this point. Nevertheless, where consent to disclosure is not forthcoming from the third party to whom the duty is owed, the Office-holder commonly resorts to an s236 application. This reduces the risk to the accountant of an exposure to an action for breach of confidence. It is worth adding that where the accountant does seek consent to disclosure from the third party, the accountant should first seek the agreement of the Office-holder to informing the party concerned of the Office-holder's request.

---

[22]*Tournier* v *National Provincial and Union Bank* [1924] 1 KB 461.

Powers of the Court to inquire and require production under sections 236 and 237

Under s236(2), the Court may on the application of an Office-holder (defined for these purposes as under s235), summons to appear before it:

(a) any officer of the company;

(b) any person known or suspected to have in his possession any property[23] of the company or supposed to be indebted to the company;

(c) any person whom the Court thinks capable of giving information concerning the promotion, formation, business, dealings, affairs or property of the company.

Accountants who have performed any services for, or in relation to, the company (possibly for its directors, creditors or shareholders) are very likely to fall within category (c) if no other.

Such persons who are summonsed under s236(2) may be required by the Court under s236(3) to:

• submit an affidavit containing an account of their dealings with the company, or

• produce any books, papers or other records in their possession or control relating to the company or any of the matters referred to at (c) above,

and may be examined on oath either orally or in the form of interrogatories (written questions and answers).[24] Examinations are normally held in private.[25]

Where a person fails to appear without reasonable excuse or absconds, the Court may issue a warrant for arrest of the person and for seizure of any books, papers, records, money or goods in their possession.

The Office-holder may apply to the Court for an order under s237(1) for the delivering up of company property by any person, where it appears to the Court, on consideration of any evidence obtained under s236 or s237, that the person has such property in their possession.

Section 236 is often described as creating an 'extraordinary power'. However, the granting of an application for an order under s236 is subject to the Court's discretion. Furthermore, the purpose of the power

---

[23]'Property' may include documents belonging to the company.

[24]Section 237(4).

[25]*Re Property Insurance Co* [1914] 1 Ch 775.

is to gather information about the company, in part to enable the Office-holder to decide whether or not the company has a claim against any persons, and not to discredit the person providing the information. Depending on the circumstances, it may be legitimate for the person to be asked for information which will enable the Office-holder to decide whether or not to bring a claim against that person, but it may not be legitimate to make an enquiry which is designed to 'furnish evidence to support a claim' against that person, e.g., where Office-holders seek to obtain explanations or admissions in relation to information already in their possession.[26] By way of an example, asking whether an accountant had given a particular piece of advice may be a reasonable enquiry to make, but the Office-holder risks going too far in asking the accountant to justify his actions and explain why he failed to give a particular piece of advice.

Although there is no clear legal authority on the point, it is unlikely that the Office-holder is entitled to know the accountant's opinion on a particular issue at the time of questioning, as opposed to the accountant's opinion held at the material time.

The procedure for an s236 application is set out in the Insolvency Rules 1986 at Rule 9.2.[27] While an application under s236 may be made 'ex parte' (in other words, without the opportunity for the person concerned to be heard), there must be good reason for excluding the person's right to be heard in this way.[28] The application should state what manner of information is sought (examination, interrogatories, affidavit or documents) and identify the general areas that are to be the subject of any interrogatory or affidavit, or specify the documents sought. It is important to note that the relevance of the information which is the subject of the duty under s235 or which may be the subject of an s236 application is very widely (and loosely) defined. The information to be given is not limited to information to which the company may at one time have enjoyed a right of access. Consequently – and contrary to the law prevailing ten years ago – the purpose of an order under s236 is not to reconstitute the records of a company.[29] However, in order for the Office-holders to obtain information which relates to other companies connected with the insolvent company or to a particular wrong-doing, they will need to show that the particular information also relates to the insolvent company.[30]

---

[26]*Re PFTZM Ltd* [1995] 2 BCLC 354.

[27]SI 1986/1925 r9.2.

[28]See *Re Maxwell Communications Corporation plc* (No.3) [1995] 1 BCLC 521.

[29]*British and Commonwealth Holdings plc* v *Spicer & Oppenheim* [1993] AC 426.

[30]See *Re Mid East Trading Ltd, Lehman Bros Inc* v *Philips & Others* [1998] 1 All ER 577.

The Office-holder applying for the order must satisfy the Court that, after balancing all the relevant factors, there is a proper case for such an order to be made. The Court must carefully balance the reasonable requirements of the Office-holder to carry out their functions with the need to avoid making an order that is 'wholly unreasonable, unnecessary or "oppressive" to the person concerned'.[31] An element of oppression may not prevent an order being made if it is outweighed by the importance of allowing the Office-holders to complete their enquiries.[32]

A common misconception is that the sheer volume of documents involved, the time that will be taken in any examination and the diversion of the accountant from his own business, will automatically constitute grounds for the Court refusing to make an order on the basis of oppression. While all of these circumstances will be factors in the Court's exercise of its discretion, they are not an absolute bar to an order. In *British & Commonwealth* v *Spicer & Oppenheim*[33] for example, the accountants concerned were ordered to disclose hundreds of files.

Factors which have been identified as potentially relevant (but not necessarily conclusive) to the balancing exercise to be undertaken by the Court in deciding whether to exercise its discretion include:

- Whether the Office-holder has commenced proceedings against the person[34] or anyone else and is simply fishing for information to assist him in those proceedings. Alternatively, it may be relevant to consider whether the Office-holder has yet firmly decided to pursue a claim, particularly where proceedings have been commenced merely to avoid the expiry of any limitation period.

- Whether any further information is needed by the Office-holder to make a decision to sue.[35]

- Whether the information is readily available elsewhere.

- Whether the order sought is for an oral examination (such an order is more likely to be oppressive than an order for the production of documents).

---

[31]Per Lord Slynn in *British & Commonwealth Holdings plc* v *Spicer & Oppenheim*. See also above under s235 regarding the requirement of reasonableness.

[32]See *Re Arrows Limited* (no. 2) [1992] BCC 446.

[33][1993] AC 426.

[34]See *In Re Castle New Homes Limited* [1979] 1 WLR 1075, which held that the Court may well refuse an order in such circumstances unless special grounds could be shown. See further details in main text.

[35]In *Re Cloverbay No. 3* [1990] BCLC 471.

- Whether the person is under a s235 duty (if so, an order is more likely to be made).

- The risk of exposure of the person concerned to a fraud claim (an oral examination may be oppressive in such circumstances).

- Whether the company is the subject of a members' voluntary liquidation.[36]

One of the most contentious and difficult issues which arises in relation to an s236 application concerns the risk of unfairness to a person who is a probable target of litigation. This situation will require consideration of the first and second factors identified above. In *Re Castle New Homes Limited* an order was made even though the liquidator had reached the view that there was a valid claim for it to bring, since it appeared that the liquidator's lawyers were not satisfied that there was sufficient information on which to issue proceedings and that no decision to commence proceedings had been reached. There has been at least one instance in which the existence of a draft statement of claim has not been sufficient to prevent an order being made. In *Re Cloverbay no.3* it was held that it would be oppressive to order an examination of certain officers of the company's bankers to take place where no further information was required by administrators to take a rational decision to sue, after extensive documentation had been provided to them. In view of the wider scope recently given to pre-action disclosure under Part 31.16 of the new Civil Procedure Rules,[37] it remains to be seen whether Office-holders who are considering litigation against accountants will increasingly resort to applications under Part 31.16 of the Civil Procedure Rules as an alternative or (more likely) a supplement to s236. Part 31.16 applications may appear particularly attractive to Office-holders facing difficulties in persuading a Court to exercise its discretion under Insolvency Act, s236 (perhaps due to the possibility that on the facts of the case they will be perceived to have formed an intention to sue).

Public examination of officers under section 133

Where a company is the subject of a winding-up by the Court,[38] the Official Receiver may apply to the Court under s133 for the public examination of any person who is or has been an officer of the company, and is normally under a duty to make such an application when a particular proportion by value of creditors or contributories so requests.

---

[36]This is likely to incline the Court against an order. See *Re Galileo Group* [1998] 2 WLR 364.

[37]See Chapter 10.

[38]Under Pt IV Chapter VI of the Insolvency Act.

On the application being made, the Court will[39] direct that a public examination be held, and the person will be examined by any of the Official Receiver, the liquidator, creditors or contributories as to:

- the promotion, formation or management of the company;

- the conduct of its business or affairs;

- the person's conduct or dealings in relation to the company;

The Court may enforce the person's presence in a similar fashion to its powers in relation to s236.

Inspection of books

After a winding-up order is made, the Court may make an order under s155 for inspection of the company's books and papers by creditors and contributories, but this power is limited to documents in the company's possession and does not extend to documents in the possession of accountants. However, there is nothing to prevent a company from asking for an accountant to provide it with the documents which the company owns.

5E.3   Bankrupts

Duty to deliver up

Under Insolvency Act, s312(3), any agent[40] or other person who holds any property to the account of or for the bankrupt person is under a duty to deliver to the trustee in bankruptcy ('the trustee') all property in his possession or under his control which form part of the bankrupt person's estate and which he is not by law entitled to retain.[41] This duty is backed up by penalties for non-compliance without reasonable excuse.[42]

Warrants

Furthermore, any property comprised in the bankrupt person's estate and any books, papers and records relating to the bankrupt person's estate or affairs may be seized from such persons under a warrant issued by the Court on the application of the Official Receiver or the trustee.[43]

---

[39]No discretion is allowed in the statute.

[40]As to circumstances in which accountants act as agents rather than as principals, see 4.2.1 above.

[41]As to ownership of documents, see 4.2 above.

[42]Insolvency Act 1986, s312(4).

[43]Ibid., s365. A warrant may be issued at any time after the bankruptcy order.

This power of seizure only arises where the property and documents fall within the duty under s312. For the purposes of seizing the property and documents in the course of executing the warrant, there is power under s365(2) to break open any premises where anything that may be seized is (or is believed to be) located.

A warrant may also be issued under s365(3) authorising a search of premises which do not belong to the bankrupt where the Court is satisfied that any property comprised in the bankrupt person's estate or any books, papers and records relating to the bankrupt person's estate or affairs are concealed there. This power is directed at obtaining documents relating to the bankrupt's affairs, regardless of ownership. The key requirement is that the documents are being concealed on premises which the bankrupt person does not own.

Powers under sections 366 and 367

Under s366, the Official Receiver or the trustee in bankruptcy may apply to the Court to summons persons to appear before it, including:

- any person believed to possess any property comprised in the bankrupt person's estate or to be indebted to the bankrupt person;

- any person appearing to the Court to be able to give information concerning the bankrupt person or the bankrupt person's dealings, affairs or property.

Such persons may be requested to submit an affidavit to the Court concerning an account of their dealings with the bankrupt person, or to produce any documents in their possession or control relating to the bankrupt person or the bankrupt person's dealings, affairs or property.[44]

Similar powers exist as under s236 and s237 for the Court to examine such persons on oath, to order delivery up of property comprised in the bankrupt person's estate, and to enforce attendance.[45]

In relation to a bankrupt person, issues of duties of confidentiality owed to third parties may arise where information is held concerning the bankrupt person's relatives or in relation to companies owned by the bankrupt person. See the commentary above on Insolvency Act, s235 for guidance on this issue.

---

[44]See above for commentary on parallel provisions in s236.

[45]Section 366(2)–(4), s367.

5E.4   General points

The following comments are made with particular reference to Insolvency Act 1986, s235 and s236, but also apply generally to s366 in cases of bankruptcy.

Preparing for the examination

Accountants are often asked to attend meetings with Office-holders at short notice in order to answer their questions. When agreeing to a meeting or participating in any examination, an accountant should:

- consider having his legal adviser present at any meeting;

- ask for advance notice of the areas on which he will be asked questions;

- ask the Office-holders to identify in advance any documents on which he will be asked questions so that the accountant may refresh his memory and be better placed to assist;

- review his files so as to refresh his memory of the work performed.

Depending on all the circumstances, some or all of these steps (and in particular the first and second) may justify delaying any meeting or examination called at short notice. It is important that sufficient time is available for any legal adviser retained to be fully instructed and in a position to advise the accountant as to any particular issues that are likely to arise in the course of the examination or meeting.

In *Re Norton Warburg Holdings*,[46] liquidators sought an order for the oral examination of the audit partner previously responsible for the audit of the company in liquidation, and the audit manager involved in the audit of a subsidiary which had entered into receivership. Both persons applied to defer the examination which would have related to work undertaken a few years previously. The judge decided on the facts of the case that an oral examination which was not preceded by an indication of the topics which the liquidators wished to pursue would be a waste of time. He directed that the liquidators should first be provided with the documents requested, and should then serve a written questionnaire setting out questions arising out of their review of those documents, before proceeding to an oral examination. In advance of the examination, the liquidators were to specify 'in as detailed terms as they are able' the topics on which they required clarification and the documents to which they would refer each person being examined.

---

[46]There is no automatic entitlement to such documents under the Insolvency Rules, but the courts may recognise such a need–see *Re Norton Warburg Holdings* [1983] BCLC 235 at 242.

These directions will not be applied in every case; in particular, it is clear that the judge in *Re Norton Warburg Holdings* considered the practicality of proceeding first by written questionnaire against the degree of oppression and unfairness to the auditors (who were not under suspicion of wrongdoing) in the particular circumstances. In another case (involving the proposed examination of a chairman who had been charged with criminal offences) the same judge decided that a written questionnaire would serve no purpose.[47]

In addition to the above steps, it may be appropriate for the accountant concerned (or another person within the same firm with relevant experience but unconnected to the particular engagement) to review any work undertaken with a view to identifying and investigating within the firm possible concerns relating to the work performed. It is imperative that any such review is carried out, and can be shown to have been carried out, for the dominant purpose of obtaining legal advice, so as to attract privilege from disclosure, and accountants should ensure that the necessary arrangements are in place, in conjunction with their lawyers, before conducting such a review. It is not advisable to volunteer the existence of the review to the Office-holder (and that information will be privileged if carried out for the purposes of obtaining legal advice) and in any case it is unlikely that such a review would constitute a justification for delaying access to papers, or a meeting or examination.

Precise compliance

As noted in relation to s235, it is important for the accountant to identify the existence of any duties of confidentiality to third parties. Although these duties will be overridden by an order under s236, the accountant may well risk breach of the duty of confidentiality if more material is disclosed than that to which the Office-holder is entitled under the order made. Furthermore, the accountant's interests (in the context of managing the risk of litigation arising from the disclosure of information and documents) lie in ensuring that the Office-holder is given no more material than that to which he is entitled, although this is not a justification for providing less than a full and frank response to an enquiry which the Office-holder is entitled to make. For these reasons, it is important that the accountant attempts to ensure that any order, enquiry or request with which he is complying is sufficiently clear in its scope and that there is an adequately detailed record on file (preferably the order itself or a written request from the Office-holder), so that there is no doubt as to whether the accountant is under an obligation to provide information in relation to a particular topic of enquiry or to provide a copy of a particular set of files.

---

[47]See *Re Arrows Limited* (no. 2) [1992] BCC 446.

Volunteering cooperation

When faced with the prospect of a s236 application, which would clearly result in an order being made, it is common for persons to submit voluntarily to requests made by the Office-holder without any order being made by the Court, because of the greater procedural informality and flexibility of such an examination. In such circumstances, it should be possible to negotiate, to some extent, the terms on which the information will be provided. For example, the accountant may require that an advance indication is given of the general issues or topics on which the person will be examined, and that the examination be limited to those. It may also be appropriate to agree the extent to which the procedural rules in Insolvency Rules 1986, Rule 9 are to apply to the voluntary examination.

In volunteering cooperation in preference to the making of a s236 order, it is important to pay regard to any duty of confidentiality owed to a third party (see above in relation to s235). Such duties of confidentiality may not be overridden by volunteering information in this way where no s235 duty applies, even if an order under s236 would undoubtedly be made, and it is recommended that consent is sought from the party to whom the duty is owed.[48]

Privilege

The Insolvency Act is silent as to whether legal professional privilege will be effective against the Office-holder exercising his powers under the Act. There has been no decision clarifying whether or not such privilege has been impliedly removed (as a number of legal writers have previously suggested). However, recent cases suggest that courts will always be reluctant to find that Parliament must have intended to remove the privilege.[49] In practice, a valid claim to legal professional privilege is likely in the majority of cases to constitute a reasonable excuse for withholding information and documents covered by the privilege.[50] While no set procedure exists for asserting privilege or for relying on other 'reasonable excuse', it is submitted that where information and documents

---

[48]If the duty is owed only to the company itself, no such difficulty arises in respect of a request by an Office-holder (other than where the request is made by the Official Receiver where an Office-holder has been appointed and remains in office).

[49]See *R* v *Secretary of State for Home Department ex parte Leech* [1994] QB 198 and *General Mediterranean Holdings SA* v *Patel* [2000] 1 WLR 272.

[50]The Human Rights Act 1998 is a possible further source of support for such a view in relation to compulsory production. To remove any legal doubt when agreeing to volunteer production of documents, the accountant may wish specifically to exclude from the agreement any documents subject to the privilege.

are being withheld, that fact (and the justification relied on) should be communicated to the party requesting disclosure.

Use of information obtained

The use to which records of examinations may be put underlines the importance of properly managing the accountant's passage through the process. Statements or records of examinations made pursuant to s236 may be used in evidence in any civil proceedings brought against the person concerned by the Office-holder. Such statements or records are (generally speaking) confidential.[51] Where the accountant holds such documents (or has or had a right of inspection), such documents will be disclosable by the accountant in subsequent proceedings brought against the accountant by any third party, as will any documents received from the Office-holder in the course of his enquiries, subject to the duty of confidentiality and the Office-holder's privilege.[52]

However, the confidentiality attaching to information provided under s236 to the Office-holder may be overridden by a statutory obligation of disclosure on the Office-holder, e.g., to the SFO in response to a notice under Criminal Justice Act 1987, s2.[53] It is not clear to what extent information which has been provided under s235 or volunteered in response to an approach from the Office-holder may be protected from such onwards disclosure by public interest immunity.[54]

---

[51] Insolvency Rules 1986, Rule 9.5, which states that leave of the Court is required to enable inspection of such documents or the production of copies (including by or for the person making the statement) except by the Office-holder or potential s236 applicants. Confidentiality exists against individual creditors.

[52] Where an obligation to disclose arises in litigation, inspection of documents which are confidential to the Office-holder as against the other litigating parties should in the first instance be withheld unless the Office-holder's consent is forthcoming and any privilege belonging to the Office-holder asserted. Furthermore, in civil proceedings inspection of affidavits, interrogatories, and transcripts of examinations made pursuant to the Insolvency Act should be withheld unless leave is ordered by the Court. See *Re a Company No 005374 of 1993* at 1993 BCC 734.

[53] *Re Arrows* no.4 [1994] 3 WLR 656, which established that an objection to disclosure of statements made under Insolvency Act s236 on the basis that such statements should always attract public interest immunity from disclosure would not succeed.

[54] In *R v Clowes* [1992] 3 All ER 440, a claim to public interest immunity in relation to information obtained from third parties under s235 was rejected in criminal proceedings based on particularly grave charges of fraud. The position in a less serious circumstance and in civil litigation remains unresolved.

5F   Regulators

5F.1   Introduction

This section covers requests for assistance made to accountants by regulatory bodies (such as, for example, the DTI and the FSA). The provisions under which different regulators operate are often complex, and to set them out in detail in a book of this nature would be unduly burdensome. Moreover, the Financial Services and Markets Act 2000 is intended to unify regulation of financial services and markets and, from the date on which it comes into force, will replace a number of different regimes currently in operation. Accordingly, this section concentrates primarily on setting out some general considerations applicable to requests from regulators, followed by a short summary of the powers available under the existing regimes and of those to be brought into force under the new Act.

Accountants may also on occasion be approached by their clients for help in responding to regulatory requests which the clients themselves have received. In such circumstances, unless there is prior agreement providing otherwise, the only obligations on the accountant will be to deliver to the client any papers belonging to the client[1] and, depending on the circumstances, to extract information relating to the client's affairs. The restricted nature of these obligations may be significant in circumstances in which the regulator does not have the power to require the accountant himself to provide assistance.[2]

5F.2   General

When dealing with regulators' requests, particularly until the Financial Services and Markets Act comes into force, it is important to recognise that powers to obtain information and documents vary between each regulator. In some circumstances, certain regulators can obtain information and documents from any persons possessing relevant information about the regulated client. In other cases, powers can be exercised only against agents, auditors or officers of a company.

It is also important to distinguish between the different types of investigation that a particular regulator may be able to conduct. These may include general investigations into the entire affairs of a company,

---

[1]For ownership of documents see 4.2 above.

[2]For example, investigations by the Stock Exchange under Chapter 14 of its Rules.

or investigations limited to particular matters, or special investigations under separate powers into particular areas defined by the relevant statute. In addition, regulators may also enjoy powers to obtain documents and information which can be exercised irrespective of whether an investigation is underway.

Duties of confidentiality

When faced with a request for assistance it is important that the accountant considers any duty of confidentiality owed to clients or third parties. Such duties are overridden where a disclosure requirement is imposed by law. While for various reasons (not least to maintain the client relationship) accountants might nonetheless prefer to seek consent from those to whom the duty is owed before disclosing material, the sensitivity of many such investigations and the risk that the accountant could become guilty of the offence of 'tipping off' mean that he should always consult the regulator before contacting the client or anyone else (other than a legal adviser) about what is going on.

At the same time the duty of confidentiality means that the accountant must be wary of not disclosing information or documents to which the regulator is not entitled. Difficulties can arise, for example, where an accountant acts for various related companies, only some of which are under investigation. The accountant first needs to establish the extent of the investigators' powers.[3] If they are limited to some of the companies only, the accountant will need to be careful when answering questions and providing documents not to disclose information relating to the affairs of the others.

Accountants will generally assume a fresh duty of confidentiality in respect of information that they receive from regulators. Care should be taken to observe this as breach of such a duty may also be a criminal offence.[4]

In addition, regulators will often ask those from whom assistance is sought to sign confidentiality undertakings. There is usually no obligation to sign such an undertaking, and indeed signing one would add little to the duty of confidentiality which arises anyway. If an undertaking is signed it is important to ensure that the accountant retains the right to disclose to his lawyers the content of the interview and any material provided by the regulator.

---

[3]See, for example, Companies Act 1985, s433 referred to below.

[4]See Companies Act 1985, s449; Financial Services Act 1986, s179; Banking Act 1987, s82; Building Societies Act 1986, s53; Insurance Companies Act 1982, s 47A; Financial Services and Markets Act 2000, s348.

The accountant may risk an action from his client for breach of confidentiality if he discloses the existence of investigations into the client's affairs to third parties without consent. This is an issue of particular relevance to enquiries by the DTI under Companies Act 1985, s447, which are designed to be conducted in a manner that preserves their confidentiality in order to avoid harming the company's business. Information obtained under a s447 enquiry cannot be disclosed without the company's consent (except in certain exceptional cases, such as for the purposes of criminal investigations).[5]

Identifying the risk of future use of statements

When responding to regulators' requests it is important for the accountant to recognise that any statement made by him may be available for use in subsequent proceedings.[6] In response to concerns about the contravention of human rights, the Financial Services and Markets Act 2000[7] now provides that no evidence relating to a statement made to an investigator under that Act may be adduced in criminal proceedings. The Financial Services and Markets Act also provides that such evidence will be admissible in other proceedings only if it 'complies with any requirements governing the admissibility of evidence in the circumstances in question'. This provision is intended to deal with the concern that a limited category of disciplinary proceedings, principally that relating to the offence of market abuse, may be categorised as criminal proceedings and hence that evidence obtained under compulsion from the defendant should not be permitted to be adduced against him.

The accountant should also be aware that any statement supplied under an obligation is likely to be disclosable by the accountant when a party to civil proceedings. Furthermore, while information and documents provided are normally subject to confidentiality provisions whereby the regulator cannot disclose this material to another party,[8] there are statutory exceptions (commonly called 'gateways') that may variously enable regulators to pass information to each other, to other authorities such as professional disciplinary bodies, or to other interested parties such

---

[5]Companies Act 1985, s449.

[6]For example, statements made under Companies Act 1985, s434(5) and 447(8), and Financial Services Act 1986, s105.

[7]In s174.

[8]For example, Companies Act 1985, s449; Financial Services Act 1986, s179; Financial Services and Markets Act 2000, s348.

as the person under investigation.[9] In *Soden* v *Burns*[10] the liquidators of British and Commonwealth Holdings Plc were able to use their Insolvency Act powers (see **5E** above) to obtain transcripts of interviews conducted by DTI inspectors.

General approach to requests from regulators.

It has always been the case that any person faced with a request from a regulator is generally best advised not only to be frank and open but also to avoid being dilatory in dealing with requests. The accountant will be best placed to address any request received by opening a line of communication with the regulator, indicating his willingness to cooperate, identifying early on any problems he faces in providing information and documents (e.g., duties of confidentiality, delays in retrieving archived documentation, departed staff), and in return trying to learn as much as possible about the scope of the investigation, and in particular the matters in relation to which he is being asked to provide information. It is to the accountant's advantage to establish as precisely as possible the subject matter of the information or documents to be disclosed, so that he may limit the extent to which material is passed out of his control. This is particularly important where there is a possible risk of future litigation. The accountant should always review documents before disclosing them to ensure that he has fully complied with any request but has not disclosed material surplus to the regulator's requirements.

Before providing information or documents to a regulator, the accountant should be clear that what is being sought falls within the regulator's powers of compulsion. It will usually be appropriate to seek legal advice on this. If an interview is to take place, the accountant should review relevant documents in order to refresh his memory and identify any difficult issues that he may need to address as it proceeds. Additional points to be borne in mind when participating in an interview are addressed at **5A** above in relation to interviews conducted by the SFO.

In certain circumstances accountants (in particular auditors) may be asked to explain not only their own documents but also documents produced to the regulator by others. In that event, the accountant may never have seen the documents before, in which case this should be made clear immediately (although it does not present a basis for refusing an explanation if the accountant is able to provide one based on other matters within his knowledge).

---

[9] See, for example, Companies Act 1985, s451A (5).

[10] [1996] 1 WLR 1512.

Privilege

The statutory powers exercised by regulators referred to below are often (but not always) subject to explicit statutory protection from production of privileged information.[11] Even if no such protection is built into the legislation it will generally be assumed to exist unless there is a clear indication that privilege is not to apply.[12]

Rather than explicitly preserving legal privilege, the Financial Services and Markets Act 2000 protects instead specified categories of documents ('protected items') which a person may not be required to produce. The definition of protected items under s413 of the Act is broadly comparable to the general definitions used for documents that are the subject of legal professional privilege.

Where privilege does exist, it is up to the accountant to assert it by reviewing his papers in order to identify and remove any privileged material before handing the papers to the regulator. It is prudent to make clear to the regulator that a claim to privilege has been asserted over certain documents which would otherwise be subject to the regulator's requirements.

Powers of entry

Certain regulators enjoy powers to obtain a warrant from a Justice of the Peace enabling them to enter premises, search for and seize documents, take copies and require explanations of them from the recipients of the warrant.[13] Other regulators enjoy powers of entry without the need to obtain a warrant.[14] An accountant is at greatest risk of being the subject of these powers where there are reasonable grounds for the regulators to believe that documents have not been produced in accordance with requirements or where there is material relating to an offence which may otherwise be destroyed (a scenario which could arise where an accountant – possibly ignorant of his statutory duties – appears to be about to return material to a client who is under investigation). Although

---

[11]See, for example, Companies Act 1985, s452, Financial Services Act 1986, s105(6), Competition Act 1998, s30.

[12]*R v Sec of State for Home Department ex parte Leech* [1994] QB 198 and *General Mediterranean Holdings SA v Patel* [2000] 1 WLR 272.

[13]Companies Act 1985, s448; Financial Services Act 1986, s199; Building Societies Act 1986, s44A; Financial Services and Markets Act 2000, s176; Competition Act 1998, s28.

[14]Banking Act 1987, s40; Building Societies Act 1986, s52A; Insurance Companies Act 1982, s44; Competition Act 1998, s27.

161

in practice a warrant is likely to be a last resort, the accountant might conceivably be faced with a warrant if he carelessly fails to make full disclosure and the surrounding circumstances are such that he falls – however wrongly – under suspicion of concealing material.

Documents lost or held elsewhere

It should be noted that where regulators have powers – whether under a warrant or otherwise – to require production of specified documents, they also commonly have powers if the documents cannot be produced to require explanations as to where such documents might be found.[15]

Penalties

Statutory penalties (including imprisonment and fines) exist in relation to regulators' powers, for example in cases of:

• failing to provide documents, information and assistance;

• failing or refusing to attend before inspectors/investigators or to answer their questions;

• obstructing the exercise of a warrant;

• knowingly or recklessly making false statements;

• destroying, concealing or falsifying documents;

• breaching restrictions on confidentiality.

The particular penalties and offences vary according to each statutory regime.[16]

5F.3 Types of regulator

The following is a brief overview of the powers exercisable by the major UK regulators against accountants holding information relating to third parties (including clients).

---

[15]See, for example, Companies Act 1985, s448(3)(d) and Financial Services and Markets Act 2000, s175(3). These additional powers have not been specifically identified in the text that follows; reference should be made to the relevant statute.

[16]See Companies Act 1985, ss 436(1), 444(3), 447(6), 448(7) and 451; Financial Services Act 1986, ss105(10), 178, and 200; Banking Act 1987, ss39(11), 40(3), 41(9), 42(4), 43(5) and 44; Building Societies Act 1986, ss52 (10) and (12), 55 (4) and (5) and 57 (6); Insurance Companies Act 1982, s71; Financial Services and Markets Act 2000, ss177 and 398; Competition Act 1998, ss 42–44.

Corporate regulators -The Companies Act 1985

The DTI has wide powers to investigate companies under the Companies Act 1985, Pt XIV. The DTI enjoys general powers of investigation in relation to the affairs of a company as a whole (under s431 and s432), in addition to having more specific powers to investigate the membership of a company (s442) and particular share dealings (s446). The accountant will need to establish the scope of the power being exercised in order to judge the extent of any obligation attaching to him. Examples of situations in which the general powers of investigation may be exercised is where there is an appearance of fraud, misconduct or unscrupulous practices. The accountant may wish to refer to the brief guide 'Company Investigations–How they work', available from the DTI.

DTI investigations are normally conducted by the Companies Investigations Branch ('CIB') and commence with the appointment by the Secretary of State of one or more Inspectors to conduct the investigation and report. Their powers reach beyond the company itself, extending to the investigation of any present and former subsidiaries, holding companies and certain other related companies.[17]

When the Inspectors are appointed under s431 and s432, all past and present officers or agents of the company (including auditors) are under a duty to produce on request *all* documents belonging or relating to the company, to attend before the Inspectors when required and to give all assistance which they are reasonably able to provide (s434 (1)). The accountant who falls within this duty should therefore be ready to comply with such a request, since delay is likely to be less excusable than where no such duty exists.

In addition, the Inspectors may specifically require any past or present officer or agent, or any other person who may be in possession of information relating to a matter which the Inspectors believe relevant to the investigation, to do the same, in which case a duty to comply will arise. It is essential that the accountant has a clear understanding of the precise details of the matters concerned in order to match his response to the request, and it may be necessary to clarify the relevant details with the Inspectors. The Inspectors may examine on oath any person who is required to attend before them (s434(3)).

The duties and powers under s434 outlined above apply in respect of investigations under s442 (company membership investigations) to any person whom the Inspector has reasonable cause to believe possesses

---

[17]Companies Act 1985, s433.

relevant information. In the case of an investigation under s446 (share dealings), only past and present officers will be subject to these powers.

The accountant who is subjected to an interview or examination on oath may need to prepare for this ordeal in advance, and should consider whether it is appropriate to seek legal advice and representation. The possibility of future litigation or disciplinary proceedings will obviously be a major factor in reaching a view on this point. Subject to the requirement to act fairly, DTI Inspectors have a wide discretion as to the way they conduct interviews and handle their investigation. Similarly, the extent to which the Inspectors will provide information that will enable witnesses to prepare for interview may vary. There is no automatic entitlement to this information. The role of the lawyer at interview is also limited but they are permitted to intervene on such matters as the clarity of the question and to make representations on their client's behalf either orally or in writing. The witness will normally be provided with a transcript of his interview for comment.

The Inspectors' conclusions are not required to be measured against any civil or criminal standard of proof. It is, however, standard procedure to allow those who may be affected by the report to have advance notice of provisional criticisms and to be allowed to reply to or comment on them. On receipt of the Inspectors' report the Secretary of State has the discretion as to whether or not to publish its findings.

There are other powers available to the Secretary of State under the Companies Act that are not connected with the DTI investigations referred to above. The Secretary of State may require production 'forthwith' by any person of documents belonging to the company, and take copies of them, and require an explanation of them from that person or a past or present officer of the company (s447). This power is much more commonly exercised than the investigation powers referred to above, and is often used to decide whether disqualification proceedings should be brought against directors or whether a winding-up petition should be presented. The Secretary of State also has a separate power to obtain information as to past and present share ownership from any person in possession of or able to obtain that information (s444). Since these powers can be exercised in the absence of any DTI investigation, the subject matter of the enquiry may not always be readily apparent and it may be appropriate to clarify whether the DTI requires, for example, every document belonging to the company or only a set of particular documents.

Financial regulators: the old regime

The Financial Services And Markets Act 2000 is intended to unify the regulation of financial services and markets and create a more comprehensible system so that responsibility for direct supervision is in the hands of a single regulator, the Financial Services Authority ('FSA'). Until such time as this comes into force[18] the regimes which it is intended to replace will apply as follows.

Financial Services Act 1986

FSA 1986 regulates investment business, insurance business and friendly society business.

The FSA enjoys a general power under FSA 1986, s105 to investigate the affairs (or any aspect of the affairs) of any person carrying on investment business. This power can be exercised by the FSA in relation to directly authorised firms, and in certain circumstances in relation to members of the Self-Regulating Organisations ('SROs'). The SROs have their own rules which govern investigations conducted by them.

The FSA's general investigatory power under FSA 1986, s105 enables it to require any person to produce (and explain) specified documents which appear to the FSA to relate to any matter relevant to its investigation. The FSA enjoys further powers over 'connected persons', a term which is defined to include agents and auditors of the person under investigation, who may be required to attend and answer questions or otherwise furnish information with respect to any matter relevant to the investigation. Furthermore, agents and auditors of any person producing a document may be required to provide an explanation of the document.

There are also two principal types of specific investigation for which Inspectors may be appointed by the FSA.

The first concerns investigations in relation to the affairs of collective investment schemes (s94), in which case the Inspectors' powers are defined to correspond to the powers of DTI inspectors under Companies Act 1986, s434 and give rise to duties on the part of agents for the managers, operators or trustees of the scheme.

The second type of investigation (under s177) arises where it appears to the FSA that an insider dealing offence[19] may have been committed. The Inspectors may require any person who may be able to give information concerning any such offence to produce documents which appear to them to be relevant to the investigation, to attend before the Inspectors

---

[18]April 2001 is a probable date.

[19]Under Criminal Justice Act 1993, Pt V.

when required, and to give all assistance which they are reasonably able to provide. There is a statutory duty to comply with such a requirement. The Inspectors may also examine such a person on oath.

Certain matters (for example, the exercise of intervention powers) are referred by the FSA to the Financial Services Tribunal. This has the power to summon any person to give evidence or to produce any document which the Tribunal considers it necessary to examine.[20]

Banking Act 1987, Building Societies Act 1986 and Insurance Companies Act 1982

All of the relevant powers under these Acts are to be swept away by the Financial Services and Markets Act 2000 when it comes into force. In the meantime, the supervisory powers previously exercised by the Bank of England under the Banking Act 1987 have already been transferred to the FSA (by the Bank of England Act 1998). The powers of the Insurance Directorate under the Insurance Companies Act 1982 are currently exercisable by the FSA under contract with the Treasury.

The Building Societies Act 1986[21] and the Insurance Companies Act 1982[22] created general powers for the regulators concerned to obtain specified documents and information (and explanations of them) about specified matters from the regulated entity's 'officers and agents'. In addition, under the Insurance Companies Act, officers may be required to explain documents produced under the general power exercisable by the FSA, even if produced by another party.[23]

In contrast, under the regulatory regime of the Banking Act, the FSA only has a general power on written notice to obtain documents under the control of authorised institutions that are in the possession of other persons.[24]

The regulators under each regime enjoy a connected right of entry for the purpose of obtaining those documents.[25] Under the Insurance

---

[20]Financial Services Act 1986, Sch 6, para 5.

[21]Building Societies Act 1986, s52.

[22]Insurance Companies Act 1982, s44. The documents to be provided must be specified by the regulator.

[23]Insurance Companies Act 1982, s44(4)(a)(ii).

[24]Section 39. A similar power exists under Building Societies Act 1986, s52.

[25]Banking Act 1987, s40; Building Societies Act 1986, s52A; Insurance Companies Act 1982, s44.

Companies Act 1982, it is also possible for the FSA to obtain a search warrant (s44A) in order to exercise its general power to obtain information and documents under that Act.

Each of these statutory regimes includes powers of investigation. The FSA may conduct general investigations under Banking Act, s41 to report on the nature, conduct or state of an authorised institution's business (or any aspect of it) or the ownership or control of the institution. The Building Societies Commission may conduct investigations into the affairs or conduct of a building society under Building Societies Act, s55 and s56. Such investigation may be either wide or narrow in scope and it is important for the accountant to establish its extent in order to consider the nature of any obligation that he may be under. The regulators may extend the investigation to other 'undertakings' or partnerships that have particular relationships with the entity under investigation (e.g., parents and subsidiaries).[26]

The FSA has the power to appoint investigators under the Insurance Companies Act in order to consider the fulfilment of the criteria of sound and prudential management.[27] Agents and auditors are under a duty in such an investigation to produce all documents relating to the company, to attend before the Inspectors when required and to give all assistance which they are reasonably able to provide.

A general investigation under the Banking Act or the Building Societies Act will normally be of concern only to agents and auditors of the banking institution (or the agents[28] and officers of the building society) which is being investigated. These persons will fall within the class of persons who are under a duty to produce all documents relating to the body concerned (which it should be noted is a very wide obligation indeed), to attend before the Inspectors when and where required and to give all assistance which they are reasonably able to provide. Under the Building Societies Act, persons other than officers or auditors may be subjected to the same duties if so required by Inspectors appointed in a section 56 investigation who consider that they are or may be in possession of information concerning the society's affairs.[29]

---

[26]See Insurance Companies Act 1982, s41(2) and (3).

[27]Insurance Companies Act 1982, s43A.

[28]Agents are specifically defined under Building Societies Act 1986, s55(6)(a) to include the building society's accountants.

[29]Building Societies Act, s57(3).

Under the Banking Act, in addition to this general investigatory power under s41, the FSA has specific investigative powers in relation to more serious matters. These powers arise under s42, where it has reasonable grounds for suspecting an offence of unauthorised deposit-taking[30] or fraudulent inducement to make a deposit.[31] Under these specific powers, the FSA may serve written notice on any person requiring them to provide such information or specified documents as may reasonably be required, or to attend to answer questions relevant for determining whether such a contravention has occurred.

Sections 39, 41 and 42 of the Banking Act and s52 of the Building Societies Act restrict the degree to which production of documents can be refused on the basis of legal professional privilege.

The Financial Services and Markets Act 2000

This Act, passed in June 2000, makes provision for the regulation of all financial services to be carried out by a single regulator (the FSA) who will be responsible for authorising those persons who may carry out such activities. Hence, the Act will complete the process of transferring regulatory functions from the SROs and other regulatory bodies to the FSA. The Act also provides for the transfer to the FSA of responsibility for regulating building societies, friendly societies, industrial and provident societies and certain other mutual societies. Lloyd's will become an authorised person under the Act and will be subject to supervision by the FSA.

This Act will affect accountants in two important respects. First, accountants who carry on mainstream regulated activities will henceforward be authorised and regulated directly by the FSA and will be subject to the various investigatory powers of the FSA contained in s165–s176. Secondly, accountants may also be 'connected persons' for the purposes of investigations and enquiries into other authorised persons.

Where the accountant is or has been an auditor under the Companies Act to an authorised person which is a body corporate the FSA may seek information under Pt XI, s165 directly from the accountant since the definition of 'connected' under this section includes (under Pt I of Sch 15) 'an officer or manager of [the body corporate] or of a parent undertaking'. The FSA must specify the information and documents which are the subject of their request, and this power is limited to such

---

[30]Banking Act 1987, s3.

[31]Banking Act 1987, s35.

information and documents as are reasonably required in connection with the exercise of the FSA's functions.

Under s167 the FSA may conduct general investigations into the nature, conduct or state of the business of an authorised person or an appointed representative. The FSA may limit the investigation to a particular aspect of the business. It may also investigate the ownership or control of an authorised person. As previously stated, given the degree of flexibility in this provision, it is essential that the accountant understands the scope of the investigation when dealing with requests for information.

The FSA may also conduct specific investigations under s168 where it has reasonable grounds to suspect the existence of any one of a particular set of circumstances (including specific offences and statutory breaches) as defined either at s168(1) or at s168(2) and (4). These offences include insider dealing, misleading statements, market abuse, breach of the general prohibition on the conduct of regulated activities other than by authorised or exempt persons, and restrictions on promotion.

An investigator appointed to conduct a general investigation under s167 exercises powers specified at s171 of the Act. Any person may be required to produce specified documents. In addition, provided the investigator reasonably considers the information to be relevant, any person 'connected' with the person under investigation may be required under s171 to attend for interview or otherwise provide the investigator with such information that the investigator considers to be relevant. The definition of 'connected' in these circumstances includes (as well as officers) agents and auditors of the person under investigation or its parent or connected subsidiaries.[32]

Investigators appointed on specific grounds under s168 have separate powers (under s172 and s173). The application and extent of those powers depend on the grounds on which the investigators have been appointed. In essence however, these powers extend to interviewing persons and requiring documents from persons who need not be connected to the person under investigation.

Failure to comply with a requirement made by the FSA under the above powers may lead to a warrant for entry, search and seizure (s176).

The Act replaces the provisions which existed under the Financial Services Act 1986 relating to Unit Trust Scheme investigations and provides a new range of powers (s284).

---

[32]Financial Services and Markets Act 2000, Sch 15, Pt II.

5G   Witness summonses and non-party discovery

The accountant may be in a position to provide evidence in either civil or criminal proceedings. These documents might be working papers or any other documents having some bearing on the issues in dispute. In either case, if the Court is satisfied that the accountant is likely to be holding material evidence and that he will not voluntarily provide it, the Court will, subject to various requirements, provide the means for the evidence to be disclosed.

5G.1 Criminal

Even though he might not be actively monitoring the case, it would be unusual for the accountant not to be conscious that a criminal prosecution which touched upon issues he knew about was underway. In most cases, if it was considered that he had information material to the prosecution it is likely that an approach would be made by them well in advance of trial. If the case were being prosecuted by the SFO, for example, the accountant might well be called upon to produce a number of documents at an early stage pursuant to the SFO's investigative powers.[1]

The ability of defendants to criminal proceedings to obtain access to information and assistance from the accountant is much more limited: the only available procedure is the witness summons. While a witness summons may be issued if necessary during the trial itself, in practice the defence will try to ensure that it is issued sufficiently far in advance for any issues over its validity and the admissibility of the documents sought to be resolved and for the usefulness of the documents to be assessed before the presentation of the prosecution case.

For confidentiality and other reasons, the accountant should be wary of allowing the defendant access to documents simply in response to a threat that a witness summons will be issued. He should satisfy himself that all the necessary procedures have been followed and that the requirements for the production of documents have been met.

Save with the consent of all those to whom duties of confidentiality are owed, the accountant should not in response to a summons or threat of one embark upon discussions with the defence about what documents are in existence. Even with such consent, from the accountant's own risk management perspective, this is seldom a practice to be recommended.

---

[1] See 5A.

If a witness summons is issued more than seven days before the commencement of a trial, it must be made by written application and supporting affidavit and copies of these must be served on the person (the witness) to whom the summons is directed. If the application is made within the seven-day period or during the trial itself, it need not be served on the witness in advance but the application is referred to the judge for appropriate directions.

In either case, it is open to the recipient to resist the production of the documents on certain grounds. If he has been served with the application then any objections must be made at the hearing of the application. If the application has already been granted then it is necessary to seek an order that the witness summons is of no effect.

Where documents are held by an accountant, the summons might be directed to the relevant audit partner or possibly the senior partner. It is important for that person to be aware that he is responsible for responding to the summons and attending Court as directed unless a different arrangement is reached either through agreement with the defence (confirmed by the Court) or as a result of a Court Order following a challenge to the summons. It is a contempt of court to disobey a witness summons without just excuse.[2]

The more common grounds for opposing the issue of a witness summons or seeking an order that the witness summons is of no effect are as follows.

Lack of particularity

An effective summons must specify what is sought with reasonable particularity. A summons may not be effective in whole or in part if it requires the recipient to make judgements about which documents are relevant, or if it is plain that the applicant is simply making assumptions or guessing about whether documents actually exist. The applicant must also explain the basis upon which he believes the documents exist. A summons would be unlikely to be effective if, for example, it required an accountant to produce all working papers relating to a particular engagement. The purpose of the witness summons procedure is to enable a party to put before the Court material evidence, not to enable a search to be conducted through voluminous paperwork in an attempt to find evidence.[3]

---

[2]Criminal Procedure (Attendance of Witnesses) Act 1965, s3.

[3]See, for example, in the civil context, *MacMillan Inc* v *Bishopsgate Investment Trust Ltd* [1993] 4 All ER 998.

Inadmissibility

The material which is sought to be produced by summons must be admissible in Court as evidence in accordance with the law governing admissibility of evidence. For example, evidence which would be used for the sole purpose of contradicting a witness in cross-examination, and thereby damaging his credibility, is not admissible evidence.[4]

Relevance

The purpose of a witness summons is to produce evidence which is likely to be material to the proceedings in question. If the documents sought to be produced are not relevant in that they do not assist in proving or denying the charges brought, the summons will be set aside. On the face of it the chances of the witness having sufficient knowledge of the issues to further this argument effectively may often be small, but the affidavit in support of the application should make a clear case for production. If the witness does not believe this test has been passed, he may find that he will be assisted in his arguments by other parties and it is open to the judge to examine the evidence himself.

Legal professional privilege and public interest immunity

It is not possible to compel the production of privileged material by means of a witness summons unless for some reason the privilege has been waived. The accountant needs to take care in this respect to identify not only documents in which he himself can claim privilege, but also to tell the Court if there are documents in which his client or another party may be able to claim privilege.[5]

In rare circumstances it is also possible that a claim to public interest immunity could be made.

Confidentiality

Confidentiality is not in itself a reason for objecting to a witness summons but it is a factor which the Court may take into account in considering objections. While there is probably no direct legal obligation

---

[4]Thus, in *R v Cheltenham JJ, ex parte Secretary of State* [1977] 1 All ER 460, the Court set aside a summons served on an Inspector appointed under Companies Act 1948, s165 to produce transcripts of evidence obtained during the investigation. The Court held that as this evidence was required only for use in cross-examination to contradict the statements a witness might make by reference to what he had said previously, the evidence was not admissible.

[5]See, in the civil context, *Robertson v CIBC* [1994] 1 WLR 1493.

on the accountant to raise objections based on his client's or another party's confidentiality, the prudent course will usually be to notify the person concerned so that they have the opportunity to object.[6]

5G.2 Civil proceedings

If an accountant is a party to civil litigation he must give standard disclosure of documents to the other parties to the litigation as required by the Civil Procedure Rules ('CPR').[7]

Where the accountant is not a party to proceedings but has working papers or other documents in his possession or power which are likely to be relevant to the issues in the proceedings, there are two principal ways in which he may be required to produce them:

(i)   The Court may order the accountant to give non-party disclosure; or

(ii) The Court may issue a witness summons requiring the accountant to produce documents to the Court. Similar principles apply to witness summonses in civil proceedings as in criminal proceedings.

Non-party disclosure

Under the CPR a party to proceedings may apply to the Court for an order requiring a person who is not a party to the proceedings to give disclosure of documents.[8] The application must be supported by evidence to persuade the Court that the documents of which disclosure is sought are likely to support the case of the applicant or adversely affect the case of one of the other parties to the proceedings and that disclosure is necessary in order to dispose fairly of the claim or to save costs.

Any order for disclosure by a person not a party to the proceedings must specify the documents or the classes of documents which the non-party must disclose.[9] This automatically means that an order for non-party disclosure can be made in wider terms than a witness summons, but its scope is still much narrower than standard disclosure as between the parties to proceedings. Thus, the Court is unlikely to require an accountant who is not a party to proceedings to disclose all of his files relating to a particular engagement. The Court will require the applicant

---

[6]*Robertson* v *CIBC* [1994] 1 WLR 1493.

[7]CPR Rule 31.6. See Chapter 10.

[8]CPR Rule 31.17.

[9]CPR Rule 31.17(4).

to identify particular documents or classes of documents which are relevant to the proceedings and explain why they are relevant and why their disclosure will assist in the disposal of the proceedings.

An example of an application for non-party disclosure against a firm of accountants is *Anselm v Anselm*.[10] The parties to the proceedings were two brothers who had worked together in a clothing business operated through a limited company. HW Fisher & Co ('Fishers') acted as accountants to both parties, the company through which the business was run and other companies owned by one or both of the parties. Fishers had agreed to disclose specific documents but one of the parties sought an order for further disclosure of a large number of files.

Mr Justice Neuberger refused the application. He held that it was not in accordance with the modern approach to disclosure or fair to a third party not involved in the litigation to order disclosure in such wide terms. The judge said that Fishers were entitled to a more specific identification of which documents were sought and an explanation as to why they were helpful. Save in the most exceptional case, the Court should not make an order as wide as that sought. He also considered that the Court should be concerned to protect Fishers' own privacy and interests. While he dismissed the application, the judge indicated that the applicant could amend his request to be more specific about the documents he wanted disclosed and make a fresh application to the Court if necessary.

There is a presumption that the Court will award to a non-party the costs of complying with any order made.[11] Disclosure is required to be made in the same manner as by a party to the proceedings, by providing a list of the documents in question in the prescribed form.[12]

Witness summonses in civil proceedings

Now that it is possible to obtain non-party disclosure in all civil proceedings, litigants who are mainly interested in the production of papers are likely to follow that route rather than seeking the issue of witness summonses to obtain documents. However, it remains possible for a party to civil proceedings to request the Court to issue a witness summons requiring a witness to attend Court to give evidence or to produce documents to the Court.[13] A witness summons may require a

---

[10]Unreported, Chancery Division, 15.12.99, Neuberger J.

[11]CPR Rule 48.1(2).

[12]See Chapter 10.

[13]CPR Part 34.

witness to produce documents to the Court either on the date fixed for a hearing or on such other dates as the Court may direct.[14]

A person can be required to produce a document at the hearing only if the document is admissible as evidence at the hearing.

Provided that the witness summons is issued more than seven days before the date of the trial and requires a witness to give evidence at or produce evidence at the trial, a party does not need the permission of the Court to request the Court to issue a summons. This differs from criminal procedure where a written application, on notice to the intended recipient, is required. However, permission is required if a party wishes to have a summons issued less then seven days before the date of the trial, or to have a summons issued for a witness to attend Court to give evidence or to produce documents on any date other than the date fixed for the trial or at any hearing except the trial.[15]

At the time of service of a witness summons the witness must be offered or paid a sum reasonably sufficient to cover his expenses in travelling to and from Court.[16]

The CPR provide no guidance as to the approach the Court should adopt to an application to set aside a witness summons. However, the principles relating to subpoenas under the old rules are likely to apply save that the Court will take into account the overriding objective of the CPR including the new factor of proportionality.

A case involving accountants under the old rules was *Re Global Info Ltd*[17] where three accountants served with *subpoenae duces tecum* applied successfully to have them set aside. The six principles identified by the Court were:

(i)   The documents must be specifically identified.

(ii) A subpoena must not be used as an instrument to obtain discovery.

(iii) A subpoena must not be of a fishing or speculative nature.

(iv) Production must be necessary for the fair disposal of the action or to save costs.

---

[14]CPR Rule 34.2(4).

[15]CPR Rule 34.3.

[16]CPR Rule 34.7.

[17][1999] 1 BCLC 74.

(v) The Court has the discretion to refuse to order disclosure of confidential documents.

(vi) The Court has the power to vary the terms of a subpoena.

The case involved disqualification proceedings issued by the Secretary of State for Trade and Industry against a director of Global Info Limited. The director served a subpoena on each of three accountants who had audited the company's accounts, produced management and end of year accounts and been appointed liquidator when the company went into voluntary liquidation.

Each subpoena listed categories of documents which the recipient was required to produce. Most of the categories followed the formula, 'All correspondence with . . . [a named person] . . . in relation to the affairs of [Global] . . . '.

The Court held that each subpoena infringed the first four principles. The above formula was too widely drawn, failing to identify specific documents and amounting to an attempt to obtain discovery. It was also a fishing expedition in the sense that the director could not state which or what proportion of the documents would be relevant to which issues in the case.

Furthermore, the Court held that categories of documents relating to correspondence with the ICAEW infringed the principle in relation to confidentiality in that it was confidential and had no bearing on the qualification proceedings.

It is unlikely that the outcome of the *Global* case would be materially different under the CPR.

6 Resignation and ceasing to act

6.1 Introduction

An accountant may act for a multitude of clients in a multitude of roles. For the most part, there is no professional guidance or other statutory framework setting out what is required when he resigns or ceases to act. There might, however, be some provision in the letter of engagement regulating the termination of the relationship, with which the accountant should comply.

It is also important for the accountant to consider whether he is dealing with third parties as agent for the client. For example, he acts as agent whenever he submits a tax return or a tax computation to the Inland Revenue on behalf of a taxpayer client. In those circumstances, the accountant should notify third parties, such as the Inland Revenue or HM Customs & Excise, with whom he is already dealing as agent for the client, that he has ceased to act and that all future correspondence or other communications should go to the client direct or any successor.[1] If the accountant continues thereafter to receive communications from third parties, he should not refuse to respond and ignore the position altogether – this is likely to have serious consequences for the client and could prejudice the client's position and thereby his own. The accountant should inform the former client of the further communications and forward all relevant post to them. It would also be wise to inform the third party again that the accountant has ceased to act for this client.

Where the accountant is acting as auditor, however, the position is more complex. This Chapter is primarily devoted therefore to consideration of the position in which an auditor wishes to resign from the engagement either at the conclusion of the engagement or, more rarely, before an audit opinion has been expressed on the financial statements. We shall look at:

- the time at which the auditor might want to resign;

- the statutory requirements on resignation;

- the professional guidance on dealing with any potential successor auditor; and

---

[1] See ICAEW Statement 1.306.

- the ways in which the auditor can minimise the risk of claims for defamation or breach of confidence.

6.2 Reasons for resigning

Resignation by auditors is an act of last resort. It is normally preferable and in the interests of shareholders and creditors for the auditors to remain in office to fulfil their statutory duties.[2]

This is reflected in the fact that if the auditor is unable to express an unqualified opinion, he is not, as a result, required to resign from the engagement. Indeed, the ICAEW has at times advised its members that their obligation to express an opinion 'is inescapable' and 'it would be inappropriate for auditors to seek to avoid it by resigning before the expiry of their term of office because they are dissatisfied with the position disclosed by their audit . . .'.[3] Rather, the auditor has to consider whether to reach a qualified or adverse opinion, or, in extreme circumstances, a disclaimer of opinion.

In short therefore:

- The auditor may issue a 'qualified opinion' where there is either (i) a limitation on the scope of the auditor's examination,[4] or (ii) the auditor disagrees with the way in which the matter is disclosed in the financial statements,[5] and, in the auditor's opinion, the effect of either of these matters is or may be material to the financial statements such that they may or do not give a true and fair view of the relevant matters on which the auditor is required to report or do not comply with relevant accounting or other requirements.

- An 'adverse opinion' (i.e., that the financial statements do not give a true and fair view) may be expressed where the effect of the disagreement is so material or pervasive that the auditor concludes that the financial statements are seriously misleading.

- A 'disclaimer of opinion' may be expressed where the possible effect of a limitation on scope is so material or pervasive that the auditor has

---

[2]SAS 120, para 72. Under Companies Act 1985, s385(2), the auditor is normally appointed to serve until the next general meeting at which accounts are laid.

[3]The Accountant, 3 February 1972, pp. 133–135.

[4]See SAS 600.7.

[5]See SAS 600.8.

not been able to obtain sufficient evidence to support – and accordingly is unable to express – an opinion on the financial statements.[6]

Also, if the financial statements could be affected by an inherent uncertainty which, in the view of the auditor is fundamental but adequately accounted for and disclosed, the auditor should include an explanatory paragraph referring to the fundamental uncertainty in the section of his report setting out the basis of his opinion.[7] An explanation may be required, for example, where there is litigation against the client or one of its subsidiaries. While the immediate financial effect on the client may not be known, there could be future consequences (such as an adverse finding and damages award against the client or regulatory fines), which could have a material effect on the true and fair view given by the financial statements. The purpose of an explanatory paragraph is to make it clear that this is a matter the auditor has taken into account in forming his opinion; it does not qualify the opinion. The auditor should therefore conclude his explanatory paragraph with a statement to the effect that 'our opinion on the financial statements is not qualified in this respect.'

In certain circumstances, the auditor may conclude that in addition to qualifying his opinion or expressing a disclaimer of opinion (or even despite this) it is necessary to resign. Less frequently, the auditor may reach the same conclusion mid-way through the engagement and decide to resign, having proffered no opinion at all.

At a general level, there will often be good reason for considering resignation if any of the criteria that would cause the auditor to refuse an invitation to accept appointment as auditor becomes apparent during the course of an engagement and, in particular, the first engagement for that client.[8]

Specifically, examples where there may be justification for resigning include:

- the auditor considers that the shareholders have not been given the information they require and the auditor sees no opportunity for reporting such information to the shareholders whilst continuing as auditor;

- the highest authority within the client company is suspected of involvement with a suspected or actual fraud – this may affect the reliability of management representations, cause the auditor to lose

---

[6]SAS 600.7

[7]SAS 120.10; SAS 600.6.

[8]See Chapter 2.

confidence in the integrity of one or more of the directors, and impact on the auditor's ability to undertake his responsibility to the members of the company;

- the relationship between the auditor and senior management or directors of the client has irretrievably broken down such that it is no longer possible to continue with the engagement but it might be possible for another firm of auditors to do so; or

- the directors of a company refuse to issue its financial statements, or the auditor wishes to inform shareholders or creditors of the company of his concerns and there is no immediate occasion to do so.[9]

Resignation may also be motivated by professional considerations such as the discovery of an impediment to the auditor's independence – resignation in these circumstances could become increasingly common in light of the strict requirements of the Securities and Exchange Commission regarding independence. The auditor's position may also be affected by doubts about his ability to provide a satisfactory quality of audits (although we would seldom expect an auditor to reach this conclusion!).

An auditor may wish to resign if he suspects that his client is involved in money laundering. However, an added complication arises from the tipping off provisions in the money laundering legislation.[10] Disclosing the fact that a money laundering suspicion has been reported is an offence liable to fine or imprisonment if the disclosure is likely to prejudice an investigation. The auditor must be very careful not to fall foul of these provisions in his audit report, his statement of circumstances, or in any statement to successor auditors (see below). In these circumstances, the auditor should consider discussing the matter with the National Criminal Intelligence Service ('NCIS'), the organisation to whom money laundering suspicions are reported, before any decision on disclosure (and resignation) is taken.[11]

If the conclusion is reached that the auditor should resign from the engagement, it would be prudent, where possible, for an independent party (such as another member of the firm or legal advisers) to review the matters which have led to the decision that the auditor should

---

[9]See SAS 110, para 62.

[10]See Criminal Justice Act 1993, s93D.

[11]The central authority to which all UK money laundering suspicions should be reported is The Financial Intelligence Unit, National Criminal Intelligence Service, PO Box 8000, Spring Gardens, Tinworth Street, London SE11 5EN (Tel: 020 7238 8000).

voluntarily resign. In particular, the independent party should ensure that the matters in question are not matters which should more properly be dealt with in the auditor's opinion (as discussed above). Such a review will be particularly important when the decision to resign is taken during the course of an engagement, since any improper resignation may give rise to a claim for breach of contract by the client (although damages, other than the cost of replacement auditors or wasted fees, may be difficult to substantiate).

6.3 Companies Act requirements

Companies Act 1985, s392 (as amended by Companies Act 1989) provides that an auditor may resign by depositing a notice in writing to that effect at the company's registered office (the notice would usually be addressed to the company secretary or the directors of the company). The notice must be accompanied by the statement required by Companies Act, s394.[12] The company is required within 14 days to send a copy of the notice of resignation to the Registrar of Companies.

The statement required by s394 has to set out any circumstances connected with the auditor ceasing to hold office which he considers should be brought to the attention of members or creditors of the company,[13] or, if he considers that there are no such circumstances, a statement that there are none.

The auditor must consider separately the interests of members and the interests of creditors. The members of some clients (for example, owner-managed businesses) will be fully apprised of the company's affairs and there may well be no matters for the auditor to bring to their attention. However, the creditors of such companies will be in an entirely different position and it will be especially important for the auditor to focus on their position.

Equally important, readers should remember that the statement of circumstances and the auditor's opinion are made (and read) independently of one another. So, for example, it might be possible for the

---

[12]Although this Chapter primarily focuses on the voluntary resignation of the auditor, the same statutory obligations apply when the client asks the auditor to resign. Similar statutory obligations apply when the auditor does not seek re-election: see Companies Act 1985, s394(2).

[13]Whereas the auditor's opinion is made for the benefit of shareholders, Companies Act legislation requires the auditor to take certain steps to safeguard the interests of shareholders *and* creditors. Otherwise, the auditor ordinarily owes no duty of care to creditors: *Caparo Industries plc* v *Dickman* [1990] 2 AC 605 (HL).

181

auditor to qualify his opinion or issue a disclaimer of opinion, but for there to be no mention of circumstances in the letter of resignation. However, in doing this, the auditor must be careful to ensure that he has complied with Companies Act legislation – in particular, that he has expressly considered the interests of creditors. The mentioning of matters in the auditor's opinion does not discharge the auditor's obligations to creditors under the resignation legislation.

6.3.1 Letter of resignation

The letter of resignation is self-explanatory. For example:

> The Directors
>
> [name of client]
>
> Dear Sirs
>
> In accordance with Section 392 of the Companies Act 1985 we give notice of our resignation as auditors of [name of client], registered number [company number] with effect from [date] [or with immediate effect].
>
> Yours faithfully
>
> [Auditor]

The resignation will be effective from the date on which notice is deposited at the registered office of the company, or on such later date as is specified in the letter of resignation.

6.3.2 Statement of 'no circumstances'

The statement of 'no circumstances' is similarly self-explanatory and could be included in the letter of resignation or, alternatively, set out in a separate letter (in which case good practice dictates that it should be attached to the letter of resignation). An example of the latter follows:

> The Directors
>
> [Name of client]
>
> Dear Sirs
>
> Our notice of resignation as auditors of [client name] with effect from [date] [or with immediate effect] is being deposited at the company's registered office today (see attached).

In accordance with Section 394 of the Companies Act 1985, we confirm that there are no circumstances connected with our resignation which we consider should be brought to the attention of members or creditors of [name of client].

Yours faithfully

[Auditor]

6.3.3   Statement of 'circumstances'

There is no professional guidance as to what constitute the 'circumstances' that should be brought to the attention of the members or creditors of the company. The only guidance of any relevance is in ICAEW Statement 1.206 entitled 'Changes in a professional appointment'. This deals with the matters that an existing auditor must bring to the attention of a prospective auditor in order to allow the latter an opportunity to decide whether, in all the circumstances, it would be proper for him to accept the appointment.

Having regard to Statement 1.206, it seems that 'circumstances' would include the following:

- the publicity surrounding the change in auditor and/or information provided by the client to members, creditors or prospective auditors is misleading and does not reflect the true position as regards the reasons for the auditor's resignation;

- the auditor and the client are unable to reconcile differences of principle and/or practice which the auditor regards as fundamental;[14]

- any aspect of the conduct of the client, its directors or employees which leads the auditor to suspect there has been an unlawful act or default and/or which the auditor believes should be investigated further by the appropriate authority;

- serious concerns and doubts regarding the integrity of the directors and/or senior managers of the client;

- the withholding of information from the auditor, shareholders, creditors or a prospective auditor.[15]

---

[14]In a recent case, the resigning auditor indicated in the Statement of Circumstances that he regarded his inability to agree appropriate fee proposals with the client's management as a limitation on the necessary scope of the audit.

[15]See Companies Act 1985, s389A. In addition, where the client refuses to grant the existing auditor consent to provide relevant client information to a prospective auditor, this will usually be a matter of interest to the members and creditors and should be included in the statement of circumstances, if one has not yet been made.

We are also aware of circumstances in which a resigning auditor has disclosed in his statement of circumstances the fact that the client has refused to pay the auditor's fees. The existence of unpaid fees is unlikely of itself to be a matter of interest for members or creditors and we question whether this is sufficient reason on its own to justify resignation, and whether it should be included in the statement of circumstances.[16] It may, however, be appropriate to disclose the non-payment of fees where this fact is indicative of a matter which is of direct concern to members and creditors such as where the client stops paying the auditor's fees during the course of the audit engagement and the auditor suspects the client's position may be symptomatic of cash flow problems or a breakdown of the necessary professional relationship between client and auditor.

It is difficult to provide a pro-forma letter of circumstances since the relevant circumstances will vary in each case. Careful thought will need to be given to what should be said in light of the specific facts that have arisen. We set out below one example that might provide some guidance as to the depth of information which could be disclosed in the letter of circumstances.[17]

One point the resigning auditor should bear in mind when preparing the statement of circumstances is that in many cases the deadlock that has been reached with the client is specific to the existing client/auditor relationship. While the resigning auditor may see the problems as insurmountable, often a new auditor with a fresh approach and perspective can get past the deadlock and resolve matters to his satisfaction – and also to the satisfaction of the members and creditors. The auditor should therefore be careful not to paint too dark a picture and should stick strictly to the facts. For example:

> The Directors
>
> [name of client]
>
> Dear Sirs
>
> Our notice of resignation as auditors of [client name] with effect from [date] [or with immediate effect] is being deposited at the company's registered office today (see attached).

---

[16]Nor is the existence of unpaid fees of itself a reason why a prospective auditor should not accept appointment.

[17]While the statement of circumstances may itself be quite brief, the existing auditor will be required to provide further detail to a prospective auditor in accordance with ICAEW Statement 1.206; see also the next section. Any additional information does not have to be made available to shareholders or creditors.

As required pursuant to Section 394 of the Companies Act 1985, this letter constitutes a statement of the circumstances connected with our resignation which we consider should be brought to the attention of members or creditors of [name of client].

Statement

Subsequent to the directors' approval of the financial statements of the Company for the year ended [insert date], we were informed that certain payments may have been made which might give rise to liability for tax on the part of the Company. We requested certain information from the directors in order that we could assess whether these payments, if any, created any tax obligation on the Company. The directors informed us that in their view no such obligations had been created. However, they did not provide the information requested by us to enable us to form our own view.

In all the circumstances, we consider that the professional relationship between us and the company has irretrievably broken down and we have concluded that we cannot continue to act as the company's auditors.

Yours faithfully

[Auditor]

As referred to in the above example, the auditor is entitled to request from the company's officers such information and explanations as he thinks necessary for the performance of his duties.[18] Where the company's officers have failed to provide this information the auditor may be justified in concluding that the relationship with the client has irretrievably broken down.

6.3.4   Further procedural requirements

Within 14 days of the statement of circumstances being deposited, the company must either send a copy to every person entitled to copies of the accounts under Companies Act, s238, or apply to the Court on the basis that the auditor is using the statement to secure needless publicity for defamatory matter.[19] If the company does apply to the Court, it must notify the auditor of the application in advance of the hearing. Once on

---

[18]See Companies Act 1985, s389A.

[19]See Companies Act 1985, s394.

notice, the auditor will usually have the opportunity to put his views before the Court.[20]

In the (presumably rare) case where the Court is satisfied that the auditor is using the statement to secure needless publicity for defamatory matter, the Court will direct that the company should not send out copies of the statement and it may further order that the auditor pay part or all of the company's costs of the application, even though the auditor is not a party to the application. In these circumstances, the company is obliged to send out a statement setting out the effect of the Court's order to the persons mentioned above who fall within Companies Act, s238.

If the Court is not persuaded that the auditor's statement is an abuse of process, the company is required to send out a copy of the statement of circumstances to the s238 recipients and notify the auditor of the Court's decision. The auditor has a further seven days from receipt of such notice to send a copy of his statement to the Registrar of Companies.

Where the auditor does not receive notice of a Court application within 21 days of depositing the statement of circumstances, the auditor must, within a further seven days, send a copy of his statement to the Registrar of Companies. There is no requirement for the auditor to send his statement to the Registrar of Companies if there are no circumstances to report.

6.3.5   When the resigning auditor wants to say more

When the resigning auditor deposits a letter of circumstances with the company setting out circumstances that he considers should be brought to the attention of the members and creditors, the auditor can, if he so wishes, call on the directors to hold an extraordinary general meeting of the company for the purpose of discussing and explaining the circumstances connected with his resignation. The auditor may also request that a statement of the circumstances connected with his

---

[20]There has been limited judicial consideration of these provisions. On 14 July 2000, however, Lightman J handed down judgment in the case of *Jarvis Plc* v *PricewaterhouseCoopers* LTL 14/7/2000. The Judge stressed the importance of the auditor's duty under s394 in the public interest and remarked that the Court would assume that the auditor was acting in faithful discharge of that duty, and not in pursuit of any private or collateral interest, unless the contrary is shown. He also observed that the process should not be abused by the company concerned in an attempt to delay dissemination of statements of circumstances.

resignation be circulated to members prior to any such meeting.[21] The full procedural requirements are set out in Companies Act, s392A.

Worthy of note in this context is the right of the company to make an application to the Court to prevent the auditor's statement from being circulated to members or read out at the meeting. As above, the auditor must be given notice of this application and will usually be entitled to be heard on the application. If the Court is satisfied that the auditor is abusing the process in order to secure needless publicity for defamatory matter, the Court may order that all or part of the company's costs of the application be paid by the auditor, even though he is not a party to the application.

6.4   Communicating with the successor auditor

In the interests of both the public and the existing and prospective auditors, the Institute considers it necessary for the existing auditor to communicate with a prospective auditor concerning any considerations which might affect the prospective auditor's decision whether or not to accept the appointment.

6.4.1   Responding to the request for information

It is incumbent upon the prospective auditor to write to the existing auditor and ask him whether there are any matters which could influence the prospective auditor's decision whether or not he should properly accept the appointment as auditor of the company. The prospective auditor will usually also ask for copies of the letter of resignation and the statement of circumstances. Importantly, the existing auditor should not volunteer any information to a prospective auditor in the absence of any such request.

---

[21]A rare public example of an auditor writing to company members was seen in 1995 when BDO Stoy Hayward, who had been the auditors of the Royal Automobile Club for some 16 years, circulated a letter to RAC members to try and persuade them to reverse the directors' decision to appoint Price Waterhouse in their place. It was said that PW had won the RAC audit by tendering an audit fee almost half that which BDO had received for the previous year and which was a good deal lower than BDO's tender. BDO told members that 'it is our strongly held view that the independence and objectivity of any auditor will be at risk in circumstances where an audit has been secured on the basis of a predatory price'. PW rejected these allegations. The RAC's letter to members came down firmly on the side of PW, who later received overwhelming support at the annual meeting: see *The Times*, 21 April 1995; *The Independent*, 22 April 1995; *The Times*, 18 May 1995.

The resigning auditor must take care to act prudently and sensibly at all times in dealing with such delicate matters. For example, all too often the prospective auditor asks the resigning auditor whether there are any valid 'professional objections' to the prospective auditor accepting their appointment. This is, on one view, the wrong question in the sense that a resigning auditor will (usually) have no grounds to object to the new appointment, even though there may be matters the resigning auditor wishes to bring to their attention. Furthermore, the resigning auditor has no responsibility for the decision of the prospective auditor, and there is no 'professional clearance' which he can give or withhold.

Notwithstanding that the wrong question has been asked, it will usually be appropriate for the resigning auditor to treat the enquiry as if it were an enquiry for information which might influence the prospective auditor's decision as to whether or not he may properly accept the appointment.

6.4.2   Confidentiality of client information

As discussed elsewhere, the auditor owes duties of confidentiality to his client.[22] Therefore, before the existing auditor does anything in response to the request (other than perhaps acknowledge receipt), he should seek his client's consent to disclose the client's affairs to the prospective auditor. If this consent is not forthcoming, the existing auditor should inform the prospective auditor accordingly, who should decline appointment. The existing auditor must then refrain from disclosing any information about the client's affairs to the prospective auditor.[23]

When providing information to the prospective auditor, the existing auditor should expressly state that any information so provided is confidential.

6.4.3   Responding without delay

The existing auditor should respond to the enquiry from the prospective auditor without delay. Failure to do so may result in the prospective auditor making a complaint to the ICAEW. The existing auditor cannot refuse to respond or delay his response on the grounds that either the

---

[22]See Chapter 1.

[23]See footnote 15. Where the client refuses to grant the existing auditor consent to provide relevant client information to a prospective auditor, this will usually be a matter of interest to the members and creditors and should be included in the statement of circumstances, if one has not yet been made.

prospective auditor has been nominated in contravention of Institute Guidance, or the existing auditor believes the client is treating him unfairly.

Where the prospective auditor has combined his general enquiry for 'matters of influence' with requests for specific client information (for example, copies of previous accounts), the existing auditor may wish to inform the prospective auditor of the matters of influence first. This is so particularly where the matters of influence might be significant and cause the prospective auditor to decline the appointment, in which case there will be no need to collate the additional information.

6.4.4 No matters to be disclosed

Where there are no matters to disclose to the prospective auditor, a straightforward response can be sent. For example:

> Dear Sirs **CONFIDENTIAL**
>
> **[name of client] registered number [company number]**
>
> Thank you for your letter dated [date] relating to your proposed nomination as auditors of the above company.
>
> In our opinion there are no matters of which you should be aware that could influence your decision as to whether or not you may properly accept this appointment.
>
> We enclose a copy of our letter of resignation and a copy of the statement made under Section 394 of the Companies Act 1985. Both documents have been deposited at the company's registered office.
>
> Yours faithfully
>
> [resigning auditor]

6.4.5 Matters to be disclosed

The existing auditor is required to inform the prospective auditor of such matters that the existing auditor, in his opinion, thinks he should be aware. It is not sufficient that the existing auditor states that 'unspecified factors' exist; the existing auditor must provide more detail than this. ICAEW Statement 1.206 suggests that relevant matters would include the following:

● the reasons for the change in auditor as advanced by the client of which the existing auditor or adviser is aware are not in accordance with the facts (as understood by the latter);

- the proposal to displace the existing auditor or adviser arises in his opinion because he has carried out his duties in the face of opposition or evasion/s in which important differences of principle or practice had arisen with the client;

- the client, its directors or employees may have been guilty of some unlawful act or default. It is enough for the auditor to suspect improper behaviour, it is not up to the auditor to be judge and jury;

- any aspect of the conduct of the client, its directors or employees which is relevant to the carrying out of the audit or assignment ought, in the opinion of the existing auditor or adviser, to be investigated further by the appropriate authority;

- the existing auditor or adviser has unconfirmed suspicions that the client or its directors or employees have defrauded the Inland Revenue, Customs & Excise or others;

- the existing auditor or adviser has serious doubts regarding the integrity of the directors and/or senior managers of the client company;

- the client, its directors or employees have deliberately withheld information required by the existing auditor or adviser for the performance of his work or have limited or attempted to limit the scope of his work;

- the existing auditor proposes to bring to the attention of members or creditors circumstances surrounding the proposed change of auditor.

A statement from the existing auditor limited to a description of any of the matters listed above, although apparently acceptable, would still, on any view, be economical. What the existing auditor should ensure is that he at least provides sufficient information to the prospective auditor to allow him to ask the client for relevant information so that the prospective auditor can reach his own conclusions. In this regard, it may be appropriate for the existing auditor to refer to correspondence with the client which sets out any difficulties and concerns the existing auditor has had with the client. The prospective adviser can then ask the client for copies of that correspondence and in this way will learn of any matters of possible concern. Beyond this, while the existing auditor may offer to provide further detail in writing, from a risk management perspective it will usually be preferable to explain matters further orally to the prospective auditor, with each party making their own record of this discussion. This approach is endorsed by the Institute.[24]

---

[24]See ICAEW Statement 1.206, para 1.8.

Importantly, communication of such information to the prospective auditor does not relieve the existing auditor of his duty to continue to press on the client his views on any technical or ethical matters which may have led him into dispute with the client, nor does it affect the freedom of the client to exercise his right to a change of auditor.

6.4.6 Avoiding defamatory statements

An existing auditor who communicates to a prospective auditor matters damaging to the client or to any individuals concerned with the client's business will have a strong measure of protection were any action for defamation to be brought against him, in that the communication would be protected by qualified privilege. This means that the existing auditor should not be liable to pay damages for defamatory statements even if they turn out to be untrue, provided that they are made without malice, that is, in good faith and without spite, ill will or some other improper motive.

In order to avoid acting maliciously, the auditor should state only what he sincerely believes to be true, and he should not make reckless imputations against a client or individuals connected with the client, which he can have no reason for believing to be true. (This is of course true of all statements made by the auditor, whether in the audit report, the letter of circumstances or in communications with the prospective auditor.) It would be wise and generally helpful to seek an independent review internally as to what should be communicated to the prospective auditor, before acting; too often the individual responsible for the engagement may be so closely involved that he cannot see the wood for the trees.

Finally, the auditor should only provide such information as is known to him in his capacity as auditor (whether prior to or after resignation) and as is necessary to discharge his obligations.

For example:

Dear Sirs   **CONFIDENTIAL**

[name of client] registered number [company number]

We refer to your letter dated [date] seeking information that might influence your decision whether to accept appointment as auditors of the above company.

We have received written authority of the directors of [company] to discuss their affairs with you.

We enclose a copy of our letter of resignation and a copy of the statement made under Section 394 of the Companies Act 1985. Both documents have been deposited at the company's registered office [and the statement of circumstances has also been deposited with the Registrar of Companies].

The reasons for our resignation are set out in the enclosed statement of circumstances. Material facts which would have been relevant to our decision in [date] whether to accept the appointment as auditors of [company] were disclosed to us [explain the circumstances and refer to the existence of relevant documents so that the prospective auditor can request them from the client].

Explanations we have received from the directors of [company] are inconsistent with what is recorded in the documents which have recently been disclosed to us and which are identified above.

We have also been provided with documents by the directors as supporting documentation for the purchase of certain assets. Our enquiries suggest that these documents do not provide conclusive audit evidence insofar as the details contained therein are inconsistent with the explanations we have received from independent sources.

These matters have given rise to serious doubts in our minds regarding the integrity of the directors of [company] such that the required professional relationship of mutual trust between the directors of the company and us has irretrievably broken down.

This letter [and its enclosures] are provided to your firm in the strictest confidence in response to your letter of enquiry dated [date] and are solely for use of [enquiring auditor] in this context. The contents of this letter and its enclosures should not be disclosed to any other party.

Yours faithfully

[resigning auditor]

6.4.7 Providing access to working papers to the successor auditor

On resignation, the resigning auditor should transfer to the client or, where the client consents, the successor auditor, those papers which belong to the client (unless the resigning auditor is exercising a lien over those papers in respect of unpaid fees, as to which see **4.3** above).

It is customary for the successor auditor also to ask for access to the resigning auditor's working papers. In practice, we would expect the resigning auditor to refuse such a request – this is particularly so where there is no ongoing relationship with the client which might otherwise motivate the existing auditor to provide such disclosure. In any event, where the resigning auditor has completed the audit and provided an opinion on the financial statements, it is unlikely that he will have any further material information. On the other hand, where the auditor has resigned during the course of the engagement, he should provide sufficient information regarding the client's affairs to the successor auditor to enable him to carry out his duties and to avoid prejudicing the client's interests. Insofar as the resigning auditor does provide this information to the successor auditor (or volunteers any further information), he should follow the general guidance on providing working papers to third parties discussed in **Chapter 3**.

6.5 Other resignation issues

6.5.1 Informing the client

With the notable and important exceptions of (1) suspected money laundering activities and (2) suspected fraud or non-compliance with the law which casts doubt on the integrity of the directors,[25] it is difficult to conceive when the auditor would have good reason not to discuss his proposed resignation with his client, before he deposits a letter of resignation at the company's registered office.

Where the auditor has been in discussions with the client and it is clear that matters will not be resolved to the auditor's satisfaction, the auditor should, as a courtesy, inform the client in advance that he has no option but to tender his resignation.[26]

However, where the auditor has become aware of matters which have not yet been brought to the attention of the directors of the company, it would be sensible for the auditor to discuss his concerns with the directors so that the auditor may make an informed assessment of the significance of the matter and so that the directors may be given the opportunity to be heard. As stated at the outset, resignation is, after all, an act of last resort.

---

[25]These matters are beyond the scope of this book; refer to SAS 120 and 620 and ICAEW Statement 1.304.

[26]This could be done either orally or in writing. Where the relationship between the client and the auditor has deteriorated completely, the auditor may decide that this is inappropriate altogether; it is entirely a matter for his discretion.

All discussions with the client in these circumstances should be documented by the auditor, not least because the auditor may wish to provide a copy of any such documents to the successor auditor as part of the 'matters of influence' for the successor auditor's consideration.[27] As with all documents prepared by the auditor, but particularly so in this instance, the auditor should endeavour to record accurately what was said by the client in response to the auditor's concerns and must avoid derogatory remarks about the client, including speculation about the directors' or employees' honesty and integrity. If possible, it would be helpful to get the client to sign the document as an agreed record of the matters discussed.

If, following the discussions with the client, the auditor concludes that it is appropriate to resign, professional courtesy again suggests that the auditor should inform the client of his intention to resign, before he does so.[28] The auditor will not lose any surprise advantage by doing so and may get advance notice of the likely response from the client (that is, whether they are likely to offer any objection). Where possible, the auditor should avoid being drawn into a detailed explanation of the reasons for resignation; the client should, by this stage, have a clear idea of the auditor's views in any event. However, if pushed, the auditor might want to disclose what he intends to include in his statement of circumstances, if anything (but he should only do so where he has prepared his statement in advance).

Any courtesy call (or letter) should be followed as soon as possible by a formal letter of resignation. As set out above, this letter should be straightforward and should not include anything more than the statement of resignation since it is likely to be copied to the successor auditor in due course.

In addition to the letter of resignation, the resigning auditor[29] should consider sending a separate letter of disengagement to his client, which confirms the termination of the engagement and deals with consequential matters such as identifying:

- which services have been provided up to the date of resignation;

- what further action (if any) the resigning auditor will take after resignation;

---

[27]See Chapter 4 for general guidance on the preparation of attendance notes of discussions with clients.

[28]This is entirely a matter for the auditor's discretion – see footnote 26.

[29]In fact, this suggestion applies equally to any situation in which an accountant ceases to act.

- which services are outstanding including, for example, whether there are forthcoming deadlines which will require immediate work by the successor auditor;

- what steps, if any, the client should take;

- (perhaps most importantly) what fees are outstanding.[30]

This action should help to avoid misunderstandings with the client about the services provided during the engagement and disputes about fees for this work. Equally, this action should assist in achieving a smooth handover of responsibilities to the successor auditor, with whom the resigning auditor is required to cooperate insofar as is necessary to avoid prejudicing the interests of the client.[31]

6.5.2 Disclosure to third parties (other than the prospective or successor auditor)

While beyond the scope of this book, the resigning auditor should be aware of connected issues such as his duty to report suspected money laundering related to drug trafficking or terrorism to the National Criminal Intelligence Service ('NCIS').[32]

The resigning auditor of regulated entities must also consider whether it is appropriate to bring any matters to the attention of the regulator of the client, having regard to the auditor's special statutory reporting duties.[33]

---

[30]The auditor may wish to claim a lien over client papers in respect of unpaid fees: see 4.3 above.

[31]Refer to ICAEW Statement 1.206, para 3.0 and see also previous section.

[32]Refer to SAS 120, ICAEW Statement 1.304 and The Money Laundering Regulations 1993.

[33]Refer to SAS 620 and the associated Practice Notes.

7 Professional indemnity insurance

7.1 Introduction

This Chapter looks at some issues concerning accountants' professional indemnity insurance cover, focusing both on the stage when insurance cover is bought and on what needs to happen if the cover later has to be called upon.

Just as every accountancy practice is different in terms of its people and the types of work it does, so it will have different needs, and its own particular relationship with its insurers. Many books could be (and indeed have been) written on the subject of insurance, but this Chapter is intended as a brief practical guide, and to highlight some of the more common pitfalls.

7.2 Buying insurance

7.2.1 Minimum cover

The ICAEW has a compulsory professional indemnity insurance scheme whereby all members holding a Practising Certificate must comply with the Professional Indemnity Insurance Regulations ('PII Regulations'). An accountant must be able to provide satisfactory evidence of professional indemnity insurance cover in order to be a Registered Auditor, to be authorised under the Investment Business Regulations, or to practice as an Insolvency Practitioner.

The minimum limit of indemnity which an accountant must buy in order to fulfil the current requirements of the PII Regulations is two and a half times the gross fee income of the practice for its last financial year, subject to a minimum of £50,000 cover for a sole practitioner or £100,000 in any other case, but up to a maximum required cover of £1 million. Within these figures, firms may choose a self-insured excess of up to £20,000 per principal. It should be stressed that these are the minimum requirements and, as we shall discuss below, it would be very unwise to assume that this minimum cover is adequate for all accountants' needs.

A further requirement is that an accountant's professional indemnity insurance cover must be obtained from a 'Participating Insurer'. Whilst the policies issued by the Participating Insurers may not be worded the same way, all these insurers have agreed to meet the requirements of the ICAEW's minimum policy wording.

We shall discuss policy wordings in more detail below, but the most significant feature of the required cover is that it is on what is known as a 'claims made' basis. This means that a current policy will provide cover for claims arising from past events, even if those events occurred some years ago. Sometimes, insurers impose a cut-off date known as a 'retroactive date' for past events which result in claims, before which they will not provide cover, but Participating Insurers have agreed that this date should be at least six years before the date of the current policy (or the date of commencement of the firm's public practice, whichever is the more recent date). This is sufficient for most practices given that the limitation period in respect of professional indemnity claims is for most purposes six years.

At the other end of the timescale, when a practice dissolves, or for some other reason insurance is not renewed, a 'discovery' provision, which may already be in the policy or which may be bought separately, may extend or provide cover for a certain number of years for claims which are made during that period arising out of events which occurred prior to the 'discovery' period. This is also known as 'run–off' cover, which will also be needed for partners who have retired from an ongoing practice.

7.2.2   Using a broker

It is usual to use a broker to arrange insurance cover (only a few of the Participating Insurers will deal with firms directly) particularly since it is common for a practice's professional insurance cover to be spread amongst a number of insurers, usually with one 'lead underwriter' and several 'following underwriters'. An insurance broker will negotiate the cover on behalf of the practice, and will advise on such matters as how the insurance cover should be arranged, and on any extra terms which should be negotiated depending on the needs of the firm. As discussed below, it may be that several policies will be needed, stacked in 'layers' of cover.

Although the broker is the accountant's agent for the purposes of negotiating the insurance cover, the broker is effectively paid by the insurers for this service since the broker's commission will be a percentage of the premium paid under the policy, separately negotiated with the underwriters.

7.2.3   What insurance cover does an accountant need?

Different accountancy practices will have very different insurance requirements. Each practice must look at its individual exposures and consider the possibility of being sued should anything go wrong and the possible amount of such a claim, client by client, having regard to the maximum potential exposure of those interested in the client such as shareholders. It need hardly be said that a firm of accountants engaged as auditors or advisers to a large Plc may be exposed to shareholder claims (should anything go wrong) of up to tens or maybe hundreds of millions of pounds, whereas a practitioner dealing only with individual clients, even quite wealthy ones, will have nothing like this level of liability per claim, but may have greater exposure to numbers of smaller claims. When assessing its exposure, each practice should look at not only its current work in progress, but also its past staff, consultants and subcontractors.

The ICAEW requires each practice to return a form stating that it has carried out a risk assessment, and that it has either enough personal or partnership assets, or insurance, to cover the assessed risks. Each practice must put in place procedures to enable it to carry out this risk assessment, which will usually involve circulating all professional staff with a questionnaire designed to show such things as areas of high-risk activity, engagements relating to unusually large transactions or clients, and 'difficult' or dissatisfied clients. As we shall discuss below, a broker will need to present underwriters with a very clear picture of the practice and its exposures prior to underwriters agreeing to give cover, so this process will have to be gone through in any event as part of the process of buying insurance.

Since the insurance cover may well include costs and expenses (i.e., legal fees), the required maximum cover of £1 million may not go very far, and in many cases a practice will need to 'top up' the minimum required insurance to cover its exposure, unless it has very substantial personal and partnership assets which the partners are prepared to risk in the absence of taking out extra cover. This 'top up' insurance cover may well be divided into 'layers' of risk with perhaps one insurer agreeing to cover £5 million of liability over and above the £1 million compulsory (or 'primary') insurance and different insurers covering a further 'layer' of £5 million on top of that, and so forth.

As mentioned above, the current maximum self-insured excess is £20,000 per principal in the practice. Depending on the typical size and number of the practice's clients, the appropriate excess may be much smaller. Although carrying a high excess usually means that the

199

premiums are reduced, a practice exposed to a number of smaller claims may find cover with a high excess almost worthless.

7.2.4   Mutual, captive, or open market?

Insurance is referred to as having been bought on the 'open market' if it has been bought from an insurance company (or Lloyd's syndicate). By contrast, a 'Mutual' or 'Mutual Fund' is an arrangement whereby a group of professionals 'club together' to pay into a fund which is then used to pay out in respect of liabilities. Although there may be little difference between the terms under which the fund indemnifies its members and typical policy terms, and the contributions or subscriptions members make into the fund and premiums which might be paid under a policy, this is not technically 'insurance'. In some circumstances a practice may find it more advantageous to purchase cover from a mutual since the contributions may be lower than open market premiums (where insurance companies have to make profits) and do not attract insurance premium tax. Most practices would be best advised to explore both open market and mutual options.

Some very large practices find that it is cost (and tax) effective to set up their own insurance company, often offshore, which will either provide 'primary' cover, with the excess layers arranged elsewhere, or will obtain reinsurance protection for its exposure to claims over a certain amount.

7.2.5   What activities does 'professional indemnity insurance' cover?

Insurance policies may differ greatly in their manner of expressing the cover, varying from 'Any civil liability incurred in connection with the Practice', to the more elaborate:

> 'Any act, error, omission, breach of contract or duty or libel or slander or any allegation thereof . . . on the part of the assured firm or an affiliated firm or their predecessors in business or any other person or entity for whose act, error, omission, breach of contract, or duty or libel or slander or allegations thereof the assured firm is legally responsible whether assumed by contract or otherwise in or about the conduct of any professional business conducted by or on behalf of the assured firm . . . .'

Some policies attempt to define the types of activities that are covered by referring to 'professional business'. For example:

'Advice given or services performed of whatsoever nature...pro-
vided that the fee or a portion of the fee accruing from the work
inures to the benefit of the firm....'

Policies usually include in this description, work done in the name of the
firm, even if no fee has been charged. The different definitions of the
activities covered are always subject to other terms and exclusions
elsewhere in the policy, and cover may not be as wide as it might initially
seem. It will always be important to read all the policy documentation.

Put simply, the policy is intended to apply to situations where
accountants and/or their firms have incurred liability *as professionals*.
Professional indemnity insurance is not intended to cover the types of
liabilities which might be incurred in running any business (for
example, liability to visitors who may injure themselves on the premises
or liability as an employer, which would be covered by public liability
and employers' liability insurance policies respectively). The types of
claims envisaged would be those made by clients or those analogous to
clients relating to deficiencies in work carried out by the professional as
an accountant.

The expansion in the types of work undertaken by some accountancy
practices, and the increasing use of innovative fee arrangements (such as
taking stock in a client company in lieu of conventional fees) might mean
that some activities fall outside the intended cover. A practice would be
well advised to consult its broker and/or advise its insurers if in doubt as
to whether a particular activity will be regarded as covered.

A professional indemnity insurance policy will not cover a professional
for any criminal penalties, or fines or penalties imposed by a governing
body, and will not always cover the costs of dealing with a regulatory
investigation, or the costs of defending a professional in any disciplinary
proceedings. Where regulatory costs are covered in a policy (perhaps in
return for additional premium) this may only be in relation to regulatory
proceedings which are relevant to a claim or potential claim arising out of
the same acts or events. Occasionally, the costs of defending criminal
proceedings may be covered, again only if relevant to a potential claim
and only in the event of a not guilty verdict.

In recent years accountants' practices have expanded into an increasingly
diverse number of non-traditional activities that may not be covered,
although policy terms may vary between the Participating Insurers. If a
firm's risk assessment procedure shows up any of these activities, the
policy should be checked and the possibility of shopping around for wider
cover or negotiating extensions of cover should be discussed with the
broker. Examples include:

(a) Investment advice.

(b) Directors' and Officers' liability when serving on outside boards (often excluded).

(c) Foreign business (US/Canadian business will almost certainly be excluded).

(d) Management consulting.

(e) IT/Computer consulting.

There is no substitute for a close examination of the policy, but it should be noted that the following are likely to be excluded:

(a) Irrecoverable fees or fees which have to be repaid to the client. Sometimes, however, the costs and expenses in recovering these fees are covered under the policy if the reason behind the fees being withheld is a related professional indemnity claim. An action by an accountant for unpaid fees is often the trigger for a counterclaim against him alleging professional negligence.

(b) Employers' liability.

(c) Personal injury.

(d) Dishonest, fraudulent and malicious acts which the practice know about or ought to have known about or suspected at the time they were committed. (This is another reason to ensure that effective risk assessment procedures are in place so that dishonest activity does not go undetected.)

(e) Buying and selling investments and warranties as to investment performance.

As a general rule, insurers will only be liable to indemnify in respect of the costs of defending a claim where the claim itself is covered under the policy. In the event that a claim turns out to be unfounded, the costs incurred in the successful defence of that claim without the prior consent of insurers may not be recoverable.[1]

It is quite possible that a claim may be made which makes a number of allegations of which some may be covered by the policy and others excluded. What matters is not how the claimant happens to frame its case legally, but the factual basis behind it, and proceedings may be on foot for some time (or even concluded) before the full facts emerge making it apparent whether the liability is covered or not. To avoid the practice

---

[1] See *Thornton Springer* v *NEM Insurance Co Ltd & Ors* [2000] 2 All ER 489.

having to wait until that stage is reached to recover any of its costs, an insurer might in these circumstances give its consent to costs being incurred to the extent of the portion of the costs necessary to defend the allegations which might, if proved, be covered, or consent to the costs being incurred subject to a 'reservation of rights' as to whether the claim is one which the policy covers.

7.2.6 What should be disclosed to insurers when buying insurance?

There will invariably be a proposal form to be completed for presentation to the underwriter, who will make a decision as to whether or not he will insure the practice, and if so on what terms and at what rate of premium, based on this information and any other information which forms part of the broker's presentation to him. Although the questions in the proposal form give a good indication of the sort of information which underwriters need to know (invariably asking about the practice's claims history and practice areas), they are not exhaustive and there may well be other facts which do not fit into answers to particular questions, which nevertheless still need to be disclosed as they are material to the risk to be insured.

Unlike normal contracts, contracts of insurance are known as contracts *'uberrimae fides'* ('of utmost good faith'), which means that rather than the onus being on the insurer to enquire as to the nature of the risk, the onus is on the insured to provide all relevant and material information.[2] This is why it is not safe to rely merely on answering the questions in the proposal form. The duty to disclose material facts continues right up to the policy being issued, so information which comes to light after the proposal form has been submitted must also be communicated to the underwriters.

As part of a firm's risk assessment procedures to establish the level and type of cover needed (discussed above), systems should be put in place to make sure that all information relating to the practice's potential professional liabilities known about by the most junior staff to the most senior partners, finds its way into the hands of the person or people responsible for liaising with the broker and completing the proposal form or other information pack for the underwriters. Once this information has been gathered, those within the practice responsible for the insurance arrangements would be well advised to discuss with the broker just how much of it is material. As a general rule, if there is any doubt, it should be disclosed to the underwriters.

---

[2]See *Carter* v *Boehm* (1776) 3 Burr 1905.

If information material to the risk insured which would have affected the underwriters' decision whether or not to accept the risk (and if so on what terms) is not disclosed, underwriters have the right to avoid the whole policy. This means that the policy is treated as if it had never existed, and premiums paid under the policy are returned to the insured. This could have serious consequences, partly because the practice would then be in breach of the ICAEW PII regulations, but also because it could find itself without insurance cover just when it needs it most.

Most PII policies soften the somewhat harsh rules on avoidance for non-disclosure by providing that insurers will not exercise their rights to avoid a policy because of non-disclosure or misrepresentation in the proposal form or other placing information, provided that the insured firm can show clearly that there was no intent to deceive or fraudulent conduct. This is currently required in the approved minimum terms. Although this means that the insurance is probably still in place should information have been missed by mistake, this does not mean that firms can safely dispense with the risk assessment and information-gathering procedures for fear of un-earthing information which might have to be disclosed, not least because there may be some tough negotiations when the policy comes up for renewal if underwriters suggest that the risk assessment procedures are not effective.

7.2.7 Other policy provisions

It is sensible for every firm to have at least one person whose responsibility it is to make themselves aware of the terms of the insurance policy or policies, and for ensuring that the terms are complied with, including notifying claims. Policy wordings can change from year to year, and every accountancy practice should check its policy wordings, rather than rely on the insurers or broker to point out any changes. Rather than being something that crops up once a year on renewal, professional indemnity insurance policies often specify matters which need to be advised to insurers as and when they occur, such as new or leaving or retiring partners, change of offices, mergers of the practice, etc.

One obvious ongoing duty is to ensure that premiums are paid on time. Rather than relying on the broker to remind or chase for premiums due under the policy, someone in the practice should make sure that premiums are paid.

7.3 Claims

7.3.1 What *must* be notified to insurers?

Professional liability insurance policies generally require notice to be given in writing 'as soon as practicable' of any claim. 'Claim' is not always defined but it certainly includes the issue of proceedings, or a letter from a claimant or his solicitors indicating that a claim is being made.

Policies usually require notice to be given of any circumstances of which a firm becomes aware which 'may' give rise to a claim, or which is 'likely' to result in a claim. It is quite common for complaints to be made, or proceedings to be issued several years after the alleged negligence or breach of duty was actually committed. Most policies provide that if an insured notifies circumstances or reports an event or occurrence which it is feared will lead to a claim in the future, then the date on which the notification was made effectively locks any future claim (even if made years later) into the policy in force on that date, which will be regarded as the date of the 'claim'.

It can often be difficult even when a mistake has clearly been made, to say whether that mistake 'may' or is 'likely' to result eventually in a claim against the accountant or practice. This is especially so given the length of time it sometimes takes claimants to pursue claims against professionals, the length of time that it may take for an actual loss to crystallise even after a mistake has come to light (for example, tax liabilities contingent on future events) and the fact that not all clients pursue complaints which they may have against their professional advisers. Generally, the best advice is: if in doubt, notify. Information about potential claims would have to be provided during the renewal process in any event.

The limit of indemnity in the policy will usually be in respect of any one claim, but all claims against a practice arising from the same act or omission or series of acts or omissions are usually regarded as one claim for these purposes. The aggregation of claims under such policies can be a matter of dispute since it is often difficult to say what constitutes a series of acts or omissions. Would the same mistake repeated in the context of a number of different clients' files by the same partner be regarded as a series of acts or omissions for these purposes? It will depend on the facts of each case, but the financial consequences for an accountancy practice may be significant, depending on the size of the excess under the policy and the size and number of the claims. It may be advantageous to aggregate a number of smaller claims to incur a single excess under the policy, but conversely if related claims are aggregated to form a single claim which is then greater than the limit of indemnity afforded by the primary and top up policies, this may leave the practice with having to cover the shortfall from its own resources.

7.3.2   What *may* be notified to insurers?

The accountancy practice may be aware of some circumstances which it is fairly confident will never result in claims, but nevertheless might wish to notify insurers to ensure that in the event a claim is made in the future, there will be no trouble with insurance cover. The temptation may be to submit what is known as a 'laundry list' style of notification setting out a string of engagements from which one or more claims might ultimately result.

In some circumstances this style of notification will be valid, but much will depend on the notification provisions in the policy. For example, a policy which responds to notification of circumstances 'likely' or 'reasonably likely' to give rise to a claim may require some greater degree of certainty or specificity, compared to one which merely states that notification must be given of circumstances which 'may' give rise to a claim. A vague concern that the firm may be exposed to a number of claims arising from a particular type of activity, before any specific instances or complaints have actually come to light, might not be enough. The danger of a 'laundry list'-type notification is that the insurers will refuse to accept it as crystallising any future claims under the policy,[3] but may then reflect the exposure to such claims in the terms of the renewal, or even by declining renewal. Nonetheless, since facts material to the risk will have to be disclosed on renewal in any event, it is probably better to err on the side of caution and notify.

7.3.3   When should claims be notified?

Prompt notification (usually 'as soon as practicable') is often described as a condition precedent to indemnity under the policy, so that once an accountant becomes aware of a possible claim, he must either notify it to the insurers or immediately tell whoever in the practice is responsible for dealing with insurers. Any conceivable disadvantage to early notification will almost certainly be outweighed by the advantage of ensuring that insurers cannot complain about late notification. This is so even if it is

---

[3]See *J Rothschild Assurance plc* v *Collyear & Ors* [1999] L.R.L.R6 where this issue was discussed.

thought unlikely that a claim will go any further – for example, if it is suspected that a client is only complaining as a way to reduce or get out of paying a bill for professional fees.

7.3.4 To whom should claims be notified?

The policy should be checked first as it may state the manner in which, and to whom, claims should be notified. In some cases, a claim could be reported to the broker who will pass on the notification to the insurers. Notifying the broker does not usually discharge the duty to notify under a policy, since the broker is the agent of the accountant, not the insurers. There might be a remedy for breach of contract or duty against the broker if he fails to pass on notice of a claim to insurers, but it is best to ensure that the problem does not arise by ensuring that insurers have actually received the notification.

7.3.5 How can an accountant ensure that all claims are discovered and notified promptly?

As discussed above in the context of risk assessment procedures and information in the proposal form, it is essential that there are systems in place and a culture of early warning ensuring that the practice becomes aware of all claims and problems which might lead to claims as early as possible so that they can be reported appropriately. This will also help to ensure that the practice's defence can be conducted within the strict and time sensitive requirements of the Civil Procedure Rules.[4] In particular, effective lines of communication must be in place where the practice comprises more than one office.

7.3.6 What are the penalties for late notification?

Late notification can result in some or all of the claim not being covered if the delay has prejudiced insurer's position (for example, if a claim could have been settled for a smaller amount had insurers been involved at an earlier stage, or if some concession or admission of liability has been made where there might have otherwise been a defence, prior to insurers being notified).

A claim may be denied if the practice is in breach of warranty (for example, if it has warranted in its proposal form that there are no

---

[4]See Chapter 10.

outstanding claims, when in fact there were). The ultimate penalty for late notification might be avoidance of the whole policy and complete loss of insurance cover if the claim was known about before the insurance incepted, but was deliberately concealed from insurers.

7.3.7 Policy disputes

In the event of a dispute between the practice and its insurers concerning cover under the policy (or indeed any other dispute concerning the operation of the professional indemnity insurance), the policy may specify where and how proceedings may be served against the insurers, but it may also specify that a dispute should be resolved by arbitration. For example, the policy may provide that any dispute should be referred to the President of the ICAEW (or his appointed representative) whose decision will be binding on both parties. It will often be possible to explore alternative methods of resolving problems such as early mutual evaluation or mediation. If there are doubts concerning insurance cover, the practice must continue to defend claims, acting as if it were what is known as a 'prudent uninsured' until such doubts are removed. If it fails to act prudently, and increases the loss or unreasonably incurs costs as a result, insurers may refuse to indemnify the practice to the extent that such conduct has increased the loss or costs, or caused prejudice.

7.4 Assuming the claim is covered, what happens next?

7.4.1 Cooperation

The key to resolving a professional negligence claim as speedily and painlessly as possible lies in close cooperation between the insured accountant and the insurers. Although there is a general obligation to cooperate arising out of the relationship between the insured and insurer, many policies spell out some of the insureds' obligations such as:

(a) to provide insurers with such information and documents as they reasonably require;

(b) not to make any admissions of liability, or agree to settle a claim without insurers' prior consent; and

(c) not to incur any costs and expenses in defending the claim without the insurers' prior consent. As noted earlier, without such consent, there may be no recovery for the costs of successfully defending a claim.

Once the claim has been notified, it is usually helpful to conduct an early investigation so that a strategy for the defence is agreed with insurers as soon as possible. It may be possible to resolve a complaint or a claim before the claimant and the accountant become so entrenched that litigation seems inevitable.

7.4.2 Appointing a solicitor

A solicitor may need to be appointed to represent the accountant at quite an early stage, even before a formal claim has been made. An accountant may have his own preference as to who he would like to represent him, and insurers will usually have their own panel of firms of solicitors that they prefer to use in defending claims (the policy may even provide that claims should be notified directly to a specific firm of solicitors rather than to insurers themselves). Unless the policy specifically states who will make the decision, the appointment of a solicitor to defend a claim will usually be the result of a joint decision between the accountant and the insurers.

The solicitor will act on behalf of both the insured accountant and the insurers. One of the first things that the solicitor will check is that the claim is covered under the policy. If differences arise between the accountant and the insurer as to whether or not the claim is covered under the policy, then the solicitor may have a conflict of interest making it impossible to act for both parties. The letter of engagement which the solicitor should send to both the accountant and the insurer when first involved in the matter should provide for what happens in this event.

7.4.3 Settling claims

As mentioned above, policies usually provide that claims may not be settled without the prior consent of the insurers. Likewise, if the insurers want to compromise or settle a case, they cannot do so without the consent of the insured accountant. As a matter of professional practice, the solicitor will be on the record for the accountant client and will not settle the case without that client's consent.

A situation can arise when the insurer wishes to settle a case (perhaps because the costs of defending it are becoming disproportionate to the amount claimed), whereas the accountant against whom the case has been brought feels strongly that he did nothing wrong and wants to defend it. Some policies provide that where the costs and expenses look as if they might exceed the amount of the claim, the insurer is entitled to offer the insured the amount of the claim and any costs already incurred in settlement of the claim under the policy, leaving it to the accountant to decide whether to fight on at his own expense.

Conversely, it can happen that an accountant wishes to settle a claim (perhaps because of adverse publicity or embarrassment), which would otherwise have a very strong defence. Policies sometimes contain a provision that the insured is not required to contest a claim unless a Counsel (mutually agreed by the accountant and the insurers) advises that such a claim should be contested. This is commonly known as a 'QC clause'.

7.4.4   What if the insurer is insolvent?

There is a statutory scheme in the UK which has been set up to provide assistance to policyholders in the event that insurers become insolvent or otherwise unable to meet their liabilities under policies.[5]

The scheme, which is administered by the Policyholders' Protection Board ('the PPB') and funded by levies on the insurance industry, applies to private policyholders (which includes partnerships but not companies or partnerships containing companies) holding policies issued by UK insurers or issued in the UK by EC insurers.

If an accountant has an outstanding claim against an insolvent insurer under a professional indemnity policy at the date of the insolvency, he may be entitled to recover 90 per cent from the PPB, and will have a claim in the liquidation of the insurer for the balance. What constitutes an 'outstanding claim' for these purposes has been the subject of much debate. Whilst it certainly includes claims which have been settled and on which payment is due and claims which have been notified by the date of insolvency, it may also include claims which have not yet been made but which arise out of events which took place before the insolvency.

If there are no outstanding claims at the time the insurer became insolvent, then a claim should be made in the liquidation for the 'value of the policy', usually a return of the premium attributable to the unexpired portion of the policy at the date of the insolvency.[6]

---

[5]See the Policyholders Protection Act 1995 and 1997.
[6]See the Insurance Companies (Winding-Up) Rules 1985.

8 Handling complaints and claims

8.1 Initial complaint handling

It is inevitable in the life of a busy practice that from time to time problems will arise in the handling of a client's affairs. Many of these problems will be relatively trivial and mundane: a query over a bill for example, or a terse reminder about some overdue advice. Others will be more serious. Usually, the accountant's first and instinctive aim will be to try to manage the problem so as to secure a satisfactory outcome both for the firm and for the client. But good risk management requires that issues of this type are also considered from another perspective: is there a possibility of the problem going further and turning into a claim for professional negligence?

The ICAEW's Bye-laws place a duty on firms to investigate complaints. Guidance in this area is provided by Section 1.112 of the *ICAEW Members' Handbook* ('The Duty on Firms to Investigate Complaints'). It is not compulsory to have a formal complaints procedure, but most medium and large sized firms will have one. The ICAEW's guidance suggests that a good complaints procedure is likely to include the following elements:[1]

- review by a principal other than the engagement partner;

- reference to the client where the facts are not clearly established;

- prompt rectification of the error, with apology and offer of waiver or reduction of the fee if appropriate;

- full explanation to the client if the complaint is unjustified;

- notification to the client of his right to complain to the ICAEW if he remains dissatisfied;

- drawing serious complaints to the attention of the senior partner.

It is essential, however, to focus also on what lies behind the client's dissatisfaction. If there is the possibility that the client may claim that he has lost something tangible as a result of anything the firm has done or failed to do, some modification of approach is likely to be called for.

---

[1] *ICAEW Members' Handbook 2000*, Section 1.112, para 3.

In particular, it will then be inappropriate to make any offers to try to resolve the problem without considering potential insurance and other implications.

The ICAEW's experience has been that client complaints tend to fall into one of five broad categories:[2]

- fee disputes;
- delay;
- failure to respond to correspondence;
- failure to carry out duties;
- poor work or advice.

In all cases the first objective must be to ascertain what the client regards as the problem and what he wants to see done about it. It is important at this stage not to be adversarial but to make a real attempt to understand the client's position so that consideration can be given to the best solution. In simple cases the solution may well be obvious: an agreement to reduce the bill or to prioritise the outstanding work or advice. In other cases the position may be less clear-cut.

Where fee disputes are concerned, the most important issue to gauge is whether the client is simply saying that the work cost too much or that he did not expect to pay for it at all, or whether he is saying that it was not done properly. If the latter is the case, is the client suggesting that this has given rise to some tangible adverse consequences so far as he is concerned, or is it possible that he could do so? If there are or might be some adverse consequences for him, the matter should be treated as a potential claim for professional negligence and the steps set out in **8.2** below should be followed.

If, on the other hand, all that is and could ever be in issue is simply the level of fees, and the client has been provided with all the information to which he is entitled,[3] the matter will be one of commercial judgement. In appropriate cases, where a satisfactory compromise cannot be reached, it may be necessary to consider referring the matter to the ICAEW's fee arbitration service or some similar scheme, or perhaps pursuing court action or exercising a lien.[4]

---

[2]*ICAEW Members' Handbook 2000*, Section 1.112, para 7.

[3]*ICAEW Members' Handbook 2000*, Section 1.112, para 14; see more generally ICAEW Statement 1.210.

[4]Guidance on the availability and exercise of liens is given at **4.3** above.

Where the complaint is not directly about fees but about delay or poor work or other failures, again the most important issue to gauge is whether the client contends, or might be able to contend, that he has lost something tangible as a result. If there is any real likelihood of this, the matter should be treated as a claim and the steps set out in **8.2** should be followed. In other cases, the matter will again be one of commercial judgement. Further practical guidance for use in such situations appears in Section 1.112 of the *ICAEW Members' Handbook* at paras 13 19.

8.2 What to do when a claim may arise

As soon as it can be identified that there is scope for a claim to be made against the accountant or his firm for damages for professional negligence, the following steps need to be taken:

- Ascertain how likely it is that a claim will be made. This needs to be done quickly: other steps, possibly urgent, will depend upon the outcome. In some instances it will be obvious that a claim is likely, or indeed one may already have been made; in other situations, it may be helpful to find out more information so as to establish whether there really is some risk of a claim or not. In these latter situations, however, two further rules should be borne in mind:
  - (i) First, where the prospect of a claim being made cannot quickly be ruled out, it is wiser to proceed on the assumption that one will be made rather than not.
  - ii) Second, great care is needed in dealing with the client or other potential claimant at this stage so as to avoid making the problem worse or prejudicing the insurance position.[5]

- Notify insurers, if this has not already been done. What must or may be notified to insurers is covered at **7.3** above. Again, the wiser course in cases of doubt will be to notify insurers rather than not.

- Consider the appointment of a solicitor. Where a claim has been made or is very likely to be made, this is likely to follow as a matter of course: indeed insurers may well respond to a notification by appointing a solicitor to investigate the position and, subject to any questions about policy coverage, act for the accountant or his firm. In any event, it is sensible to liaise with insurers before appointing a solicitor, not least because the insurers are likely to be asked to pay the solicitor's fees in due course.

- Where the claimant is a continuing client, consider whether it is appropriate to continue acting. This is an area which sometimes gives

---

[5] See 7.4 above.

rise to particular difficulty. The natural wish of the accountant will often be to continue acting for the client while trying to resolve the problem. Sometimes this will be possible, but great care is needed to ensure that continuing to act does not compound the problem. The effect of an outstanding claim by a client on the accountant's independence should also not be underestimated: so far as an auditor is concerned, for example, the issue of proceedings by the audit client claiming damages for professional negligence is regarded by the ICAEW as certainly impairing the auditor's independence.[6] It should also be borne in mind that what may help a client in a given situation will not necessarily help, or be acceptable to, insurers. Thus, in circumstances in which the accountant wishes to continue acting, and the relevant ethical guidance permits this, great care should be taken to ensure that a close dialogue is maintained with insurers so as to be sure that they agree with what is proposed.

- Locate and safeguard all the relevant papers. All files and documents relating to work which may be subject to a claim should be located and kept secure. This includes personal files and papers of individual partners and staff and material stored by electronic means. Any temptation to add new material to the papers or amend them in any way should be resisted: it is almost impossible not to get caught out if this is done, and the inevitable outcome will be that the person responsible for the changes will have to explain why he made them in any Court proceedings which follow. The temptation to destroy or hide papers should likewise be resisted. It is important to bear in mind that while there may be some embarrassment initially in making available to others papers which show that a mistake has happened, the consequences will nonetheless be manageable. If the papers are tampered with, though, the likelihood is that the mistake will still be found out and – much worse – the attempt to conceal it will also be discovered. The consequences of this situation may be far less manageable, and in a serious case might include severe disciplinary sanction.

- Do not permit clients or others to have access to the papers or to those who did the work. This general rule applies at all times but particularly when a claim has been made or is possible. In certain circumstances of course, various bodies may be in a position to obtain access to the papers, or to individuals, using statutory powers.[7] In such cases, care should be taken to ensure both that these powers are properly exercised and that appropriate preparations and other safeguards are put in place before access is given. In all such cases, insurers should be

---

[6]ICAEW Statement 1.201: 'Integrity, Objectivity and Independence', paras 4.16–19.

[7]See Chapter 5.

consulted and appropriate legal advice taken. It should be borne in mind that releasing potentially damaging information to outsiders when there is either no obligation to do so or appropriate safeguards are not in place is likely to worsen the accountant's position in relation to a prospective claim. It will be a term of the policy that nothing which might prejudice the position is done without the insurers' permission, and failure to observe this is likely to cause insurers to consider whether coverage under the policy should be reviewed.

- Do not create new disclosable material which may confirm that mistakes have occurred. Documents relevant to the issue in a claim will have to be disclosed to the claimant if Court proceedings are pursued, and very likely even before proceedings are begun.[8] The files and papers created when the work in issue was done will tell their own story, and it is important not to add to any weaknesses in them by creating new documents which may tend to confirm that problems exist. For this reason, any internal memoranda identifying possible problems should be purely factual and be couched where possible in terms of the claimant's actual or possible allegations rather than the author's perceptions of weaknesses in the work. Once insurers and lawyers are involved they will advise on any further steps necessary, with a view to ensuring that documents generated from then on in connection with the investigation and defence of the claim will attract legal professional privilege and hence be protected from disclosure.

- Within the limits of the other rules above, share the problem! The natural reaction of any professional faced with potential criticism of his work is to go on the defensive. It is important that, wherever possible, others in the firm get involved in the potential problem, not only to provide support to the individual concerned but also to introduce a measure of objectivity. The problem may be smaller or bigger than the individual most directly affected thinks it is. There may be issues about whether it is appropriate to continue acting for the client which that individual does not himself see. In some circumstances it may be helpful, as a tool to assist the firm and its insurers and solicitors, to have a review conducted by another individual independent of the problem to identify the strengths and weaknesses of the work that has been done.[9] Most important, however, is to ensure that the problem is viewed in proper perspective from the outset: if it is serious it must be recognised as such, but even the most serious problems can potentially be contained provided the proper steps are taken.

---

[8] See Chapter 10.

[9] Care should, however, be taken to ensure that the results of such a review are privileged: see above.

9 The disciplinary process

9.1 Introduction

Virtually all professional bodies promulgate rules to promote high standards of ethical behaviour and competence and to discipline those who do not live up to them. The accountancy profession is no exception: each of the major UK professional bodies publishes guidance to members in practice and operates its own disciplinary code. While there are some differences between the disciplinary codes, each conforms broadly to the following two-stage pattern:

- an investigation stage, where a branch of the professional body enquires into circumstances which may give rise to disciplinary action in order to decide whether the member concerned has a case to answer; and

- a formal hearing stage, where an independent tribunal hears disciplinary charges against members in order to determine liability and, if need be, penalty.

In what follows we describe the pattern followed by a typical investigation, highlighting the considerations which the accountant subject to it should take into account. Reference is made to the ICAEW's disciplinary procedures and to those of the Accountants' Joint Disciplinary Scheme ('JDS').[1] It should be borne in mind that the procedures of other bodies, though broadly similar, may differ markedly in certain respects.

9.2 The initiation of a disciplinary investigation

Investigations tend to be initiated in one of two ways. Most commonly, the professional body will receive a complaint about a member or member firm from an external source, most usually a client but possibly

---

[1]The role of the JDS is to deal with more serious cases which 'give rise to public concern in the United Kingdom' and which are referred to it by participating professional bodies including the ICAEW. From a date in 2001 the functions of the JDS will be assumed by a new Investigation and Discipline Board ('IDB'). Significant changes in the new body's powers, as presently proposed, are highlighted below.

another accountant or regulator. Occasionally, however, the professional body may become aware through generally available information, such as press reports, that grounds for disciplinary action may exist, in which case it will normally itself have power to initiate an investigation.

So far as the ICAEW is concerned, the first step which has then to be taken is to gauge the likely seriousness of the matters to be investigated. At one end of the scale a very small number of cases will be such as to 'give rise to public concern in the United Kingdom', in which case the ICAEW's Investigation Committee has power to refer it to the JDS.[2] Matters of public concern in this context will include the collapse with substantial loss of funds of a listed or other public interest company and any other matter in which the conduct of a member or member firm is the subject of criticism from an official body or gives rise to widespread public discussion.[3]

The vast majority of complaints will inevitably be of much lesser significance. Where the complainant is a client, the ICAEW's Professional Conduct Department will first consider whether the matter is suitable for resolution by some form of conciliation process. In practice, many relatively minor problems and grievances are resolved in this way without the need for any formal disciplinary process. A residue of cases, however, will either not be soluble by conciliation or will be of sufficient potential seriousness as to justify disciplinary investigation in any event. These will be referred to a case officer for further enquiry.

9.3   The investigation stage

The aim of the investigation stage is to gather the available evidence so that a decision can be taken on whether formal disciplinary action is appropriate. The ICAEW conducts such investigations through case officers, who will provide the member or member firm with details of the complaint against them and invite a formal response, usually within 14 days. When such a request is received, the following points should be considered:

- Has any independent assessment been made of the work or other matters in issue so as to establish the strengths and weaknesses of the position of the member or member firm? If this has not been done, urgent arrangements should be made. Consideration should also be given as to whether legal assistance should be sought.

---

[2]Disciplinary Bye-law 12(3).

[3]Paragraph 3 of Council Guidelines on Publicity for the Disciplinary and Regulatory Processes under Disciplinary Bye-law 36.

- Where the matter has not already been notified to professional indemnity insurers, should it be notified now? Sometimes a complaint to a disciplinary body can be a prelude to a civil claim. In any event, it is worth bearing in mind that some policies will indemnify the costs of dealing with disciplinary investigations.

- In all but the simplest cases, a response period of 14 days is likely to be insufficient. Case officers will usually be receptive to requests for more time provided they are made promptly and give a realistic explanation of why it is required.

- When preparing responses, it goes without saying that the best available answers should be given to the points raised by the case officer and the complainant. Care should also be taken not to worsen the situation, either by drawing attention to other potentially problematic issues or by adopting an inflammatory style of correspondence. It should be borne in mind in this context that the case officer will normally copy the response to the complainant.

The case officer is backed by formal powers exercisable by the ICAEW's Investigation Committee to call on any member or member firm to provide information or explanation about matters in issue and access to books, records and documents.[4] Failure to comply with such calls can itself constitute grounds for disciplinary action.

Where access to papers is sought, the following points should be borne in mind:

- Provide copies, not originals: the latter should be preserved intact in their entirety for use in defending any disciplinary or other proceedings which may follow.

- Sometimes the case officer will ask to make arrangements to inspect original files at the accountant's offices. If this is to happen, it is usually better for those whose work or conduct is in issue not to be present when the inspection takes place: requests for assistance in interpreting particular aspects of the papers are better dealt with in writing after the inspection has taken place.

As to the JDS, its investigative powers are exercised by an Executive Counsel, who will normally appoint an outside accountant to assist him. The usual starting-point, once notification has been given to a member or member firm that they are under enquiry, is for a request to be made that all relevant papers be copied to the investigating accountant. The Executive Counsel then has power to call for further information,

---

[4]Disciplinary Bye-law 13.

exercisable either in writing or by the attendance of members at formal or informal interviews.[5] As with the equivalent ICAEW powers, refusal by a member or member firm to comply with such calls can itself constitute grounds for disciplinary action.

If interviews are called for, they may be conducted by the Executive Counsel himself or, more commonly, by an investigating accountant or external lawyer. Where an interview is requested, it is essential that there is sufficient opportunity for the interviewee to prepare thoroughly. This means not only that there should be enough time for him to refresh his memory of matters generally but that the Executive Counsel should indicate what specific areas the interview will cover. Normally this will be done by provision of a list of topics and a bundle of papers which are likely to be the subject of questioning. The interviewee should devote time to considering which topics and papers he can help with and the issues to which they are likely to give rise.

The interview itself can often be stressful, particularly if protracted. Care should be taken to ensure that if any aspect of a question is unclear it is clarified, but there are relatively few grounds on which answers can legitimately be refused provided what is being sought is information within the interviewee's own knowledge. It is inappropriate, however, for the Executive Counsel to use the interview as a forum for cross-examination with a view to extracting admissions.

9.4 Can investigations be stayed while legal proceedings are resolved?

Deferment of disciplinary investigations while civil or criminal proceedings are solved is rare. The general rule is that disciplinary proceedings will not be stayed while civil proceedings against the member or member firm arising out of the same subject matter are resolved. Although a JDS Investigation into Price Waterhouse's work for BCCI was stayed pending resolution of a parallel civil claim, it is clear that this was a very unusual and exceptional case.[6]

Where what is in issue is parallel criminal proceedings, the position may be different. However, there is no automatic right on the part of a

---

[5]Joint Disciplinary Scheme, para 11.

[6]*R* v *ICAEW ex parte Brindle* [1994] BCC 297. The case was distinguished in *R* v *Chance ex parte Smith* (1995) 7 Admin LR 821 (an application for a stay of an enquiry into Coopers & Lybrand's Maxwell-related work) in a way which confirms that it is very unlikely that future applications for stays will succeed.

respondent to disciplinary proceedings who faces criminal charges arising out of the same matters to have the disciplinary proceedings stayed: a stay will only be ordered if it can be shown that continuation of the disciplinary proceedings will create a real risk of a miscarriage of justice in the criminal proceedings.[7]

9.5 The decision whether to lay disciplinary charges

At the conclusion of the investigation stage, those conducting it have to decide whether there are grounds for formal disciplinary action. What constitutes grounds for such action as regards the ICAEW and the JDS is set out in **9.6**.

Within the ICAEW the decision is taken by the Investigation Committee. If prima facie grounds for disciplinary action exist, the Investigation Committee has the following options:[8]

(1) To refer formal disciplinary complaints against the member or member firm concerned to the ICAEW's Disciplinary Committee.

(2) To offer the member or member firm the chance to deal with the matters by way of a consent order.

(3) To caution the member or member firm (which may include a requirement that the member or member firm pay a sum by way of costs).

(4) To take no further action.

If no prima facie grounds exist, the Investigation Committee is required to dismiss the complaint.[9]

Where the Investigation Committee's decision is that formal complaints should be referred, the matter moves forward to the tribunal stage. However, where the Investigation Committee has found a prima facie case but offers a consent order or decides to issue a caution or take no further action, the member or member firm has a range of options.

---

[7] *Jefferson* v *Bhetcha* [1979] 2 All ER 1108; *R* v *BBC, ex parte Lavelle* [1983] 1 All ER 241.

[8] Disciplinary Bye-law 15(2).

[9] Disciplinary Bye-law 15(1). A complainant aggrieved by the dismissal of a complaint at this stage can ask (normally within six months) that the matter be referred to an independent reviewer or complaints under Disciplinary Bye-law 17. In certain circumstances, this may lead to the complaint being revived and to the Investigation Committee pursuing one of the options available to it under Disciplinary Bye-law 15(2).

Offers of consent orders have to be made in a letter or notice in prescribed form.[10] This will identify the complaint, indicate the Investigation Committee's conclusion that prima facie grounds for disciplinary action exist and state what penalties and orders the member or member firm is invited to agree to. These penalties and orders may include any of the following:[11]

- a reprimand or severe reprimand;

- a fine;

- a sum by way of costs;

- an order of waiver or repayment of fees;

- a remedial order relating to the return of documents or the clarification of fees.

Previous practice was to discourage recipients of such notices from doing anything other than accepting or rejecting them. However, perhaps prompted in particular by human rights concerns, there is now at least implicit recognition in the Bye-laws and in the prescribed form of notice that the accountant, even if in principle accepting that there are grounds for disciplinary action against him, may have legitimate reasons for contending that the penalties or orders proposed are excessive. Recipients are therefore no longer presented with a straight choice between accepting and rejecting the offer of a consent order but can make representations as to why its proposed terms are inappropriate. As before however, if the Investigation Committee is not persuaded by any representations, or if the offer is simply rejected, it will prefer a formal complaint to the Disciplinary Committee.

The 'caution' procedure is a new one that can only be applied to matters which took place on or after 7 October 1999. The procedure is set out in Disciplinary Bye-law 16A. If the recipient of a proposed caution is aggrieved by it he can serve notice of this within 28 days; but unless the Investigation Committee is persuaded by representations to modify its approach, the matter will then be referred to the Disciplinary Committee.[12]

There is provision also for anyone who is notified by the Investigation Committee that it considers that prima facie grounds for disciplinary action exist but that it proposes to take no further action, to object to the

---

[10]Disciplinary Bye-law 16; Schedule to the Investigation Committee Regulations.

[11]Disciplinary Bye-law 16(2).

[12]Disciplinary Bye-law 16A(4).

finding of prima facie grounds. It seems unlikely that such objection would often be taken, particularly as the Investigation Committee then has power to prefer a formal complaint to the Disciplinary Committee.[13]

As for the JDS, the Executive Counsel is required to notify proposed disciplinary action to the member or member firm concerned and give them an opportunity to make representations.[14] In practice, notification is given by providing a copy of the proposed form of disciplinary complaint in draft together with supporting evidence usually in the form of a report by the investigating accountant. The period stipulated for the making of representations is four weeks but can be extended by agreement.

The Executive Counsel also has the power to invite the member or member firm concerned to make admissions in respect of some or all of the matters raised in the draft complaint. If admissions are made in a form acceptable to the Executive Counsel, those making them cannot subsequently be ordered to pay anything in respect of the costs of the enquiry.[15]

Where the Executive Counsel concludes, or is persuaded by representations, that disciplinary action under the Scheme is inappropriate, he will deliver a report to that effect. In that event he has a residual discretion to request that the matter be referred back to one of the participating professional bodies to be dealt with under its own disciplinary process.[16] Otherwise, the Executive Committee of the JDS will appoint a tribunal to hear formal complaints. Where complaints are admitted, the tribunal's function is solely to determine the appropriate penalties and orders, which may sometimes be the subject of provisional agreement between the Executive Counsel and the member or member firm concerned.[17] There is no equivalent in the JDS procedures to the ICAEW's power to offer consent orders under Disciplinary Bye-law 16.

---

[13]Disciplinary Bye-law 15(7).

[14]Joint Disciplinary Scheme, para 6(h).

[15]Joint Disciplinary Scheme, paras 6(i) and 7(f) and (g). It is likely that the costs concession will be modified in the new IDB Scheme so as to relate only to costs incurred after the admission is made.

[16]Joint Disciplinary Scheme, para 6(j) and (g).

[17]Such a practice was approved by the tribunal hearing complaints against Stoy Hayward in relation to Astra Holdings plc: report dated August 1998.

9.6 The grounds for disciplinary action

The grounds on which a member of the ICAEW can be liable to disciplinary action are as follows:[18]

- Discredit: 'if in the course of carrying out professional work or otherwise he has committed any act or default likely to bring discredit on himself, the Institute or the profession of accountancy'.

- Inefficiency or incompetence: 'if he has performed his professional work or the duties of his employment, or conducted his practice, inefficiently or incompetently to such an extent, or on such a number of occasions, as to bring discredit on himself, the Institute or the profession of accountancy'.

- Any breach of Bye-laws or regulations, or any orders, directions or requirements made under them.

- Failure to comply with orders of the Investigation, Disciplinary or Appeal Committees.

- In various circumstances where his solvency is called into question.

Broadly speaking, the same grounds apply as regards member firms.[19]

The position as regards the JDS is more fluid. If formal disciplinary complaints are laid, the tribunal hearing them has to determine whether there are grounds for an adverse finding as regards 'the professional or business conduct, efficiency or competence' of the member or member firm concerned. In doing so, the tribunal is required to take into account 'the conduct or quality of work reasonably to be expected of a member or member firm in good standing in the formal conduct of their profession or business', together with a number of other matters including the importance of the work and the known or potential consequences of any shortcoming revealed in it.[20] But the threshold between what is acceptable and what is not is not made explicit: the Scheme does not state how far below normal standards of conduct, efficiency and competence a member or member firm has to fall before an adverse finding is justified. The new IDB Scheme is likely to address this omission by providing a threshold that the relevant work or conduct must have 'fallen significantly short of the standards reasonably to be expected'.

---

[18]Disciplinary Bye-law 4.

[19]Disciplinary Bye-law 5.

[20]Joint Disciplinary Scheme, paras 7(e) and 8.

9.7   The tribunal stage: preparation for hearing

Where formal complaints are referred to the ICAEW's Disciplinary Committee for hearing, the Committee will appoint three of its members to sit as a tribunal. Two of these must be members of the ICAEW and the third not. One will act as chairman of the tribunal but there is no requirement that he be legally qualified.[21] A date will then be fixed for the hearing: usually the member or member firm concerned must be given at least 42 days' notice of this.[22]

The JDS's procedures are essentially similar. A tribunal of three (exceptionally five) is appointed by the Executive Committee of the JDS. Unlike the position as regards the ICAEW, the tribunal chairman must be legally qualified and there is no standing pool of people available to sit as tribunals: members are appointed on an ad hoc basis as cases arise. A minimum of six weeks' notice must be given of the hearing date once the tribunal has been formally appointed.[23]

Depending upon how much is in issue in the case, significant work may have to be done in preparation for the hearing. Where liability is being contested, relevant steps may include some or all of the following:

- Clarification of either the prosecutor's or the respondent's case. The ICAEW is required to provide the member or member firm with a summary of its case and copies of material it proposes to rely on at the time that notice is given of the hearing date.[24] Normally, it will be reasonably apparent from this material what is in issue, but if it is in some way defective so that the respondent is in genuine difficulty in understanding what is being alleged the rules of natural justice will require that it be clarified. For different reasons, the prosecutor may require clarification of the respondent's case.[25] Similar considerations may arise as regards JDS cases, though no formal provision is made for them.

- Preparation of witness evidence, including expert evidence. Under both the ICAEW and JDS schemes, written statements or summaries of witness evidence have to be exchanged with the prosecutor in advance of the hearing.[26] This will include both the evidence of the

---

[21]Disciplinary Bye-law 19.

[22]Disciplinary Committee Regulation 4.

[23]Joint Disciplinary Scheme, para 7; Joint Disciplinary Scheme Regulations 14–16.

[24]Disciplinary Committee Regulation 5.

[25]Disciplinary Committee Regulations 7 and 10.

[26]Disciplinary Committee Regulation 11; Joint Disciplinary Scheme Regulations 18 and 19.

member concerned, if he is to be called at the hearing, and any expert evidence, although the latter will usually be presented in the form of a report.

- Obtaining of further evidence. Depending upon the nature of the case, it may be helpful to seek evidence from a variety of sources. It should also be borne in mind that a prosecutor may have in his possession material relating to the case which he has chosen not to rely on. This 'unused material' should, by analogy with the position in criminal cases, be made available to the respondent for inspection in case there is anything in it which may be helpful to his defence.

- Preparation of written submissions. This will normally be done by a legal adviser. In the case of the JDS, any written submissions normally have to be delivered at least seven days before the hearing.[27]

In more complex cases, the minimum time and notice periods specified in the rules are unlikely to be sufficient. In such cases, the problem may be solved informally by consultation at an early stage as to what would be a practicable timetable. Where this cannot be achieved, application can be made to the tribunal on reasonable grounds. ICAEW tribunals also have explicit powers to rule on other 'pre-trial' matters such as clarification of the prosecutor's case or the provision of further evidence.[28] JDS tribunals do not have equivalent formal powers, but in practice informal directions hearings tend to take place at which such issues can be dealt with.

9.8 The tribunal hearing

The normal order of proceedings at any tribunal hearing is that the prosecutor will open the case by summarising the complaints and the nature of the evidence to be called in support of them. The prosecutor's witnesses are then called one by one and the respondent is given the opportunity to cross-examine them. The process is then repeated as regards the respondent's witnesses. Next, closing submissions are made, with the prosecutor first and the respondent second.

The proceedings thus largely mirror those in a court of law, although there is likely to be a slightly lesser degree of formality. In particular, the strict rules of evidence normally do not apply and the tribunal is likely to have a greater degree of discretion to regulate its own procedure.

---

[27]Joint Disciplinary Scheme Regulation 20.

[28]Disciplinary Committee Regulation 12.

Respondents may conduct their own case and examine and cross-examine witnesses themselves before the tribunal, but more commonly a solicitor or barrister will be appointed for this purpose. There is normally no right to have legal representation funded, but some insurance policies will cover this.

9.9   Findings, orders, appeals and publicity

At the conclusion of the hearing the tribunal will either deliver its findings there and then or, in more complex cases, go away to consider them. In the event that the findings are adverse, the respondent or his legal adviser has the opportunity to address the tribunal on any matters of mitigation. These may include matters such as:

- The respondent's lack of any disciplinary record. (If previous disciplinary findings have been made against a respondent the prosecutor will make this known to the prosecutor at this stage.)

- Any explanations or other factors which help to explain how the problem which is the subject of the adverse finding came about, so as to minimise its seriousness in the eyes of the tribunal.

- Any changes which may have occurred in the member's or member firm's practices designed to prevent a repetition of the problem.

- Any other adverse consequences already suffered by the respondent, such as stress and worry, damage to reputation or requirements to pay compensation.

- In appropriate cases, evidence from colleagues or clients regarding the respondent's professional abilities.

Having heard submissions on mitigation, the tribunal will determine the appropriate orders to be made against the respondent. In the case of the ICAEW, orders available against a member include any of those which the Investigation Committee can offer as part of the consent order procedure, but may also extend in the most serious cases to suspension of the right to practise or exclusion from membership.[29] A similar position obtains as regards member firms, save that in their case the ultimate sanction is prohibition from using the description 'Chartered Accountants' for a specified period and withdrawal of any authorisation granted by the ICAEW either to conduct investment business or to operate as a

---

[29]Disciplinary Bye-laws 22–24.

registered auditor.[30] Broadly similar powers are available to JDS tribunals.[31] In any case, orders may be made that the respondent pay some or all of the costs of the proceedings.

The power to exclude from membership or otherwise restrain a respondent's ability to practise should only be exercised in very clear and serious cases. But there is no requirement that a member must have acted dishonestly in order to justify exclusion: this will also be appropriate in cases where there is such a history of failures to achieve a proper standard of competence that the member's continuation in practice is likely to pose obvious risks to the public.

If a fine is imposed, its level will reflect a number of factors. First and foremost is the tribunal's assessment of the seriousness of the failing, but the tribunal must also be careful not to set a fine at such a level that it is beyond a respondent's realistic ability to pay it. The same principle naturally applies also to orders for payment of costs.

Where a member or member firm is aggrieved by the findings or orders of a tribunal, there is a right of appeal, exercisable by giving notice within 28 days of the date of the relevant findings or orders.[32] Appeals are heard by an appeal tribunal. The procedure is attenuated: the appeal tribunal will not re-hear the case afresh but will re-examine particular issues of fact or law with a view to considering whether the tribunal misdirected itself or reached an obviously wrong conclusion. Where serious procedural flaws have occurred which are not corrected on appeal, it may also be possible to seek judicial review.

Hearings of ICAEW and JDS tribunals and appeal tribunals are in principle conducted in private, and both the prosecutor and the respondent are required to maintain confidentiality in relation to information provided to them in the course of the disciplinary process.[33] However, respondents have a right to have the public admitted to hearings if they wish, and a degree of publicity will also attach to proceedings at various stages depending upon the nature of the case. In particular, adverse findings and orders will, unless appealed within the relevant time limit, always be published.

---

[30]Disciplinary Bye-laws 22–24.

[31]Joint Disciplinary Scheme, para 7(f) and (g).

[32]Disciplinary Bye-law 26; Joint Disciplinary Scheme,.para 9.

[33]Disciplinary Committee Regulation 37; Joint Disciplinary Scheme Regulation 52.

9.10 Natural justice and human rights

The conduct of disciplinary proceedings is subject to a raft of legal rules, the full exposition of which is beyond the scope of this book. The aim, however, is to achieve fairness to those on the receiving end of disciplinary complaints. In particular, the so-called rules of natural justice require that complaints are determined by unbiased tribunals and that the respondent has notice of the case he has to meet and the opportunity to answer it.[34]

These requirements are now supplemented by the Human Rights Act 1998, which in broad terms requires courts and tribunals and other public authorities to operate in accordance with, and give effect to, the European Convention on Human Rights. So far as disciplinary proceedings are concerned, the most relevant Convention provision is Article 6 ('Right to a Fair Trial'):

'1. In the determination of his civil rights and obligations or of any criminal charge against him, everyone is entitled to a fair and public hearing within a reasonable time by an independent and impartial tribunal established by law. Judgment shall be pronounced publicly but the press and public may be excluded from all or part of the trial in the interest of morals, public order or national security in a democratic society, where the interests of juveniles or the protection of the private life of the parties so require, or to the extent strictly necessary in the opinion of the court in special circumstances where publicity would prejudice the interests of justice.

2. Everyone charged with a criminal offence shall be presumed innocent until proved guilty according to law.

3. Everyone charged with a criminal offence has the following minimum rights:

(a) to be informed promptly, in a language which he understands and in detail, of the nature and cause of the accusation against him;
(b) to have adequate time and facilities for the preparation of his defence;
(c) to defend himself in person or through legal assistance of his own choosing or, if he has not sufficient means to pay for legal assistance, to be given it free when the interests of justice so require;
(d) to examine or have examined witnesses against him and to obtain the attendance and examination of witnesses on his behalf under the same conditions as witnesses against him;

---

[34]*Ridge* v *Baldwin* [1963] 2 All ER 66

(e) to have the free assistance of an interpreter if he cannot
understand or speak the language used in court.'

The extent to which Article 6 will impact upon ICAEW and JDS
disciplinary proceedings is likely to be limited. Decisions of the European
Court of Human Rights[35] suggest that disciplinary proceedings of this
nature, while potentially determinative of civil rights and obligations, are
not usually to be equated with criminal proceedings, with the
consequence that only Article 6(1), and not 6(2) or 6(3), applies.
Moreover, the drafting of Article 6(1) largely reflects the pre-existing
English rules of natural justice. By a strange irony, when most members
subject to disciplinary complaints would probably wish to see as little
publicity for the process as possible, the most significant rule changes that
Article 6(1) has or is likely to bring about are those aimed at opening up
tribunal hearings to the public.

One final point to be borne in mind is that the rules of natural justice do
not normally apply to the conduct of a prosecutor at the investigation
stage before disciplinary charges are formulated.[36] It is unlikely that the
Human Rights Act affects this.

9.11 Practical considerations: realism, support, conflicts

It is difficult for human beings to accept that they have made mistakes,
particularly in the sphere of professional work and responsibilities. But
mistakes are commonly made, and where it is clear that they have been,
the best approach is always realism. Where errors have occurred and
there is no plausible defence to a disciplinary complaint, a refusal to bow
to the inevitable may cause the tribunal to wonder whether more serious
issues of professional competence exist. By contrast, there will often be
opportunities to contain a problem through negotiation with the
prosecutor as to the form of complaints to be accepted and the
appropriate penalty in the light of them. The only major constraints in
such circumstances are likely to be the prosecutor's views on the
seriousness of the matter and any restrictions that might possibly be
imposed by insurance coverage in circumstances where the matters
involved also give rise to a civil claim.

Whether disciplinary complaints are ultimately accepted or defended,
disciplinary enquiries are inevitably burdensome and stressful to those

---

[35]Most notably the second *Le Compte case* (1983) 4 EHRR 533.

[36]*Moran* v *Lloyd's* [1981] 1 Lloyd's Rep 423.

subject to them. It is important that firms recognise this in a number of ways: by transferring immediate responsibility for liaising with the disciplinary body away from the individuals concerned, either to another partner or to an outside legal adviser; by ensuring that those concerned are able to strike a balance between devoting appropriate time to the enquiry and getting on with the rest of their professional and personal lives; and by providing reassurance and support.

The last of these may be more difficult to provide – but by the same token is all the more important – where there are potential differences between the interests of different individuals caught up in a disciplinary enquiry, or between the interests of individuals and their firm. In principle, it is always preferable that firms and individuals maintain a common front in dealing with disciplinary matters, and legal representation is commonly arranged on this basis. It is essential however, that where there is a potential for difference, all concerned have the opportunity to take independent advice.

10 The litigation process

10.1 Introduction

The purpose of this Chapter is twofold:

- To give an overview of the litigation process.

- To consider ways in which claims can be resolved, including in particular Alternative Dispute Resolution ('ADR').

To set the context, we begin by briefly describing the philosophy and key features of the new Civil Procedure Rules introduced on 26 April 1999 (otherwise known as the 'Woolf reforms').

10.2 The new Civil Procedure Rules ('the CPR')

Two main aims underlay the introduction of these new rules: to discourage litigation where possible, and otherwise to make it less complex and hence less costly. These aims emerge clearly from the 'overriding objective', which appears at the beginning of the rules:

'These Rules are a new procedural code with the overriding objective of enabling the Court to deal with cases justly.

Dealing with a case justly includes, so far as practicable:
(a) ensuring that the parties are on an equal footing;
(b) saving expense;
(c) dealing with the case in ways which are proportionate:
   (i)   to the amount of money involved;
   (ii) to the importance of the case;
   (iii) to the complexity of the issues;
   (iv) to the financial position of each party;
(d) ensuring that it is dealt with expeditiously and fairly; and
(e) allotting to it an appropriate share of the Court's resources, while taking into account the need to allot resources to other cases.' (CPR Rule 1)

Not only must the Court seek to give effect to the overriding objective at all stages of the litigation process, but the parties are also required to help the Court to further it. Sanctions are introduced for those who do not.

10.3 Pre-action protocols

Where a claimant has definitely made up his mind to pursue a claim, he will generally be required to provide some further information to the accountant about what he is claiming and why. The CPR introduced the concept of pre-action protocols – procedures to be followed even before litigation has begun with a view to the claimant and defendant sharing information and documents relevant to their positions – the underlying aim of which is to encourage the settlement of claims without resort to litigation and, in those cases which cannot immediately be settled, make the ensuing litigation process more efficient.

The Court cannot enforce compliance with pre-action protocols before proceedings are issued, but the CPR give it teeth to attack pre-action behaviour during subsequent litigation.[1] The Court may penalise parties who have failed to comply with protocols by orders for costs, interest awards on damages and other sanctions, possibly as draconian as the striking out of a claim or defence. It is therefore desirable to be seen to be acting fully within the principles of an agreed protocol. Also, the period of time within which parties may act in accordance with agreed protocols is likely to be more relaxed and flexible than that imposed by a Court after litigation has commenced. The protocol period now becomes the time when parties should be really getting to grips with a dispute and deciding what they wish to do with it.

No pre-action protocol has yet been formally approved for professional negligence claims, but a draft has been produced by a group of insurers which it is hoped will ultimately be approved. This document is similar in form to protocols applicable to other forms of dispute and contains the following key elements:

- The party making the claim should first give preliminary notice to the other party that a claim is being considered.

- The party making the claim should then provide a letter before action setting out a concise but comprehensive summary of the claim, including an indication of its value. This should attach any relevant documents and if possible give indications of witness and expert evidence. The letter may also make an offer as to how the claim might be settled.

- The party against whom the claim is made should acknowledge the letter of claim within 21 days and then have a further period in which to respond (usually three months).

---

[1]See for example CPR Rules 3.1(4) and 3.5.

- The response to the claim should be detailed and reasoned and should set out which parts of the claim are admitted and which denied and why. This should be accompanied by relevant documents and evidence if possible. If further information is required for a response this should be sought. Alternatively, a letter with a settlement offer may be sent to the claimant.

- If a settlement offer is made a further period is provided for negotiation.

- After the detailed response to the claim, if no settlement offer is made by the party against whom the claim is made or negotiations terminate, the claimant is free to start proceedings.

- Where a limitation period for proceedings is about to expire, the claimant may issue proceedings at any time to protect its position.

Although not formally approved, the draft professional negligence protocol is now commonly followed. It should be borne in mind in this connection that parties to disputes for which a protocol has not formally been approved are nonetheless required to adopt a proportionate and reasonable attitude,[2] and what is reasonable is likely to be assessed by reference to other protocols, including drafts, already in existence.

The effect of the protocols is that those handling claims against accountants need to have systems in place to ensure that they are addressed fully and quickly. In practical terms this means having the resources available to investigate and consider the response to the claim within the relevant timetable.

It has of course always been true that efficient claims handling procedures are likely to save time and money – speculative claims can be quickly exposed; good, quick settlements can be achieved; early detailed investigation of claims may reveal vulnerabilities which would otherwise have lain undiscovered until much later. However, the necessity to reveal one's hand early makes such procedures all the more essential.

10.4 Pre-action disclosure

The protocols encourage the parties to disclose the key documents in relation to a dispute at the earliest possible date. There may be a reluctance to disclose much in the way of documents to claimants at the

---

[2]Practice Direction – Protocols, para 4.

pre-action stage. However, there is the risk that, if little or nothing is disclosed and proceedings are subsequently issued, the claimant may be able to argue that the defendant should pay the costs of the action in any event on the basis that proceedings might not have had to be issued if the defendant had complied with the protocol.

The CPR have in any event greatly widened the scope for applications to the Court for pre-action disclosure, and if a party is not prepared to disclose documents voluntarily it may be forced to do so.

Under the CPR any application for pre-action disclosure will have to be in respect of specified documents or classes of documents which will be relevant to the potential claim and the application must be supported by evidence in a witness statement from the claimant. The applicant will need to show that the specific documents sought are in the possession of the disclosing party and that there is a likelihood that the disclosing party will be made a party to the proceedings if they are initiated. The Court must be satisfied that the benefit of allowing disclosure will outweigh any cost and inconvenience to the disclosing party. The Court will only make an order for disclosure before proceedings have started where disclosure is desirable to dispose fairly of the anticipated proceedings, to assist the dispute to be resolved without proceedings or to save costs.

Generally, the approach to requests for pre-action disclosure should be to narrow the scope of document requests as far as possible by discussion with the claimant. However, the fact that certain requests may not appear to be sufficiently specific may not be determinative: the Court may take into account the reasons why claimants have been forced to make general requests. Moreover, the Court is likely to proceed on the basis that parties should, in accordance with the overriding objective of the CPR, adopt a constructive and cooperative approach.

10.5 Issue and service of proceedings

The new form of originating process under the CPR is the claim form.[3] Full particulars of the claim must be set out either in the claim form or in a separate document known as the 'particulars of claim'. The claim form must be served on the defendant within four months of its date of issue. If there are separate particulars of claim they must be served either at the same time or within 14 days.

---

[3] CPR Pt 7.

The particulars of claim must include:

(a) a concise statement of the facts on which the claimant relies;

(b) a statement of truth such as 'I believe that the facts stated in these particulars of claim are true.'

The requirement for a statement of truth is significant. It may be signed by the party itself (if a company, by a person holding a senior position, which position must be stated) or on its behalf by its legal representative. Anyone who signs a statement of truth in relation to the facts of particulars of claim without a reasonable basis for believing each and every fact is true will be liable to contempt of court proceedings. Clearly, the intention is that claimants should be extremely careful before they take the step of issuing and serving proceedings and defendants will have to take such proceedings seriously.

10.6 Response to proceedings

Once particulars of claim have been served the defendant has 14 days in which to file a defence or an acknowledgement of service.[4] The latter is a short standard form requiring basic details of the defendant and his intention to defend the claim and, contrary to practice before the introduction of the CPR, is only required if the defendant is unable to file a defence within 14 days of service of the particulars of claim. The defence need not then be served for a further 14 days. In practice, an acknowledgment is almost always filed because the extra time is needed.

In any event, there is a need to act quickly in responding to the claim. The CPR are designed to move litigation along quickly. The parties may agree to extend the time for service of the defence by up to a further 28 days, but no further extensions may be agreed without the consent of the Court, which will not necessarily be forthcoming. If there has been correspondence about the claim pre-action, it cannot be emphasised enough that the investigation work for the defence should essentially have been done then. As soon as proceedings are issued, the pressure will be on.

In the defence, the defendant must say:

- which of the allegations in the particulars of claim he denies;
- which of the allegations he is unable to admit or deny but which he wishes the claimant to prove; and
- which of the allegations he admits.

---

[4]CPR Pt 9.

A significant innovation of the CPR is that a defendant must state his reasons for denying an allegation, and if he is relying on a different version of events from the claimant he must state what it is.[5] Moreover, if a defendant fails to deal with an allegation, he is taken to admit it. Holding defences or bare denial defences should no longer be attempted: allegations that an accountant has failed to exercise reasonable skill and care will require some degree of reasoned rebuttal. This means that assistance from an independent expert is going to be important at an increasingly early stage.

The defence must be verified by a statement of truth signed by or on behalf of the defendant. It would be sensible to establish internal systems of verification so that one person can ultimately express an honest belief about the facts of a defence.

10.7 The new culture of case management by the Court

After the defence has been filed, the Court will send to the parties an allocation questionnaire for completion and return to the Court. A fee is payable. This is the first of a series of events whereby the Court is invited by the rules to control the litigation process. The document seeks information for case management purposes and in particular for consideration of the 'track' to which the case should be allocated. Allocation to a particular track largely depends upon the financial value of the claim. Claims over £15,000 and those which are not straightforward are allocated to what is known as the 'multi-track'. Most cases against accountants are likely to be dealt with on the multi-track due to their value and complexity. Thus, the remainder of this Chapter sets out the multi-track procedure to trial.

10.7.1 Case management conference

Once a case has been allocated to the multi-track, there will usually be a 'case management conference', at which the Court will set out directions for the future conduct of the action until trial and fix the trial date.

The directions given will depend on the size and complexity of the case and the information supplied to the Court in the allocation questionnaire and at the case management conference. Dealing with the detail of these

---

[5]CPR Rule 16.5.

may cause irritation. Information is sought as to all aspects of the dispute, from the parties' evidence to how much it is costing them, but they are viewed as significant in the new litigation process and failure to reply may prompt the Court to strike out the action or the defence.

The case management conference is really the last chance the parties have to persuade the Court how they wish the action to be managed. It will be at the case management conference that the Court, mindful of its powers of case management, will be likely to test the parties on the suitability of the case for settlement, the position the parties have got to in the litigation, the necessity for the directions sought by the parties and to conduct a cost/benefit analysis of the proceedings generally. It may even order summary judgment at its own initiative if it perceives a claim or defence or a particular issue to have no realistic prospect of success at trial and no other reason why a case should proceed to trial.[6] This reflects a fundamentally new approach. Previously, the Courts concerned themselves with law and procedure before trial but left matters of evidence to the trial itself. Now a Court has much greater scope, long before trial, to enquire into (and decide upon) the merits of the case. This may well allow the Court to clear claims off the Court lists but clearly throws a heavy burden on those handling claims who will have to be briefed on all aspects of the case even when taking narrow and discrete issues before the Court.

A thorough review of the case should therefore be undertaken before the case management conference. In particular, thought needs to have been given to the relevant documents and the other evidence for the case, both factual and expert. The sections below dealing with disclosure and evidence will provide more detail on what needs to be considered.

It should not be assumed that the fact that the parties are agreed on how the action should move forward will mean that the Court will accept their proposals. Examples have already been seen of judges ignoring parties' suggestions as to when they consider they might be ready for trial and ordering speedy trial dates, even for extremely complex accountants' negligence actions.

10.8 Disclosure

During the process of litigation, each party has a duty to disclose, and allow inspection of, certain documents.[7] If a party does not do so, he may

---

[6]It is also open to either party to seek summary judgment: see generally CPR Pt 24.

[7]CPR Pt 31.

not rely on documents without the Court's consent. 'Disclosure' in this respect means stating whether a document relevant to a dispute exists or has ever existed. 'Document' means anything in which information of any description is recorded and is not restricted to paper documents. The duty to disclose is limited to documents that are, or have been, in a party's control. That is to say, if:

- they are or have been in the party's physical possession;
- the party has or has had a right to possession of the document;
- the party has or has had a right to inspect or take copies.

10.8.1 Standard disclosure

In accordance with the overriding objective of the CPR, the intention is that disclosure of documents should be cost-effective and manageable. A party's duty to give disclosure of documents in litigation is usually limited to giving what is defined as 'standard disclosure'. For this, a party will be required to disclose:

(a) all documents on which he relies, and

(b) all documents which
    (i) adversely affect his own case
    (ii) adversely affect another party's case (this includes other defendants as well as the claimant)
    (iii) support another party's case.[8]

Unless a decision can be made that a document fits into categories (a) and (b) above, it does not need to be disclosed as part of standard disclosure. If another party believes that there should be further disclosure, the onus will be on them to make application for specific disclosure of documents. Such applications will be subject to similar considerations as for pre-action disclosure set out above.

The effect of this is that disclosure should be narrower than under the previous rules. It is, however, as yet unclear as to whether or not the narrow approach will work and achieve the CPR's intention. Moreover, the fact that the disclosure required may be narrower does not affect the practical need to locate and secure all relevant documents at the outset: only when the claim has been thoroughly investigated with the benefit of all the documents can decisions properly be taken as to what should be disclosed and what need not.

---

[8]CPR Rule 31.6.

10.8.2 Reasonable search for documents

Under the CPR, a party is under a duty to make a 'reasonable search' for standard disclosure documents before giving disclosure of their documents by list.[9] The factors relevant in deciding the reasonableness of a search include the following:

(a) the number of documents involved;

(b) the nature and complexity of the documents;

(c) the ease and expense of retrieval of any particular documents; and

(d) the significance of any document which is likely to be located during the search.

The extent of the search must be described in a 'disclosure statement' in the list of documents.[10] Parties are expected to explain why they have decided to exclude something from the ambit of their search.

The disclosure statement must identify the individual responsible for the list and state why he is an appropriate person. It should also expressly state that that person understands the duty of disclosure, believes the extent of the search to be reasonable and certifies that it is complete. A system of verification and inquiry should be adopted to enable the person to complete the disclosure statement as for the statement of truth in the defence: it will be helpful, for example, for a chronology of steps taken to locate and secure potentially disclosable documents to be made and updated as necessary.

It may be considered, given the size of a claim, that an extensive and expensive search is not worth attempting. Such an argument accords with the notion of proportionality within the overriding objective but it is important to be able to justify such arguments – otherwise, cost sanctions may result.

10.8.3 Inspection

All disclosed documents may be inspected subject to:

- the right or duty to withhold from inspection;
- inspection being proportionate; and

---

[9]CPR Rule 31.7.

[10]CPR Rule 31.10.

- documents still being within the party's control.

Privileged documents would come within the first of these categories. A full analysis of the law of privilege is beyond the scope of this Chapter, but essentially, privileged documents are as follows:

(i) documents reflecting communications between a party and his solicitors which are confidential and written for the purposes of obtaining or giving legal advice or assistance for the client. Once a document is privileged for this reason, it remains privileged;

(ii) documents which reflect communications between a party's solicitor and a third party coming into existence after litigation is contemplated or commenced and made with a view to such litigation, either for the purpose of obtaining or giving advice in regard to it, or of obtaining or collecting evidence which may be used in it;

(iii) documents which reflect communications between a party and a third party if the dominant purpose for which the document was prepared was for submission to a legal adviser in view of contemplated or pending litigation;

(iv) documents which form part of 'without prejudice' negotiations between the parties whether the litigation was current or not;

(v) documents which tend to incriminate or expose to a penalty;

(vi) documents which are privileged on the grounds of public policy. (Also known as public interest immunity.)

The mere fact that a document is confidential, for example that it contains information supplied in confidence by a third party, does not make the document privileged. However, under the CPR the Court may order controlled disclosure of confidential documents if reasonable arguments are put to them. There may be other reasons why particular care should be taken before disclosure is made, such as where material has been provided to the accountants by regulators. Legal advice should be taken on such matters.

Guidance on what 'proportionality' means with regard to inspection of documents involves reference to the CPR's overriding objective – consideration needs to be given to the amount of money involved in a claim, the importance of the case, the complexity of the issues and the financial position of each party.

Lost documents should be set out in the list of documents but for obvious reasons cannot be inspected. The more significant the document is, though, the more extensive the search for it needs to be, in order to be viewed as reasonable.

Parties to whom documents have been disclosed pursuant to the CPR may use the document only for the purpose of the proceedings in which disclosure is given, except where:

(a) the document has been read to or by the Court, or referred to at a hearing which has been held in public;

(b) the Court gives permission; or

(c) the party who disclosed the document and the person to whom the document belongs agree.[11]

Even when a document has been read to or by the Court, or has been referred to at a hearing which has been held in public, the Court has a discretion to make an order restricting or prohibiting the use of the document which has been disclosed if it thinks it appropriate.

10.9 Evidence

Before the case management conference, the identity of witnesses and the issues with which they will deal need to be disclosed either in statements of case or in the allocation questionnaire.

10.9.1 Factual evidence

At the case management conference the Court will order a timetable for the exchange of factual witness statements. It is a requirement of the CPR that witness statements should, so far as possible, be in the witness's own words, should not discuss legal propositions, should not comment on documents, and should conclude with a signed statement by the witness that the evidence is a true statement.[12] Nonetheless, legal advisers will continue to have an important role to play in the preparation of such statements, work on which will often begin at a very early stage.

10.9.2 Expert evidence

Expert evidence is often crucial in accountants' negligence actions Factual and documentary evidence alone may not resolve the issue of whether an accountant exercised reasonable skill and care.

The CPR largely reflect the formal position under the old rules. Experts have traditionally been used in Court to explain to the Court technical

---

[11]CPR Rule 31.22(1).

[12]CPR Rule 32.8 and Practice Direction – Written Evidence.

matters that are not within the Court's competence, or to provide opinion evidence on such matters. In recent years, however, experts have been used increasingly as an additional form of advocacy and have strayed into areas which are either strictly outside their sphere or expertise or are matters of judgement for the Court.

The CPR seek to re-assert the classical and limited role of the expert and emphasise that the admission of expert evidence is a matter for the Court's discretion. For example, they expressly state that 'the court must restrict expert evidence to that which is reasonably required to resolve the proceedings', and that 'it is the duty of an expert to help the court on matters within his expertise. This duty overrides any obligation to the person from whom he has received instructions or by whom he is paid.'[13]

Further, the CPR give the Court power to direct that expert evidence is to be given by a single joint expert. Unfortunately, the rules do not elaborate on the circumstances in which the Court may decide that a single joint expert is appropriate. The only guidance is that contained in the report of Lord Woolf which preceded their introduction.[14] The report stated that party-appointed experts were appropriate in large, complex and strongly contested cases where the full adversarial system, including oral cross-examination of opposing expert witnesses on particular issues, is the best way of producing a just result, in cases where there are several tenable schools of thought or in cases where the boundaries of knowledge are being extended. On this basis party-appointed experts are likely to continue to be appropriate in most accountants' negligence actions.

At the case management conference, directions will be given for the exchange of party experts' reports and probably also for a without prejudice meeting of the experts to attempt to narrow the issues in dispute. In addition, the CPR allow an opposing party to submit written questions (within 28 days of an expert report being served) for the purpose of clarification of the report.

The CPR further oblige experts to state in their reports the substance of all the material instructions on the basis of which their report was written, both oral and written. If the Court finds that there are reasonable grounds to consider the way in which the expert has stated his instructions to be either inaccurate or incomplete, then the expert may be cross-examined about his instructions and disclosure of correspondence between the expert and those instructing him may be

---

[13]See generally CPR Pt 35 and Practice Direction – Experts and Assessors.

[14]Access to Justice, July 1996 HMSO.

ordered. Whilst this rule is consistent with the intention of stopping the parties using experts as advocates, it is not clear how it will operate. Great care should be taken therefore when instructing experts at all stages of litigation, even pre-action, as it is not clear in what circumstances such instructions might have to be disclosed to the Court.

10.10 Offers to settle

One of the aims of the CPR is to promote the settlement of disputes without the need for litigation. Alternative dispute resolution (usually structured mediation with a third party mediator) is actively encouraged (see further below).There are rules for settlement offers to be made with consequences for non-acceptance and the Court can raise the issue of settlement during several points in the litigation process.

The CPR introduce important changes to allow a party who wants to settle to exert leverage over his opponent. Under the CPR both claimants and defendants can make what are termed 'Part 36 offers' in respect of claims, with payments into Court ('Part 36 payments') from defendants to settle money claims. The cost consequence if the claimant rejects the defendant's offer or payment into Court and fails to beat it at trial is (as under the previous rules) that the defendant will be awarded its costs from the date of the offer or payment in. If a defendant refuses a claimant's offer and the claimant is awarded more than the amount of the offer at trial, then the Court may award interest on the whole or part of the money awarded at a rate not exceeding 10 per cent above the base rate. The claimant may also be awarded more costs or interest on costs. Offers can be made on this basis to settle the whole of or only part of a claim. They will be open for acceptance within 21 days. They can also be made pre-action, open until 21 days after the commencement of proceedings.

The new system means that it is even more important than previously that early on in a dispute informed judgements as to its merits should be made and settlement strategies adopted.

It will also be important to keep accurate records of all attempts to settle disputes, since, although the negotiations themselves will be without prejudice, the parties' conduct as to settlement generally can be subject to investigation by the Court.

10.11 Trial

It has long been the case that the vast majority of civil proceedings never reach trial. The CPR, with their emphasis on resolution of disputes, should make trial even more unlikely. Proceedings will not reach trial for a variety of reasons – they may be struck out, discontinued, summary judgment may be entered or most frequently matters may be resolved by a negotiated settlement.

If, however, the issues in dispute cannot be resolved by one of these means, a trial will take place. This will be the most expensive stage of the litigation process and the most important. The accountant's role will probably be to give evidence as to events in issue, assisting counsel and solicitors and being on hand to give instructions should opportunities for settlement arise.

Most trials will take place in open court before a single judge. At the hearing the sequence of events is generally as follows:

(1) the claimant's counsel will make an opening speech setting out the claimant's case;

(2) the evidence for the claimant's case, factual and expert, will then be advanced.

Witnesses are called to the court stand where they are required to swear or affirm that they will give truthful evidence. They will be asked by counsel for the claimant to confirm the evidence given by them in witness statement or report form and may be asked some further questions either about matters in those documents or supplementary matters. This stage is termed the 'examination in chief'. The witness is then cross-examined by the defendant's counsel following which there is the opportunity for re-examination by the claimant's counsel.

Witnesses may also be asked questions by the judge;

(3) The defendant's counsel then makes his opening speech setting out the defendant's case, and the process of calling witnesses is repeated.

(4) The defendant's counsel then makes a closing speech summing up the defence to the proceedings, followed by a closing speech from the claimant's counsel.

(5) In all but the most straightforward cases, judgment is usually not given immediately at the end of the trial. The judge will seek a period of a few days or weeks in which to reflect upon the case and write a judgment. Another hearing will then be fixed at which the judgment will be handed down and costs and other consequential issues will be dealt with.

10.12 Alternative Dispute Resolution ('ADR')

Underpinning the CPR is a conviction that litigation is an inefficient and expensive method of resolving a dispute and that the parties should be encouraged to resolve their differences by other methods.

Thus, pre-action protocols will, it is hoped, allow parties and their advisers to understand the issues and evidence before they become embroiled in litigation. Once litigation has started the parties are encouraged to cooperate in the conduct of proceedings and, as we have seen, mechanisms have been put in place to allow parties who wish to settle to exert some pressure on the other parties.

These mechanisms may in themselves be insufficient to ensure that every case which should settle early does so. Litigation remains an adversarial process and may serve to entrench the positions of the parties rather than to promote a compromise. The courts are therefore required by the CPR actively to manage the litigation process to achieve the overriding objectives of fairness and economy. CPR 1.4 (2) lists matters which the judge, as case manager, should focus upon, including, at (e):

> 'encouraging the parties to use an alternative dispute resolution procedure if the court considers that appropriate and facilitating the use of such procedure.'

The ability to have legal rights adjudicated upon by a court of law is not removed by the rules and the CPR are careful to say that the Court should encourage rather than compel the use of ADR. Nonetheless it should be noted that the parties are required by CPR Rule 1.3 to help the Court to further the overriding objective and that the allocation questionnaire contains a question asking whether the action should be stayed to allow an attempt at settlement. Judges will require an explanation if settlement has not been explored at all.

In practical terms, in the course of any litigation against accountants which is not swiftly settled there will at some stage be considerable pressure to explore alternative methods of resolving the dispute. If the accountant and his advisers are well organised this is usually to be welcomed.

10.12.1 Routes to settlement

As we have emphasised, it is important that the legal advisers obtain an early grasp of the main issues and advise the accountant as clearly as possible as to the likely cost/benefit of proceeding with the litigation. The

CPR help in this process by allowing evidence to be assessed rather earlier than previously. It will be for the accountant to weigh other factors, perhaps including any continuing commercial relations with the other party to the dispute, so that a decision can be reached early in the process as to the settlement value of the action, if any. It will often then be appropriate to set out at an early stage the accountant's best case, in without prejudice letters or meetings. In many cases this process may lead to a resolution of the claim without the need for any more elaborate process.

However, experience shows that this does not always work. Resort may then be had to ADR. Strictly speaking ADR means any mechanism for resolving a dispute which is not litigation. The commonest form of ADR is mediation.

10.12.2 The mediation process

The essence of a mediation is that it should involve an impartial third party. The mediation may be structured in whatever way the parties and mediator consider appropriate, but the following steps are usual:

(1) The parties agree upon, appoint (and usually pay for) a mediator. He may be a lawyer or an expert in the field in question and may be a specialist mediator accredited by one of a number of bodies specialising in this area.

(2) Short written statements as to the issues in the case will usually be prepared by each party and provided in advance to the mediator.

(3) A day, or perhaps more, will be set aside for the mediation. At the beginning of that process the mediator will meet the parties, usually with their solicitors, in a plenary session at which each side's case will be put forward. Lengthy legal submissions or speeches at this session are unlikely to be constructive.

(4) Usually the parties will then adjourn to separate rooms and the mediator will shuttle between them seeking common ground and seeing to what extent it is possible to persuade each side of the realities of the case as the mediator sees them.

(5) The parties may, if it is helpful, meet with or without the mediator.

There are a number of advantages to this process if it is carried out properly:

(1) It compels the principals to focus on the dispute and is a good opportunity to bring home forcefully to the other party any weaknesses in his case.

(2) The parties may be prepared to concede weaknesses to a mediator without feeling they have undermined their position in the litigation. The mediator will not, without permission, pass on that information, but he will be in a position to form a view as to whether there is any common ground.

(3) The parties' investment of time and money in the process may create a momentum for settlement.

A mediation is, of course, no more than a means of trying to facilitate a settlement. If there is no common ground or if, for whatever reason, one of the parties simply does not want to settle, little will be achieved. Given that parties will now come under Court pressure to submit to mediation, they will not always come to the process with a real intention to settle, and we have already seen mediations in which the other side appear intent in doing no more than testing the strength of the opposition case. The accountant and his advisers should, while attempting to be constructive, be alert to attempts to abuse the process in this way.

In those rare cases where the other party is not prepared to be constructive, a mediation can be an expensive distraction; but if both parties have properly assessed and understood the strengths and weaknesses of their positions and have any interest in sorting out their dispute on a commercial basis, it can provide a very useful additional opportunity to create a dialogue.

11 When will claims succeed?

11.1 Introduction

In most claims made by clients the issues in dispute will include one or more of the following:

- What work was the accountant required to perform?
- Did the accountant perform that work with reasonable skill and care?
- Were the losses that the client suffered actually caused by the accountant's alleged shortcomings?
- Is the accountant able to place responsibility for any of the losses on the claimant?
- Is the accountant able to place responsibility for any of the losses on a party other than the claimant?
- Are the losses that are being claimed recoverable in law?
- Has the claim been brought within the applicable limitation period?

Where the claim is brought by someone other than a client, many of these same issues may have to be determined, but there the starting point is whether the accountant owed the claimant a duty of care. That aspect is addressed in **Chapter 3**.

11.2 What work was the accountant required to perform?

The question of precisely what the accountant is required to do to fulfil an engagement depends on:

- Any requirements that the law imposes on an accountant performing the particular engagement in question.
- The scope of the engagement as agreed with the client.

11.2.1 Requirements imposed by law on particular engagements

The accountant and his client are not always completely free to determine the scope of the engagement, since many of the most common engagements are the creation of statute and subject to detailed regulation. This is usually aimed at protecting interested parties who are reliant on the accountant's opinion, but who may have little or no input into the instructions he is given.

The most familiar example is the statutory audit, examined below, whereby shareholders rely on the auditor's report to monitor aspects of the way in which the company is being managed. Accountants also have a number of statutory responsibilities in connection with listed and unlisted securities, for example as set out in the Financial Services Act 1986 and the Public Offers of Securities Regulations 1995:[1] these are considered at **3.6.4**.

11.2.2 The audit

The Companies Acts of 1985 and 1989 impose strict requirements on companies in relation to the preparation of annual financial statements and the audit of those accounts. For each financial year, the directors are required to prepare a balance sheet and profit and loss account which respectively give 'a true and fair view' of the state of affairs of the company and of its profit or loss (Companies Act 1985, s226). More detailed requirements as to the content of the financial statements are set out in Schedule 4 of the Act, including that they must state whether the accounts have been prepared in accordance with 'applicable accounting standards'. If the provisions in Schedule 4 conflict with the 'true and fair view' requirement, the latter is to be given precedence.

The purpose of the auditor's role is twofold. First, to provide the directors with an assurance that they have fulfilled their statutory accounting obligations and have a set of financial statements upon which they can rely in running the company. Second, to ensure that reliable financial information is available to the shareholders to enable them to monitor the directors' running of the company.

In order to provide adequate protection for the shareholders, the auditor and the company are not at liberty to overrule by agreement the responsibilities placed on the auditor by statute. (Theoretically, the auditor may be granted relief from liability to the company at the discretion of the Court under Companies Act 1985, s727, but we are not aware of any case where an auditor, or indeed any accountant, has successfully argued that this provision should apply.)

---

[1] SI 1995/1537.

The auditor's report which is laid before the shareholders in general meeting is obliged to state whether the financial statements have been prepared in accordance with the Companies Act 1985 and, in particular, whether they give a true and fair view (s235). In reaching his opinion, the auditor is obliged to carry out such investigations as will enable him to decide whether proper accounting records have been kept and whether they agree with the financial statements (s237). If this is not the case, it should be stated in the auditor's report. Similarly, it should disclose any failure to access the information and records that are needed for the audit. In addition to his duties under the Act, the auditor is given various statutory rights to enable him to perform his role, such as the right to require information or explanations from officers of the company.

A variety of other statutes make detailed provision for the keeping of accounts in respect of bodies other than companies and the auditing of such bodies – for example, there is statutory regulation of the activities of the pensions, banking and insurance industries amongst others.

11.2.3 The scope of the engagement agreed with the client

If good practice has been followed there will be an engagement letter that records what has been agreed about the scope of the work to be carried out (see **Chapter 3**). As this can often be a major area of dispute, setting out the work to be performed as clearly as possible should be regarded as a central part of preparing an engagement letter.

An engagement letter that does not fully record the terms that have been agreed is likely to cause difficulties. First, there is a presumption in law that where a contract is recorded in writing, what is written down (however defective one of the parties may think it is) reflects the whole of the contract terms. Whilst there are some ways in which this presumption can be overcome, it is preferable not to have to try. Second, if a dispute arises about an aspect of the contract that has not been clearly recorded in writing, there is a high chance that the parties will disagree about what was said. The prospect of different recollections is, of course, that much greater where there is no engagement letter at all.

11.3 Did the accountant perform the work with reasonable skill and care?

The accountant is required to act with reasonable skill and care. This duty arises from two different sources. First, Supply of Goods and Services Act 1982, s13 implies into the contract with the client a term that the accountant will act with reasonable skill and care. Second, under the law of negligence, the accountant owes his client a common law duty of care. This again requires him to act with reasonable skill and care.

Thus, where the accountant is sued by his client, the client often has the benefit of two causes of action – in contract and, as a result of the accountant's duty of care, in the tort of negligence.

There are significant differences in the approach that the law applies to claims in contract and tort (for example, different rules apply as to the losses that the claimant is entitled to recover). These differences generally create no difficulties for the claimant, since he is permitted to choose to recover on the basis of the course of action that is more to his advantage.[2]

In two situations, however, the claimant will not have this choice. The first is where a valid contractual exclusion or limitation of liability exists: in that event the claimant cannot get around what is in the contract by relying only on the duty in tort. Second, the rules of limitation, which determine the time within which the claimant must commence proceedings, are different in contract and in tort.[3] If the claimant misses the deadline for bringing a claim in contract he will then have to bring the claim in tort alone, and any advantage he would have had from pursuing the claim in contract will be lost.

11.3.1 Meaning of 'reasonable skill and care'

Regardless of whether the claim rests on contract or the tort of negligence, the standard required of the accountant is indistinguishable: he must act with reasonable skill and care.

What constitutes 'reasonable skill and care'? The basic rule is that a professional is judged by the standards of his colleagues. If he acts in accordance with a practice accepted as proper by a responsible body of his fellow professionals, that is sufficient.[4]

Consistent with this approach, the inexperienced accountant would not be able to avoid liability on account of his relative lack of experience: the client is entitled to receive a service in line with the general standards of the profession. Moreover, where junior staff are allowed to perform tasks

---

[2]*Henderson* v *Merrett* [1994] 3 All ER 506.

[3]Limitation is dealt with at 11.8 TA below.

[4]*Bolam* v *Friern Hospital Management Committee* [1957] 1 WLR 582.

beyond their competence or are inadequately supervised, their firm may be held to have been negligent.[5]

11.3.2 The role of the expert

The question of what constitutes reasonable skill and care in the particular circumstances of a claim is central to many disputes, and expert evidence is often critical to whether or not the claim succeeds. Such evidence should provide the Court with an impartial opinion as to whether the actions of the defendant in the particular circumstances accord with a responsible body of professional opinion. There are, however, many grey areas where both claimant and defendant manage to produce supportive evidence from a reputable expert. The difficult task of assessing the relative merits of their opinions usually falls to the trial judge.

Over the course of time, standards change. What is at one time acceptable practice can come to seem reckless. The accountant will usually be defending his actions in the wake of a significant loss for his client and some years after the event. If the profession's approach to the area in dispute has been developing, it can be difficult for experts to recall or agree what was regarded as acceptable practice at the relevant time.

The fact that a supportive body of professional opinion exists is not by itself enough to defeat an allegation of lack of reasonable skill and care. The supportive opinion must also be credible. It is open to the Court to conclude 'that the body of opinion is not reasonable or responsible'.[6] From time to time the approach taken by a significant proportion of a profession has been held by the courts to be inadequate.

For example, there are instances where the widespread practice within a profession has been to take an obvious risk, on the basis that the chance of the risk materialising is very slight. But if the risk in question could easily have been guarded against, it may be hard to persuade the Court that the practice was justifiable, even if it had other advantages. Such a conclusion was reached by the Privy Council in the case of *Edward Wong Ltd* v *Johnson Stokes & Master*,[7] which concerned a claim brought by a finance company against their solicitors in relation to a mortgage

---

[5] *Jones* v *Manchester Corporation* [1952] 2 QB 852 and per Glidewell LJ in *Wilsher* v *Essex Area Health Authority* [1986] 3 All ER 801 (at p.831).

[6] *Bolitho* v *City & Hackney Health Authority* [1997] 4 All ER 771.

[7] [1984] 2 WLR 1.

transaction. The solicitors had paid over the loan advance to the mortgagee's solicitor in return for an undertaking to complete the formalities of the transaction and forward the relevant title documents within 10 days. Unfortunately, the mortgagees' solicitor absconded with the funds, leaving the finance company with no security. Their solicitors resisted the claim on the basis that in releasing the money in return for an undertaking they had merely followed the accepted practice of solicitors in Hong Kong.

It was accepted by the trial judge that this was indeed the standard practice and that, in the particular conditions of the Hong Kong property market, the system had advantages to both solicitors and their clients. Nonetheless, the Privy Council concluded that the fact that almost all Hong Kong solicitors adopted the practice was not conclusive evidence that it was prudent. As a matter of common sense, the practice inevitably involved a foreseeable and unnecessary risk to the finance company that could easily have been avoided. Accordingly, the defendants had failed to act with reasonable skill and care.

Whilst decisions such as this one are rare, there is unfortunately no reason in principle why the accountancy profession should be immune from them.

11.3.3 The specialist

It may become inappropriate to judge a professional by the general standard of his profession when he is carrying out a specialised task.[8] The appropriate standard in such circumstances is likely to be that of the reasonably competent professional exercising the specialist skill. This does not mean that the specialist must display accountancy skills of a higher than average standard, but there will be an expectation that he has a greater knowledge of the particular business sector and of how to identify and respond to the risks to which it gives rise.

Thus, in *Henderson* v *Merrett Syndicates*[9] the plaintiffs, who were members of a Lloyd's syndicate, alleged that Ernst and Whinney ('E&W') negligently allowed the closure of six years of account by way of reinsurance to close into the following year. In giving judgment, Cresswell J stated that the standard of care required of E&W was that

---

[8]In *Maynard* v *West Midlands Regional Health Authority* [1984] 1 WLR 634, Lord Scarman noted that 'a doctor who professes to exercise a special skill must exercise the ordinary skill of his specialty'.

[9][1997] L.R.L.R. 265.

of reasonably competent Lloyd's panel auditors. The defendants were not to be held to have been negligent if they acted in accordance with a practice accepted as proper by a reasonable body of auditors skilled in the relevant field. The defendants were required to live up to the standard of the ordinary skilled persons exercising and professing to have the relevant special professional skills.

Sometimes it may be difficult to decide whether a particular task or area should be regarded as a specialist one. In some professions such as medicine there are well-recognised divisions of expertise, but in accountancy some of the lines may be rather more blurred. However, it is always safer to assume that if, as a matter of fact, the engagement is of a type that is usually performed by those with specialist experience of a particular sector, the standard that the Court is likely to expect is that of such a specialist.

This proposition is illustrated by the case of *Fawkes-Underwood* v *Hamiltons and Hereward Philips*.[10] The defendant firm had provided advice over many years to the claimant, a Lloyd's Name. The claimant participated in a number of heavily loss-making syndicates on the advice of his managing agents. He alleged that his accountants, who had provided him with general investment advice, ought to have advised him not to participate in them. The case turned on whether it was part of the accountant's retainer to advise on whether the claimant should participate in the syndicates recommended by the managing agents. The trial judge decided that the defendants should have made it clear that they were not advising on the choice of syndicates, a choice that was described as being at the 'very heart' of the claimant's investment. Not having excluded this from the retainer, the accountants were under a duty to identify those syndicates which were high risk and thereby advise against participation.

This case highlights the dangers that can arise when even the most talented generalist provides advice in a specialist area. An accountant with a specialist knowledge of the insurance market would most likely have been much more alive to the potential issue regarding the choice of syndicates and could then either have provided appropriate advice or, having regard to the risks involved, excluded it from his retainer.

11.3.4 Can the nature of the engagement affect the standard of care?

It is also possible that what amounts to reasonable skill and care may be affected by the level of risk connected with the engagement. In part this

---

[10][1997] C.L.Y. 3809.

is no more than restating the need for specialist skill to be applied in some areas; but there is judicial comment in *NRG* v *Bacon and Woodrow*[11] to suggest that an accountant who advises on an acquisition might be required to obtain a greater level of comfort about his conclusions than an auditor. The reasoning behind this appears to have been that, while the decision taken by an acquirer is irrevocable, those relying on a clean audit opinion may be better able to review their position in the light of the next year's audit.

These comments were not central to the decision reached and were made with a particular situation in mind. In some instances what was said may hold good but it will, of course, depend on the circumstances. Important and irrevocable decisions can be made on the basis of an audit report just as much as on a due diligence report. The comments should not, therefore, be interpreted as an indication that the courts will accept a lower level of care from the auditor than from the investigating accountant. Instead, both accountant and auditor should bear in mind that where the risks underlying a particular engagement are high, the Court may consider that this should have been identified and extra care taken.

11.3.5 Proving the standard of the profession

In other than the simplest cases the provision of evidence as to practice at the time is likely to be important to the success of the defence. Documents which pre-date the events in dispute provide good evidence of practice or the state of the profession's knowledge in a particular field at a particular time and can be used to great effect by either party. Useful sources of such evidence can include:

- the professional guidance current at the time;
- material internal to the firm (such as manuals and briefings to staff); and
- contemporary comment in the media, particularly in specialist journals.

All these sources may either help or damage the accountant's defence, depending on whether the evidence that emerges is supportive.

11.3.6 The role of professional guidance

How do professional and legal standards interrelate? The close connection between the standard required by law and that required by the

---

[11] *Nederlandse Reassurantie Groep* v *Bacon & Woodrow and Ors* [1997] L.R.L.R. 678.

profession is identified in the ICAEW's *Guide to Professional Ethics*, which includes as a 'fundamental principle' that:

'A member should carry out his or her professional work with due skill, care, diligence and expedition and with proper regard for the technical and professional standards expected of him as a member.'

In deciding what constitutes reasonable skill and care the courts will take into account relevant professional standards and guidance. A claimant will almost certainly rely therefore on any failure to perform work that appears to be expected in a professional standard as being evidence of negligence. Any departure from the approach recommended in professional guidance is likely to be presented in the same light.

This interrelationship between professional and legal standards was strengthened by the introduction of provisions in Companies Act 1989, sch 4, requiring that the notes to financial statements disclose and give a reason for any material departure from applicable accounting standards. These changes were subject to analysis by Mary Arden QC in an Opinion which is attached as an appendix to the Accounting Standards Board's *Foreword to Accounting Standards*. Her conclusion was that courts will infer that:

'...accounts which meet the true and fair view requirement will in general follow rather than depart from [accounting] standards and that departure is sufficiently abnormal to require to be justified.... These factors increase the likelihood... that in general compliance with accounting standards is necessary to meet the true and fair view requirement.'

The practical result therefore is that unless a material departure from an accounting standard can be convincingly explained, an auditor is unlikely to persuade the Court that a particular set of financial statements showed a true and fair view. This is consistent with the approach taken in *Lloyd Cheyham* v *Littlejohn*,[12] where Woolf J held that standards issued by the ASC (the Accounting Standards Committee – replaced in August 1990 by the Accounting Standards Board) were 'very strong evidence as to what is the proper standard which should be adopted'.

Accounting and auditing guidelines, and pronouncements of the Urgent Issues Task Force ('UITF'), do not have the same status as accounting standards since they are not mentioned in the Companies Act. Nonetheless, the conclusion of Mary Arden QC was that since these were generally endorsed and adopted by the profession, the courts were

---

[12][1987] BCLC 303.

likely to treat them as having 'considerable standing'. Again, the conclusion to be drawn is that (absent some convincing justification) compliance is likely to be necessary to establish that the accounts showed a true and fair view.

11.3.7 Role of firms' manuals and other internal publications

As mentioned in **Chapter 4**, many firms provide manuals or other internal guidance for staff with a view to trying to ensure that work is done to a high standard and in a uniform manner. It is also common practice to hold internal meetings or circulate internal publications or newsletters with a view to keeping staff up to date. It should be borne in mind that where such internal material is relevant to a negligence claim or other investigation their disclosure may be sought. As a result, some care is needed in the preparation of such material. Those preparing manuals and other guidance need to have an eye on what is realistic and workable. The high standards that firms set themselves when producing internal publications such as audit manuals can cause problems in Court, as claimants may seek to suggest that the firm has failed to meet its own standards.[13] If a manual is pitched at the level of best (but not always attainable) practice, that fact should be made clear. Similarly, care is needed in the use of words such as 'must' or 'ought': they are best used only in relation to major steps or procedures which the firm absolutely requires to be performed.

11.3.8 Translating 'reasonable skill and care' into practical terms

What constitutes 'reasonable skill and care' inevitably depends on the particular circumstances. As we have seen in **Chapter 3**, even slight differences in the facts of different cases can be crucial in determining whether the accountant is liable. It would therefore be misleading to attempt a list of acts or omissions that fall below the required standard. Instead, we have identified a number of situations that can lead the accountant into difficulties and should, therefore, be classified as high risk.

---

[13]In the New Zealand case of *Dairy Containers Ltd* v *NZI Bank Ltd* [1995] 2 NZLR 30, the auditor concerned was judged in part against his own office manuals, on the basis that it could be assumed that these set a standard which the auditor regarded as reasonable. Whether such an assumption is a proper one may be questionable, but the case illustrates the dangers that manuals may create.

11.3.9 Client representations

There are many occasions where the accountant will draw support for his own conclusions from management. SAS 440 'Management Representations' provides detailed guidance about relying on and recording such representations in an audit context. Much of the guidance is equally applicable to other types of engagement.

Of course, it is important that there is a written record that explains – and, where appropriate, justifies – the extent to which the accountant has relied upon management representations. One reason for this is that there is always a danger that there will be a misunderstanding between accountant and client about the representations made. The risk of this can be reduced by ensuring that any such representations are recorded in writing. Depending on the individual circumstances, it may be appropriate for the representation to be in formal Board minutes, or for the accountant to set out his understanding in a letter to be countersigned by management. Sometimes it may be desirable to refer to the representations in the report itself. In any event, the accountant should ensure that the necessary confirmation is in place before issuing his opinion or report.

It is also crucial that the weight given to representations is no more than is appropriate. The accountant must therefore assess such information critically. In particular, the accountant should ensure that, where possible, work has been done to verify the representations. Apparent contradictions between the outcome of other investigations and the picture painted by management should be considered carefully.

11.3.10 Losing objectivity

While most accountants would pride themselves on their objectivity and independence, it is not uncommon in defending claims to find that the accountant's objectivity and independence seems to have been undermined, in that the client's views and explanations seem to have been accepted too readily. This risk increases with the length of the client–accountant relationship. Over time the accountant will inevitably develop stronger links with the client. Whilst this may have positive effects on the relationship, there is a danger that the accountant may lose some of his independence of mind.

A common example is where the accountant is assisting a long-standing client to obtain capital investment. There is an understandable inclination to do all that is possible to ensure that the outcome for the client is favourable. Where the client owes the firm a significant amount in fees (which may well not be paid if the client fails), the necessary degree of objectivity can easily be lost. In such a scenario, the accountant should take extra care to be independent and rigorous. If the resources exist within the firm for an uninvolved partner to take a second view this can be helpful in identifying whether partiality may have crept in.

The dangers of not standing back and taking a robust view are illustrated by the case of *Yorkshire Enterprises Ltd* v *Robson Rhodes*[14]. Robson Rhodes ('RR') were the auditors of a shopfitting company, Modernisation Limited ('ML'). The claimants, Yorkshire Enterprise Limited ('YEL') and its subsidiary, Barnsley Investments Limited ('BIL') invested £250,000 in ML by way of equity and a loan, but lost most of their investment when ML went into receivership. YEL and BIL sued RR, alleging that their investment had been made in reliance on misstatements made in the audited accounts and letters of advice addressed to YEL. In particular, YEL had asked RR to advise on the amount of bad debts that should be written off and on the level of doubtful debt provision that was required. RR suggested a figure of £10,000, when provisions amounting to £269,000 should have been recommended. As a result ML appeared profitable when in fact it was not.

It was recognised by all parties that ML had a poor track record when it came to collecting debts. It was known that the directors tended to be very optimistic in their assessment of which outstanding invoices could ultimately be collected. RR acknowledged that what the directors said about doubtful debts needed to be taken with 'a pinch of salt'. Nevertheless, the directors succeeded in persuading RR not to circularise debtors, even though the need for (and amount of) a bad debt provision was central to their work.

11.3.11 Lack of continuity

One of the ways in which the dangers of over-familiarity with a client are mitigated is the periodical rotation of partners and senior staff engaged on the client's affairs. This is good practice in all long-term audit relationships and is a requirement in the case of listed companies. That said, a balance has to be struck: the dangers of lack of continuity in the staffing of an engagement are just as real as those of over-familiarity. There is sometimes no choice about staff changes, but if the client is thought to be high risk, any changes (particularly at partner and manager levels) should be carefully planned.

---

[14]LTL 14.9.98.

11.3.12 Sample testing

In some types of engagement, such as audit, sample testing is routine. If a problem escapes notice, the client may later allege that the sample tested was not an adequate basis for the opinions drawn, even if the approach was agreed between client and accountant at the planning stage. It may be alleged that:

- areas were not selected for testing when any reasonably competent accountant would have tested them;

- the method used for selecting the sample was inadequate;

- the level of testing was inadequate; and/or

- the accountant failed to respond appropriately to the results of the sample, for example by failing to order a more thorough investigation of areas where the initial sample suggested problems.

Complaints about sample testing is not uncommon in cases where the client is suing as a result of the auditor's failure to detect a fraud. The allegation that the sample chosen was inadequate and that a proper sample would have revealed the fraud can be tricky to deal with. It can be easy to pick holes in the testing with the benefit of hindsight and the auditor needs to be aware of the need to be able to justify the choices made.

11.3.13 Detecting fraud

Where an audited company has been the victim of a fraud, the auditor is often the only 'deep pocket' available to sue.

The auditor is not, of course, necessarily lacking in reasonable skill and care if he fails to spot the existence of a fraud. As the old adage has it, the auditor is 'a watchdog but not a bloodhound'.[15] Thus, 'an auditor is not bound to be suspicious where there are no circumstances to arouse suspicion'.[16] Once suspicion should reasonably have been aroused, however, the auditor is obliged to investigate further.

Even in the absence of such suspicions, the claimant may allege that there were weaknesses in the company's controls and systems of such magnitude that more should have been done to alert the board to the opportunity for fraud. The claimant company will usually maintain that

---

[15]In *re Kingston Cotton Mill Co.* (No. 2) (1896) 2 CH 279, CA.

[16]In *re Kingston Cotton Mill Co.* (No. 2) (1896) 2 CH 279, CA.

had such steps been taken they would have acted swiftly to tighten up procedures.

Where the auditor has suspicions, but no firm evidence, or where there is no evidence of fraud but a serious flaw in the systems and controls exists, it can be difficult to decide at what point to voice concern. The answer must be 'the earlier the better'. If the Board decide not to put in hand further investigations or to tighten up procedures, they cannot later complain that they were not on notice of the risk they were running.

The problem was addressed by the Court of Appeal in *Sasea Finance Limited* v *KPMG*.[17] Sasea was part of a group of companies (with its main base in Switzerland) that went into liquidation in 1992. Sasea and other companies in the group had been used as a vehicle for fraud by at least one shadow director. KPMG had audited Sasea's accounts for 1988–1990. Sasea's liquidator alleged that the auditors had been negligent in relation to the 1989 audit. The 1989 accounts were not signed off until November 1990, but it was alleged that had the auditors acted with reasonable skill and care they would have informed the directors and, if necessary, various outside authorities that they suspected fraud well before this date. Had this step been taken, Sasea contended, then losses suffered as a result of fraud between September 1990 and early 1991 (amounting to some £11 million) would have been avoided. The duty to warn was said to extend to informing the police, the DTI, the SFO and the equivalent Swiss authorities.

The auditors applied to strike out the allegations on a number of grounds. One issue was whether the auditors had a duty to blow the whistle on suspected fraudulent conduct prior to the date that they certified the accounts. If they did not, that part of the losses that would have incurred if KPMG had warned at the time of certification could not be placed at their door. Whilst at first instance some claims were struck out, the judge, Mr Justice Collins, was clear that:

> 'If auditors...come across matters which satisfy them that, unless they are disclosed, for example to directors or even to regulators, the company is suffering and will continue to suffer losses, I do not think it would be right to say that they have no duty to take action until the audit is completed.'

The Court of Appeal endorsed the view that in certain circumstances auditors would be obliged to report concerns without delay. If, for example, it was discovered that a senior employee had been defrauding the company 'on a grand scale and was in a position to go on doing so', it

---

[17]First instance: [1999] BCC 857. Court of Appeal: [2000] 1 All ER 676.

would normally be the duty of the auditors to report what had been discovered to management at once. That duty would also include reporting direct to regulators in appropriate circumstances.

It is worth noting that Mr Justice Collins described as 'highly speculative' Sasea's contention that had warnings been given by KPMG the company would have taken steps that would have avoided further losses. Determining whether warnings should have been given and what the response to them would have been puts both parties in the unenviable position of trying to persuade the Court that their hypothetical version of events is more credible than their opponent's. This is uncertain ground for both sides, although the more alarming the warning should have been the more reasonable it is to assume that the company would have responded swiftly. A company whose controls and systems were ineffective may, however, have some difficulty in persuading the Court that they would have responded without delay, or in an extreme case, at all.

11.3.14 Missing time limits

Many claims arising from tax work relate to a failure to keep within time limits. Some of these errors could be avoided by implementing computerised diary systems and ensuring that all staff appreciate the importance of such systems to enter deadlines and timely reminders of their approach.

A further risk is that a misunderstanding exists about whether the responsibility lies with the client or the accountant to provide the notification or information required by the Revenue to satisfy a time limit. The respective responsibilities of accountant and client should always be clearly recorded in writing to avoid such problems.

11.3.15 Unrealistic deadlines

A not uncommon cause of work falling below the required standard is that the engagement has to be performed within an unrealistic time-scale. This is an easy trap to fall into given the pressures of competition and the short time-scales imposed by certain types of work. The phenomenon of an over-stretched and exhausted team churning out work to meet a tight deadline is all too familiar. There is an inevitable risk that work of an acceptable standard will not be produced in such circumstances.

A false expectation on the part of the client about what can be achieved in the time available is an unnecessary risk. It is therefore important that, where appropriate, the engagement letter is clear about the level of the investigations that the accountant is able to undertake in the time available.

Problems can arise where developments during the engagement mean that additional work is needed or if delays on the part of the client (or others involved in the project) run the accountant short of time. It is important that the impact of such events on the engagement is clearly explained to the client. If additional time is needed to complete the engagement in a satisfactory way this should be sought. If this is not forthcoming the accountant should record the position in a letter to the client, and appropriate caveats or qualifications should be included in any report that is then produced.

The onus is firmly on the accountant to seek extra time if needed. A defence based on the fact that the client had unrealistic expectations (which the accountant did not dispel) is not likely to succeed, particularly where the accountant has statutory duties to fulfil. Such a defence was put forward in the case of *In re Thomas Gerrard & Son Ltd*[18] in which the auditor had failed to uncover a fraud achieved by falsifying the level of stock and sales in successive accounting periods. At trial, the defendant's expert conceded that the auditor had had information that should have caused him to make further enquiries but contended that the deadline imposed by the directors for completion of the audit had not allowed sufficient time for these investigations to take place. The trial judge thought this reasoning was flawed. The auditor should either have refused to make his report or should have qualified it. Lack of time could not justify the release of a flawed report.

11.4 Were the losses that the client has suffered actually caused by the accountant's alleged shortcomings?

For the claimant to succeed, he must not only be able to identify and quantify the loss he has suffered but also be able to demonstrate a sufficient connection between the loss and the accountant's fault. If the necessary connection is lacking, the accountant will not be liable. Causation can assume particular importance in claims against accountants because the financial loss suffered by the client may well have been contributed to by a number of different parties and causes.

---

[18][1967] 3 WLR 84.

The connection that the claimant needs to prove to establish causation is expressed in similar terms in contract and in tort. In tort, the claimant will only recover where the accountant's breach was the dominant and effective cause of the loss. It need not, however, be the only cause. In contract the principle applied is essentially the same: the breach of contract has to be the effective cause of the loss.

Courts in the UK and elsewhere have tended to treat the question of whether a particular loss can in law be said to have been caused by a defendant's negligence as one to be answered by applying common sense to the facts of the particular case.[19] Inevitably, however, there is no guarantee that different courts will agree about the common sense conclusions to be drawn. Much will also depend on whether the lawyers advising the claimant are in a position to identify connections between loss and negligence and present them to the Court in a compelling manner.

In some cases reference is made to what is known as the 'but for' test. This asks whether the claimant would have suffered the loss in question 'but for' the defendant's wrongdoing. If the answer is affirmative, the loss will not be recoverable from the defendant, but it does not follow that where the answer is different the loss will automatically be recoverable: this test is better regarded as an initial filter.

Providing the 'opportunity for loss'

More important than the 'but for' test in establishing whether a claimant's loss will be recoverable is the issue of whether the defendant accountant can truly be said to have caused it or whether his negligence merely provided the opportunity for it to be suffered. Thus, a claim based on no more than the allegation that had it not been for the accountant's shortcomings a company would not have been able to continue trading – and so would not have incurred losses – will fail.

This point arose in *Galoo Ltd & others* v *Bright Grahame Murray & Another*,[20] where it was alleged that if the auditor of Galoo and its parent (Gamine) had not been negligent, the insolvency of both companies would have been revealed and they would not have continued to trade. The Court of Appeal agreed that a claim on this basis disclosed no reasonable cause of action. The fact that negligence provided an opportunity for loss to be sustained was not enough. The auditor's negligence had to be the 'effective and dominant cause' of the loss claimed.

---

[19]See for example Glidewell LJ in *Galoo*, below.

[20][1995] 1 All ER 16.

One of the decisions referred to with approval by the Court of Appeal was an Australian case, *Alexander* v *Cambridge Credit Corp Ltd,*[21] where the Court of Appeal of New South Wales dealt with similar facts. Auditors failed to note that provisions for bad debts in their client company's accounts were inadequate. Had they done so, a receiver would very probably have been appointed. Instead, the company was not put into receivership until some years later. In the meantime, losses of A$145 million were sustained. The NSW Court of Appeal concluded (by a majority) that there was no causal connection between the breach of contract and the loss. The mere fact that the claimant company continued to exist was not the cause of its trading profits or losses. In order to recover, the claimant would have to establish some clearer connection between the loss and the accountant's fault.

The approach taken in *Galoo* was applied in a first instance decision of Mr Justice Laddie in the litigation that followed the collapse of BCCI.[22] One of the defendants, Ernst & Whinney, sought to strike out certain claims that arose from audits they had performed of various BCCI companies. The losses claimed were amounts invested by the parent company in its subsidiaries and affiliates, and losses made on guarantees of loans to such companies. The judge considered that these losses arose from legitimate but loss-making business activities. They could not be laid at the door of the auditor simply on the basis that a competent audit would have revealed the true state of the business and that this would have led to an immediate end to trading. The causal connection was insufficient and such a finding would turn the auditor 'into an insurer against all future trading losses'.

It is not correct to say, however, that trading losses will never be recoverable. If an audit should have revealed a damaging course of conduct or state of affairs, loss which then occurs as the specific consequence of that course of conduct or state of affairs will in principle be recoverable. A good parallel is the situation where an auditor should have detected a fraud being committed by a senior employee of his audit client: losses resulting from the fraud continuing unchecked will in principle be recoverable from the negligent auditor.

This is illustrated by the case of *Sasea Finance Ltd* v *KPMG.*[23] As outlined above, Sasea had gone into liquidation as a result of fraudulent

---

[21][1987] 9 NSWLR 310.

[22]*Bank of Credit and Commerce International (Overseas) Ltd & Others* v *Price Waterhouse & Another (No. 3)* TLR 2.4.98.

[23][2000] 1 All ER 676.

behaviour on the part of a shadow director. Negligence was alleged against the auditors on the basis that they should have alerted the company (and if necessary outsiders) to the fraud and that, had this been done in a timely manner, a number of fraudulent transactions would not have taken place.

The Court of Appeal drew a distinction between the position in *Galoo*, where the negligence allowed the company to continue in existence and incur losses occasioned by the ordinary risks of business, and that in *Sasea*, where the claimant suffered fraud, the risk of which the auditors should have reported. In *Galoo*, the auditors were not under a duty to warn against the possibility of losses of the type incurred. In *Sasea* they were.

Nor did it make any difference that some of the transactions in issue in *Sasea* were, at least initially, of a type that were in the normal course of Sasea's business. The auditors tried before the Court to draw a distinction between fraud which took the form of simple thefts and those cases where the fraudster had caused Sasea to sell shareholdings and then diverted the proceeds. The argument was that since the sale of shares was a transaction of a type normally entered into by Sasea, the losses should be regarded as arising from the normal activities of the company and hence not recoverable. Not surprisingly perhaps, the Court of Appeal rejected this distinction: all the transactions were irregular or fraudulent and there was therefore a clear link between the risk against which KPMG should have warned and the losses suffered.

The same principle can apply in non-fraud cases. An example is provided by the case of *Grant Thornton* v *Pendigo*.[24] Pendigo was sued for unpaid audit fees and counterclaimed in respect of trading losses. Grant Thornton applied to strike out the claim on the basis of Galoo. Their position was that, even if they had been negligent (which was denied), this could only have provided Pendigo with the opportunity to continue its unprofitable trading: it had not caused the trading to be unprofitable.

The Court refused to strike out the claim. The engagement at issue was a review of interim accounts. Pendigo contended that this had been commissioned against a background of past systems' weaknesses and unprofitable trading, with the purpose of giving comfort that trading was now profitable. Pendigo alleged that the weaknesses in the systems remained and the review should have shown a major loss (rather than a small profit). The Court held that if these allegations could be proved at trial a sufficient causal link would have been established between breach and loss. If there had been a breach, this would then have had the

---

[24]1996: unreported.

foreseeable consequence of causing Pendigo to believe it was trading profitably when it was not, with the further foreseeable consequence that it had continued to trade in a way which was, in fact, very unprofitable.

It would, therefore, be overstating and simplifying the decision of the Court in *Galoo* to regard it as authority for the proposition that trading losses made in the normal course of business are never recoverable. Subsequent authorities have underlined the fact that a claim for such losses may be successful, though only where a clear causal connection can be shown between the defendant's breach and the losses for which compensation is sought.[25]

What is the type of loss in respect of which the duty is owed?

The need for a causal link between the loss and the wrongdoing was re-emphasised by the House of Lords in the case of *South Australia Asset Management Corp.* v *York Montague Ltd* ('SAAMCO').[26] Lord Hoffman, giving the lead judgment, stressed the importance of identifying whether the defendant's duty (whether in contract or tort) related to the kind of loss which the claimant has suffered.

The defendants were professional valuers who had negligently over-valued properties being considered by the claimants as security for loans. Had it not been for the valuations, the loans would not have been made. The loans were defaulted on and the claimants sued to recover the amount of the loans plus the unpaid interest, less the amounts recovered from selling the properties.

Lord Hoffman's approach was to distinguish between the professional who has a duty to advise on the course of action that the claimant should take and one who is only providing information:

> 'If the duty is to advise whether or not a course of action should be taken, the adviser must take reasonable care to consider all the potential consequences of that course of action. If he is negligent, he will therefore be responsible for all the foreseeable loss which is a consequence of that course of action having been taken. If his duty is only to supply information, he must take reasonable care to ensure that the information is correct and, if he is negligent, will be

---

[25]To similar effect is *Sew Hoy & Sons Ltd* v *Coopers & Lybrand* [1996] 1 NZLR 392, a decision of the New Zealand Court of Appeal refusing to strike out a claim for trading losses.

[26][1996] 3 All ER 365.

270

responsible for all the foreseeable consequences of the information being wrong.'

Their Lordships decided that the valuers were only providing information about the value of the properties as security. Their duty did not extend to advising whether or not to advance the loans. The defendants were not, therefore, liable for the consequences of any risks that the lender would, in any event, have taken on himself had the advice been sound. This was of particular significance because the claimants' losses had been substantially worsened by a drop in property values that had occurred after the loans had been made. The result of their Lordships' approach was that the defendants were not liable to compensate the claimants for this element of their loss.

While the distinction between a professional who is advising and one who is providing information is useful in a valuation context, it is less helpful outside that context, where it can be difficult to apply. It was, however, used in a case where accountants were responsible for providing a valuation: *Law Debenture Trust Corp.* v *Hereward Philips.*[27] There the auditors of a pension fund were instructed to provide a valuation of a company to be purchased by the fund. The auditors admitted overvaluing the target by £2.5 million and it was agreed between the parties that, following SAAMCO, the maximum amount that could be recovered from the auditor was £2.5 million, even though the total loss on the transaction was considerably higher (this case is considered further at p 284 below).

The adviser/informer distinction is of no obvious application in the audit context. In other roles, the accountant may be either adviser or informer depending on the nature of the engagement. In many instances, the accountant's advice will be one of a number of factors that contributes to the making of a commercial decision, and in such cases the accountant may well be classed as providing information rather than advising on a course of action. Reaching this conclusion, however, does not assist where it is difficult to identify which of the losses suffered were the result of the information being inaccurate. An illustration of the difficulties is provided by the case of *Yorkshire Enterprise Ltd* v *Robson Rhodes.*[28]

The claimants had invested capital in a business ('ML') in reliance on valuation work performed by the defendants, who were the auditors of ML. The trial judge, Mr Justice Bell decided that Robson Rhodes' task had been 'to supply information amounting to a valuation of ML's assets,

---

[27][1999] PNLR 725.

[28]LTL 14/9/98. See also the discussion at 11.3.10 above.

debtors and un-invoiced sales, and profit dependent thereon'. They were not advising the investors on what course of action they should take.

The judge was satisfied that at the time of the investment ML was trading at a loss. As a result of the information given by Robson Rhodes, the claimant thought ML was profitable and proceeded with an investment that was lost in a huge hole in ML's balance sheet as soon as it was made. Therefore, the whole loss could be linked to the negligent information supplied, since it occurred immediately upon the investment being made.

Robson Rhodes argued that the failure of the business was caused by factors for which they could not be held responsible: mismanagement by ML after the investment together with the effects of recession. The judge did not accept that these factors had caused ML's collapse. Although they had had some effect, he concluded that Robson Rhodes' information had been so inaccurate that it was reasonable to assume that the loss suffered had been suffered as a result of the information's inaccuracy, unless there was cogent evidence to the contrary. In other words, the facts of this particular case were such that it was justifiable not to distinguish the contribution that the inaccurate information had made to ML's loss from that made by other factors.

Nonetheless, the case illustrates the difficulty that the courts may have in distinguishing the consequences of an accountant's negligence from other factors, particularly in the context of a business which fails some time after the negligent advice has been given. In the circumstances of this case, the judge did not need to quantify the effect of the other factors (poor management and the effects of the recession) which Robson Rhodes pointed to as contributing to the loss; but had this been necessary it would have been difficult (perhaps impossible) to quantify each of those elements individually.

11.5 Is the accountant able to place responsibility for any of the losses on the claimant?

One feature of claims against accountants is that, where they are found liable, they are very often being held responsible for losses that have their origin in the acts and omissions of others. Problems in a business are often the result of the mismanagement or worse of directors, management or staff. The accountant's fault may to some degree consist of failing to warn about issues of that nature that should have become apparent during the course of his work.

This is particularly true in an audit context. The auditor may fail to identify that a fraud is being committed when he reasonably should, or fail to respond effectively to signs of inadequate internal control within the company. The auditor may feel, with some justification, that even if it is established that the audit work was not what it should have been, the company should shoulder some of the blame. The means established for achieving this appears in the Law Reform (Contributory Negligence) Act 1945, Section 1 of which provides that:

> 'Where any person suffers damage as a result partly of his own fault and partly of the fault of any other person or persons, a claim in respect of that damage shall not be defeated by reason of the fault of the person suffering the damage, but the damages recoverable in respect thereof shall be reduced to such extent as the court thinks just and equitable having regard to the claimant's share in the responsibility for the damage.'

Where Section 1 is applied the Court will order a percentage reduction in the damages to be paid by a defendant to take into account the responsibility that the claimant should himself bear for his losses.

This section opens the way for significant reductions in the level of damages paid by an accountant where his shortcomings are only one cause of loss which has also been contributed to by the claimant. There are, however, some difficulties which can arise in practice.

11.5.1 Fault

The first area of difficulty is the scope of the term 'fault'. Section 4 of the Act defines 'fault' as:

> 'Negligence, breach of statutory duty or other act or omission which gives rise to a liability in tort or would, apart from this Act, give rise to the defence of contributory negligence.'

Uncertainty arose both in the UK and in other countries such as Australia and New Zealand where similarly worded provisions are in place about the meaning of the phrase 'other act or omission'. Was it intended that a breach of contract would count as an 'act or omission'? If so, this was a fundamental change to the previous general rule that a party was liable for his breach of contract regardless of any contribution made to it by the other party.

Particularly problematic was the position of defendants, such as accountants, whose acts or omissions were both a breach of contract and a breach of a co-extensive duty in tort to take reasonable skill and care. Were such defendants able to reduce their liability by relying on the contributory negligence of the claimant only if he chose to claim on the basis of tort rather than in contract? Such an interpretation would accord with the principle that it is open to the claimant to choose the course of action that most favours him. However, a position where the defendant's liability varies significantly depending on whether the claimant chooses to treat the defendant's wrongdoing as a breach of a contract or as a tort is bound to be criticised as lacking fairness and common sense.

In England this debate is more or less settled in favour of the defendant, although the issue has not come before the House of Lords. In *Forsikringsaktiesleskapet Vesta* v *Butcher*[29] the Court of Appeal endorsed the view that where the defendant's liability in contract was the same as his liability in the tort of negligence (independent of the existence of any contract), the defendant was entitled to rely on the defence of contributory negligence.

This interpretation has received support in a number of subsequent cases. Moreover, the Court of Appeal has explicitly confirmed[30] in the context of a professional negligence claim against a firm of solicitors that where the contract term that has been breached is of the implied term of skill and care (under Supply of Goods and Services Act 1982, s13), it is open to the defendant to claim contributory negligence.

The same conclusion as that endorsed by the Court of Appeal has been reached in a number of Commonwealth countries when considering similar legislation.[31] However the High Court of Australia (Australia's highest court) took the opposite view in *Astley* v *Austrust Limited*.[32] This was a professional negligence claim against a firm of solicitors where the trial judge allowed a 50 per cent reduction in liability because of the claimants' own negligence. On appeal, the High Court (by a majority of four to one) decided that contributory negligence could not be pleaded as a defence to a breach of a contractual duty of care even where that duty was co-extensive with the common law duty of care in tort. The claimants were entitled to succeed on their best case (i.e., the contractual claim in preference to that in tort) without any reduction. It is unlikely – though not impossible – that the approach favoured in *Astley* will be followed by the House of Lords should the availability in English law of the contributory negligence defence in cases such as these ever have to be determined in that forum.

---

[29][1988] 2 All ER 43.

[30]*UCB Bank plc* v *Hepherd Winstanley & Pugh* TLR 25/8/99

[31]Including recently in the High Court of South Africa in *Thoroughbred Breeders Association of South Africa* v *Price Waterhouse* 1999 (4) SA 968 (W) – see 11.5.5 below.

[32][1999] HCA 6.

11.5.2 What acts and omissions will be imputed to the company?

Assuming that English law on the availability of contributory negligence in claims based on reasonable skill and care remains unchanged, an accountant (and particularly an auditor) sued by a corporate client rather than an individual, may nonetheless face difficulties in claiming contributory negligence. The problem arises from the fact that although a company is regarded as a separate legal entity, it can only act through natural persons. The difficulty lies in determining which acts, omissions and knowledge of the individuals involved with the company are to be treated as the acts, omissions and knowledge of the company itself.

Where the contributory negligence takes the form of an act of the board of directors, or a decision of the members in general meeting, there is no difficulty since these are clearly decisions of 'the company itself'. More problematic are the acts and omissions of individual directors, management or employees. Which of these are to be attributed to the company for the purposes of assessing contributory negligence?

In most cases, the principles of the law of agency will resolve the issue. As a general rule, the company will be bound by any act of its servants or agents that falls within their authority. This authority encompasses not only the powers that the servant or agent has been expressly granted, but also those that it is reasonable for him to exercise given his position within the company and those that the company has held him out to outsiders as possessing. Thus, a finance director would be assumed to be acting on behalf of the company insofar as his acts fell within the normal remit of the role generally exercised by finance directors.

The one exception to the principle just stated is that the law does not fix the company with any knowledge of a fraud on it committed by an employee or a director, beyond what (if anything) is actually known to the board of directors.[33] In most cases, the basic principle and this exception are then all that are needed in order to determine what acts, omissions and knowledge are to be treated as those of the company itself and can therefore be relied upon for the purposes of an allegation of contributory negligence. Occasionally, however, the courts pose a slightly different question: of whether a particular individual is to be regarded as the 'directing mind and will of the company'.

---

[33]This does not, however, preclude the possibility of an allegation that individuals within the company have been negligent either in failing to uncover the fraud or to create an environment that reduced the risk of fraud.

The 'directing mind' concept originally arose in criminal cases and was concerned with instances where one (or a small number of individuals) could be identified as being 'the very ego and centre of the personality of the corporation'.[34] An illustration in the civil context is provided by the case of *Berg Sons & Co. Ltd* v *Mervyn Hampton Adams & Others.*[35] The former auditors of Berg, a small company in liquidation, were sued by its liquidators who alleged that the company had suffered loss as a result of the auditors' negligence and breach of contract. The ultimate beneficial owner of all the shares in Berg was a single individual (a 'Mr Golechha'), who was a director of Berg and in effect its sole proprietor. He was 'the directing mind and will of the company', such that 'his knowledge was the company's knowledge'.

The essence of the claim made by Berg against its auditors was that the auditors ought not to have accepted various assurances and representations made by Mr Golechha. It was not being said that Mr Golechha at any time relied upon anything said or done by the auditors or was misled. Nor were there any other directors or shareholders to be misled as a result of the auditors' failures. Nor was there any fraud on the company. Not surprisingly, Berg's claim failed.[36] Whether Mr Golechha was classified as the directing mind of the company which he controlled or as its agent, the company was in no position to disclaim full knowledge of his activities.[37]

11.5.3 The auditor and contributory negligence

It has been suggested in the past that since the auditor's statutory duty is to report to the company's members in general meeting, only matters brought to the attention of the general meeting should be attributed to the company. Thus, one member of the Court of Appeal of New South Wales in *Simonius Vischer* v *Holt Thompson*[38] stated:

> 'It is difficult to see how the conduct of any servant or director could constitute the relevant negligence, so as to defeat the claim against

---

[34]Lord Haldane in *Lennard's Carrying Co. Ltd.* v *Asiatic Petroleum Co. Ltd.* [1915] AC 705.

[35][1993] BCLC 1045.

[36]The parties who stood to benefit from Berg's claim were, of course, Berg's creditors. Some of those creditors also brought claims in their own right alleging negligence, but these claims failed for different reasons.

[37]Whether resort was needed to the 'directing mind' concept in order to decide *Berg* is debatable. More recently, the Privy Council have suggested that the concept should only be used in circumstances where other rules of attribution (such as agency) do not assist: *Meridian Global Funds Management Asia Ltd* v *Securities Commission* [1995] 3 WLR 413.

[38][1979] 2 N.S.W.L.R. 322, per Moffit P at p. 329.

the auditor, whose duty is to check the conduct of such persons, and where appropriate report it to the shareholders.'

The practical result of this approach would, in the majority of cases, be to deprive the auditor of the possibility of successfully alleging contributory negligence, since the failings that he is likely to wish to rely on will not be those of the Board, individual directors and management. No English Court has had to rule specifically on whether the *Simonius* approach should be adopted but it seems unlikely that it would now find favour here. Indeed, subsequent Australian decisions (particularly *AWA* v *Daniels* below) have shied away from it.

What is perhaps more uncertain is how much broader the approach taken by the English courts would be. One option would be to treat only matters known to the Board as known by the company, so that any negligence on the part of the Board would be treated as that of the company.

In many cases, however, such an interpretation would not be wide enough to assist the auditor, since the acts, omissions or knowledge that the auditor wishes to rely on by way of contributory negligence may well be those of an employee (often a senior manager) or an individual director. A broad approach allowing a claim for contributory negligence based on the failings of senior management was upheld in *AWA* v *Daniels*, the facts of which are set out below.

In what follows we consider some of the practical contexts in which claims for contributory negligence have succeeded and the amount by which the liability of the defendants was reduced.

11.5.4 Over-delegation and failure to supervise

The allegation made against the company will frequently be that it has brought its losses on itself or contributed to them by failing to monitor certain aspects of the business or the activities of particular individuals. A broad approach allowing a claim for contributory negligence based on the failings of senior management was upheld in two notable commonwealth cases. *AWA* v *Daniels* (a decision of the New South Wales Court of Appeal) and *Dairy Containers Ltd* v *NZI Bank Ltd* (a first instance decision in New Zealand).

AWA v *Daniels*[39]

The claimant suffered severe financial losses as a result of an employee's foreign exchange hedging transactions. Responsibility for the foreign

---

[39] [1995] 16 ACSR 607.

exchange operation had been almost wholly delegated to senior management, who had allowed the exchange operation to operate without proper records or controls. As a result, an employee was able to conceal substantial losses. The auditor was aware of the weaknesses, but failed to report them to the board of directors. The company sued the auditor, alleging a negligent failure to report the weakness in controls and the losses. The auditor's claim for contributory negligence succeeded because the NSW Court of Appeal found that there had been an almost wholesale delegation by the AWA board to senior management of the task of setting up and operating the foreign exchange operation. The NSW Court of Appeal commented that a company is not entitled to abdicate all responsibility for proper management of the financial aspects of its operation and then seek to attribute the entire blame to its auditor when loss was suffered. The auditor's liability for damages was accordingly reduced by one third.

Dairy Containers v *NZI Bank Ltd*[40]

In this case the auditor failed to uncover frauds on the part of three senior executives who managed the claimant company. The Court found that there had been a significant failure on the part of the company's directors to monitor the exercise by senior management of powers delegated to them by the Board, which amounted to contributory negligence. The directors could not rely on the failures being those of senior management rather than the Board, since management were exercising the delegated powers of directors; nor did the fault of the company have to be causally connected to the negligence of the auditor. The auditor's liability was reduced by 40 per cent.

11.5.5 Failure to avert a known risk

An allegation of contributory negligence may also be made where the claimant has deliberately taken a risk and has failed to alert the accountant to that risk.

Thoroughbred Breeders Association of South Africa v *Price Waterhouse*[41]

The claimant engaged Price Waterhouse ('PW') as its auditors. PW failed to detect that substantial amounts of cash resulting from auctions had not been banked and that a promissory note had been cashed without

---

[40][1995] 2 NZLR 30.

[41]High Court of South Africa, 1999 (4) SA 968 (W).

authorisation. The culprit was the claimant's financial manager. On being sued, PW raised a number of defences including contributory negligence, arising from the fact that the claimant knew that the financial manager had been convicted of three counts of theft some years earlier, but had failed to inform PW.

The Court declared that the claimant's behaviour in appointing the manager to a position where he was responsible for large amounts of cash, failing to monitor his activities adequately and not informing PW of the situation amounted to 'extremely gross negligence'. Whilst PW's audit was found wanting, their shortcomings were adjudged to be far less serious than those of the claimant, resulting in a reduction of PW's liability for damages by 80 per cent.

11.5.6 Summary

While there are still very few English cases dealing with contributory negligence in claims against accountants, the cases just set out support the proposition that directors have a responsibility for the proper running of their company's business and that failures by them in this regard should result in a reduction in the level of damages properly claimable from the auditors if they too were at fault. It is likely, and certainly to be hoped, that the English courts will specifically endorse this view in due course. In the meantime, however, availability of the defence appears to be widely recognised by claimant and defendant lawyers alike.

11.6 Is the accountant able to place responsibility for any of the losses on a party other than the claimant?

We have so far focused on attributing responsibility to the client, but it may also be open to the accountant to seek to reduce his liability by claiming that a party other than his client should bear responsibility for some of the client's losses. Under the Civil Liability (Contribution) Act 1978, s1:

'Any person liable in respect of any damage suffered by another person may recover contribution from any other person liable in respect of the same damage (whether jointly with him or otherwise).'

The amount of the contribution is 'such as may be found by the court to be just and equitable having regard to the extent of that person's responsibility for the damage in question', and may amount to a complete indemnity (s2).

As long as both wrongdoers are liable in respect of the same damage, it is immaterial whether their liability is in contract or in tort. Nor is a defendant barred from seeking a contribution from another party simply because he has negotiated a settlement of the claimant's action against him. Provided the compromise is reached in good faith, the defendant is entitled to seek a contribution without regard to whether or not he himself is or was liable in respect of the damage, provided he would have been liable had the factual basis of the claim against him been proved (see s1(4)).

A defendant can make a claim for a contribution up to two years after the judgment against him is given, or in the case of a settlement, the date on which the amount to be paid under the settlement is agreed.

As a result of these provisions, in cases where the accountant is seeking to blame the directors of the claimant company for the losses the company has suffered, the accountant may succeed in a claim for contribution against the directors even if he fails to persuade the Court that their activities should be attributed to the company and treated as contributory negligence.

In such situations, the accountant will face a choice as to whether to claim contributory negligence or contribution and at trial will have to make an election as to which he intends to pursue. The accountant will usually prefer to claim contributory negligence, because this is expressed as a reduction in the damages payable to the claimant. By contrast, on most occasions where the accountant succeeds in obtaining a contribution, he will be responsible for paying the whole of the claimant's damages and will have to attempt to recoup the appropriate share from the contributing party. The result is that any inability or unwillingness to pay their contribution will be visited on the accountant rather than on the claimant, the law taking the view that it is more fitting that these problems be fitted on another wrongdoer than on the claimant.

We have so far dealt with parties 'internal' to the claimant company from whom the accountant may seek a contribution, but there are also 'outside' parties whom the accountant may seek to blame. In *Dairy Containers*,[42] for example, the auditor sought to blame the parent company of the claimant on the basis that the parent had failed to monitor adequately the activities of its wholly owned subsidiary. This claim did not succeed, on the basis that the usual control that a parent

---

[42]See 11.5.4 above.

exercises over its subsidiary was an insufficient basis for a duty of care to be owed by the parent to the subsidiary. Nonetheless, it is possible to envisage situations in which a parent company does play a particularly active role in the running of the subsidiary and where such an argument could therefore succeed.

More successfully, the Auditor-General sought a contribution in *Dairy Containers* from banks who had honoured fraudulent cheques without due enquiry. Given that the banks owed a duty to DCL to make proper enquiries and had failed to do so, there was no reason why the Auditor-General should not seek a contribution from them. Nor was the amount of the contribution limited to the value of the cheques in question.

Another occasion where the accountant may seek to spread liability for the claimant's losses is where he is one of two or more advisers on the same proposed transaction, such as where the accountant and other professionals advise on the due diligence process of a proposed acquisition. If the claimant subsequently sues some or all of the advisers alleging that they were negligent, they will investigate whether they can successfully contend that, to the extent that they are liable, they are entitled to a contribution from their fellow advisers.

As previously outlined, a contribution can only be sought if the party seeking the contribution and the potential contributor are liable in respect of the 'same damage'. This phrase has been narrowly interpreted by the courts and imposes a substantial limitation on the availability of contributions under the Act. An example in a non-accountancy context is *Birse Construction* v *Haiste Ltd*[43] where the Court of Appeal had to consider a claim arising out of the design and construction of a water reservoir by Birse for Anglian Water. Haiste were instructed by Birse as consulting engineers to assist in the design of the reservoir and the tendering process. 'N', an engineer employed by Anglian, had administered the project. When defects in the reservoir emerged, Birse rebuilt it at its own expense and then sued Haiste alleging negligence. Haiste claimed a contribution from N. The Court of Appeal struck out the claim for contribution on the basis that the damage allegedly caused to Anglian by N was not the 'same damage' as that caused by Haiste to Birse. The damage suffered by Anglian had been the physical defects in the reservoir, whereas that suffered by Birse had been the financial loss of constructing the replacement reservoir.

---

[43][1996] 1 WLR 675.

11.7 Are the losses that are being claimed recoverable in law?

11.7.1 Loss that is too 'remote'

The law recognises that it is not always appropriate to hold the defendant financially responsible for all of the losses that he has caused. Therefore, even where it can be said that harm has been caused by the accountant's shortcomings, the loss suffered by the claimant may be 'too remote' to be recoverable.

The line as to what losses are too remote to be recovered is drawn somewhat differently in contract and in tort. In contract, the purpose of awarding damages is to place the claimant in the position they would have been in had the contract been properly performed. The basic principle is that a loss will only be compensated if it either:

- arises naturally from the breach of contract, or

- may reasonably be supposed to have been in the contemplation of the parties at the time the contract was made as the probable result of the breach.[44]

In tort, the purpose of awarding damages is to return the claimant (as far as possible) to the position he would have been in had the tort not occurred, and loss is recoverable if it was reasonably foreseeable.[45] It is not necessary for the precise form or extent of the harm to be foreseeable. What must be foreseeable is the type of harm that has been suffered.[46]

11.7.2 The claimant's duty to mitigate his loss

The claimant has an obligation to minimise the damage that he suffers and will not receive compensation for any losses that he could reasonably have avoided. Accordingly, it is important that the defendant carefully reviews the items of loss that are claimed and challenges any element of loss that the claimant could reasonably have taken steps to avoid. The onus of showing that the claimant has failed to minimise his losses falls on the defendant. The defendant will be liable to pay the cost of any mitigating steps that the claimant reasonably takes.

---

[44]*Hadley* v *Baxendale* [1854] 9 Exch 341.

[45]*Overseas Tankship (UK)* v *Morts Dock and Engineering Co. (The Wagon Mound)* [1961] AC 388.

[46]*Hughes* v *Lord Advocate* [1963] AC 837.

Take the example of a company that has falsely believed itself to be profitable on account of the accountant's negligence. If the company has made an overpayment of tax as a result of its mistaken belief, it is arguably then obliged to take steps to recover the overpayment from the Inland Revenue.

Another example of mitigation would be that of a company which is the victim of a fraud that the auditor has negligently failed to identify. As soon as it becomes aware of the fraud, the company is obliged to take whatever steps it reasonably can to ensure that no further losses are sustained and to investigate whether any recovery can be made from the fraudster.

There are, however, limits on what claimants are expected to do to protect their own interests. In *Pilkington* v *Wood*[47] it was decided that it was not reasonable to require a claimant 'to embark on a difficult piece of litigation' in order to recover losses that would otherwise be recoverable from the defendant, even if the defendant is prepared to indemnify the claimant against his costs.

11.7.3 Giving credit for benefits that flow from the defendant's wrongdoing

Since the damages paid to the claimant should not put him in a better position than he would have been in if the defendant had properly performed his obligations, the defendant is entitled to the benefit of any positive consequences that his wrongdoing has had on the claimant's position. Otherwise, the claimant would recover more than his net loss. If, for example, a company suffers losses as a result of unauthorised transactions that the auditor should have detected, his liability will be for the net amount of the losses, after credit has been given for any of the unauthorised transactions that were profitable.

Another example is that of taxation. If the claimant is being compensated for a loss that would in the normal course of events have been subject to taxation, the accountant's liability should be calculated net of tax.

11.7.4 Calculating how amounts recovered by the claimant reduce the defendant's liability

Where the claimant has recovered part of his losses from a source other than the defendant, an issue may arise as to how that recovery affects the

---

[47][1953] 2 All ER 810.

extent of the defendant's liability. This will only be a problem where the defendant is not liable for the full amount of the claimant's loss.

The point was dealt with in the case of *Law Debenture Trust Corp.* v *Hereward Philips.*[48] The claimant was the independent trustee of the Belling pension fund, appointed after Belling had gone into liquidation. Prior to Belling's collapse, but at a time when it was desperate for an injection of cash, the fund (which was then controlled by Belling's directors) had purchased a company from Belling for £5.5 million. The company was ultimately sold by the fund for £1.43 million, resulting in a loss of £4.07 million.

The claimant sued the liquidators of Belling to recover the fund's loss, alleging that the transaction had been improper and entirely for the benefit of Belling at the expense of the pension fund. The liquidators paid £1.5 million in settlement of the claim. The claimant then brought proceedings against the auditors of the fund, alleging that they had given negligent advice at the time the company was purchased, having overvalued it by £2.5 million.

A settlement of the claim against the auditors was reached, but the court was asked to consider the question of whether their liability should be reduced by some or all of the £1.5 million compensation received from the liquidators. The auditors contended that credit should be given since the compensation received from the liquidators would not have been received but for the auditors' negligence and because some or all of the sum was compensation for the same loss. Both arguments were rejected.

The Court decided that the correct starting point was the maximum amount of the claim against the liquidators. Since there was no reason why the full loss of £4.07 million should not have been claimed, the £1.5 million recovered from the liquidators fell to be deducted from the total loss of £4.07 million, leaving an unrecovered loss of £2.57 million. This exceeded the maximum that could have been recovered from the auditors (£2.5 million) and there was therefore no reason to reduce their liability.

11.7.5 Particular types of loss

In what follows we consider various types of loss that are commonly claimed in cases against accountants and whether they are likely to be recoverable.

---

[48][1999] PNLR 725.

Losses associated with false profits

Many claims are based on the contention that as a result of the negligence of the accountant, the claimant company appeared to be profitable (and believed itself to be so) when it was not. There are a number of losses that claimant companies (and their liquidators) commonly claim have flowed from a mistaken belief in the fact or extent of the company's profitability.

Dividends

An obvious example is dividends paid out of illusory profits. It was established in *In re Thomas Gerrard & Son Ltd*[49] that these losses can be recovered. In this case the managing director had successfully falsified the company's stock records over a number of years, with the result that the directors declared dividends for these years when the company was not genuinely profitable (despite appearances to the contrary). The frauds were discovered when the company went into liquidation. The company's liquidator brought an action against the auditors who had allegedly been negligent in failing to respond to certain information that should have made them suspicious about the figures for stock. The Court decided that the dividends paid other than from available profits were recoverable from the negligent auditors. The auditor's breach of duty in not investigating when suspicions should have been aroused was accepted as being the direct cause of these losses.

It made no difference that the dividend was only paid on the recommendation of the directors and after approval by the members. These decisions were taken purely because of the false picture that the auditor's negligence had allowed to persist.

Some doubt was thrown on this decision by *Galoo*,[50] where the Court of Appeal struck out the claim for recovery of a dividend together with the claim for trading losses. It is very doubtful whether this aspect of *Galoo* is correct and it has subsequently been queried by both commentators and judges alike.[51]

---

[49][1967] 3 WLR 84.

[50][1995] 1 All ER 16.

[51]See Collins J's comments in *Sasea Finance Limited* v *KPMG* ([1999] BCC 857) supporting the doubts expressed in Jackson & Powell *Professional Negligence* (4th Edition) at para 8–132 (note 22) that the £500,000 dividend claim in *Galoo* 'appears to have been overlooked...and wrongly struck out'.

It would therefore seem established that dividends paid out of illusory profits which have arisen as a result of negligence on the part of accountants are recoverable. When faced with such a potential claim, it is important to examine the factual circumstances on a case by case basis. The accountant may be able to argue that the company would have chosen to pay the dividend, even if the true picture had been known. For example, where the company's position is shown to be less favourable than was thought, but nonetheless profitable, the accountant may contend that a dividend would have been paid in any event. It may, however, be difficult for the accountant to bring forward convincing evidence to establish whether any dividend would have been paid and, if so, how much to counter the directors' account of what they would have done in hypothetical circumstances.

In addition, the defendant should investigate whether any other circumstances existed which should have prevented a dividend being paid. For example, there may have been transfers of cash or assets between a parent and a subsidiary with the purpose of disguising the fact that one or both were insolvent. Any dividend paid out to the parent as a result of such a transaction may well be irrecoverable.

Next, the defendant should check the timing of the decision to declare a dividend. It may be that the decision was taken prior to the time at which the accountant would (or should) have expressed an opinion on the company's finances.

Directors' bonuses

The same considerations that apply to dividends also apply to directors' bonuses. Bonuses paid as a result of a false idea of profitability caused by (or which persists as a result of) the accountant's negligence will usually be recoverable.

Overpayments of tax

As has previously been referred to, a business suffering from a false impression of its profitability may well have made overpayments of tax. These are recoverable, together with interest thereon, subject to the fact that the claimant may be expected to mitigate the loss suffered by taking reasonable steps to recoup the overpayment from the Inland Revenue.[52] The costs associated with obtaining repayment are recoverable from the defendant.

---

[52]*In re Thomas Gerrard & Son Ltd* [1967] 3 WLR 84.

Does issuing shares count as a loss?

More difficult is the situation in which the company has issued shares in itself that would not have been issued had it not been for the negligence of the accountant. In this situation it is arguable whether there is any 'loss' at all. Even if there is, how is it to be measured?

The contention that issuing shares does not constitute a loss was supported by the decision of the South Australian Supreme Court in *Health and Life Care Ltd* v *Price Waterhouse ('PW')*.[53] PW were retained to advise on a proposed acquisition. After the purchase had been completed the claimant alleged that the value of the assets acquired was far less than it had been led to believe by PW. The claimant sought to recover damages corresponding to the value of the shares it had issued, but this was disallowed. The judge ruled that whatever rights attached to the newly issued shares did not give rise to any immediate liability on the part of the claimant company. A company's capital is not a debt of the company. Nor could a claimant recover damage for a potential future loss as distinct from an actual loss.

This decision was later contradicted in another Australian case: *Duke Group Ltd (in Liquidation)* v *Pilmer and Others*.[54] Duke, a listed company, made a successful bid for another listed company and successfully acquired the whole of its share capital. The defendant firm of accountants had provided a report (in accordance with Australian stock exchange requirements) that concluded that the takeover price was fair and reasonable. The target turned out to be worthless. Part of the purchase price for the target had been paid in the form of shares in Duke. The judge accepted that Duke had suffered loss by the issue and allocation of shares in the takeover. The loss was to be measured by reference to the value of those shares at the time they were allocated.

Although the *Duke* decision was upheld on appeal,[55] the position remains uncertain. A better answer to the problem may be that where a company issues shares without getting proper value for them, it does suffer a potential loss because its ability to issue shares is, from a commercial point of view, finite. However, it would be for the claimant to show that it could have issued those shares to others, and that full value would have been obtained. In some circumstances this would not necessarily be possible.

---

[53][1997] SASC 6240.

[54][1998] SASC 6529.

[55][1999] SASC 97.

Loans

A similar issue arises in cases where a company has obtained a loan on the strength of an over-optimistic assessment of its financial health. The problem for the company is that it cannot be said to have suffered a loss merely by having accepted a loan, since it receives the benefit of the money advanced. This position was confirmed by the Court of Appeal in *Galoo*,[56] where a claim in respect of a loan secured on the strength of allegedly negligent audited accounts was struck out on the basis that the mere acceptance of the loan could not amount to a loss to the borrower. This does not, however, mean that a recoverable loss could not flow from the use to which the money was then put, if that use was foreseeable.

Trading losses

As discussed above, trading losses are only recoverable if a sufficient link can be shown by the claimant between the loss and the accountant's wrongdoing. Without this connection, the accountant may have provided the opportunity for the company to continue to trade but he is not regarded in law as being the cause of the trading losses.

Thus, where an auditor fails to identify that a company is no longer a going concern, with the consequence that it trades on, a liquidator will not on this basis alone succeed in reclaiming the losses that have resulted from the continued trading. On the other hand, where an auditor negligently fails to detect a fraud on the company, the company may be able to seek compensation in respect of amounts defrauded after the auditor should have blown the whistle. Equally, where the accountant is asked to consider a particular aspect of the client's business or systems and fails to identify problems, thus enabling further trading, losses arising from the inadequacy of the areas reviewed may prove to be recoverable.[57]

Losses in acquisition cases

Where a reporting accountant has produced a due diligence report for a client that proceeds to acquire a target company, he may well face a claim if the client later concludes that the acquisition was a bad bargain. The allegation will usually be that the accountant failed to give adequate advice about the target and that had he done so the acquisition would either not have been proceeded with or would only have gone ahead at a lower price.

---

[56][1995] 1 All ER 16.

[57]See generally 11.4 above

As discussed at **11.4** above, if the accountant provides a valuation of the target, the maximum that is likely to be recoverable from him is the amount by which the target was overvalued;[58] but where a valuation is not provided, it may be more difficult to assess what losses are to be regarded as flowing from the accountant's negligence

Fees

The accountant who is sued will habitually face a claim that some or all of the fees charged for the work done should be repaid to the claimant. Where only part of the work performed is at fault, the accountant is entitled to be paid on a *quantum meruit* basis, which simply means that he will receive that proportion of his fees which reflects the value of the work performed. Where the whole engagement is fundamentally flawed, the claimant will contend that there has been a total failure of consideration (in other words that no work of value has been performed) and that none of the accountant's fees should be payable.

Where the *quantum meruit* basis is applied, the accountant will be in a better position to recover an appropriate proportion of his fees if the billing records show an accurate breakdown of the amounts payable for different aspects of the engagement and the number of hours worked.

The claim for interest

The Court has the power to award interest on damages from the date at which the cause of action arises until the date that judgment is paid. Where a settlement is agreed between the parties after proceedings have begun, it will usually include an amount for interest equivalent to the amount that would have been awarded by the Court.

When the Court orders the payment of interest, it draws a distinction between interest awarded up to the date of judgment and interest that accrues from then until the judgment is paid. The Court has discretion over whether and how much interest to award for the period up to the date of judgment, but in most instances will award simple interest at a rate prescribed from time to time by statutory instrument, which currently stands at eight per cent per annum.

An unpaid judgment will almost always accrue interest automatically under statute, the current rate again being eight per cent per annum.

---

[58] *Law Debenture Trust Corp.* v *Hereward Philips* [1999] PNLR 725.

11.8 Has the claim been brought within the applicable limitation period?

The law requires a claim to be commenced within a specified period of time, known as the limitation period. If a claim is started after that deadline, the defendant will usually have a complete defence.

The length of the limitation period depends on the type of claim made and the particular facts of the case. It is not the intention here to give a comprehensive account of the law in this area, but to outline the basic position which will cover the majority of cases.

A claim for breach of contract must usually be brought within six years of the alleged breach. This is the case regardless of whether or not damage is suffered at that time; indeed, the date at which the damage occurs is of no consequence. Although it may sometimes be difficult to decide precisely when the breach of contract occurred, logic dictates that it cannot have been after completion of the engagement. As far as a claim in tort is concerned, the period is six years from the date at which the damage occurs.

Most claims against accountants allege both a breach of contract and the tort of negligence. Where the claimant has both a claim in contract and in tort arising from the same facts, the essential requirement in tort that relevant loss must be suffered for the cause of action to arise can result in the cause of action in tort accruing later than that in contract. The result of this, of course, is that a claimant who is slow to start proceedings will sometimes find that whilst it is too late to pursue his claim in contract, he can still proceed with the claim in tort.

In relation to a claim in tort, it can sometimes be difficult to pinpoint the date at which the damage occurred. This is a question of fact to be decided in each case. The courts have held that the cause of action does not arise until the claimant has suffered some loss which is more than merely trivial[59] and that it must be 'real damage as distinct from purely minimal damage'.[60] In *Nykredit Mortgage Bank plc v Edward Erdman Group Ltd*,[61] a case where the claimant advanced a loan on the strength of a negligent valuation, the House of Lords stated that a claimant has a cause of action the moment he can show that he is worse off than he would

---

[59]*Pirelli General Cable Works* v *Oscar Faber and Partners* [1983] 2 AC 1 HL.

[60]*Cartledge* v *E. Jopling and Sons Ltd* [1963] AC 758.

[61][1997] 1 WLR 1627.

have been but for the defendant's negligence. It is not necessary for the claimant to be able to quantify the loss he expects to suffer more precisely in order for a cause of action to accrue.

In most cases therefore, it is possible to measure the limitation period in tort from the time at which the client acts to his detriment in reliance on the allegedly negligent advice. Where the claim is being made by a client rather than a third party, it will usually be the case that reliance occurs at or around the end of the engagement. Where, for example, the client alleges negligent due diligence work, the period would be measured from the date on which the client bought the target company. In the case of a third party who relies on a negligent audit opinion however, the reliance might not take place until several months after the opinion was signed.

There are special provisions that apply where the fact that damage had been suffered was not known to the claimant, with good reason, for a number of years.[62] This may be the case, for example, in relation to negligent tax advice: if the advice is wrong, the consequences may not be apparent for some time. The effect of this is to defer the cut-off point for a claim for negligence to as much as 15 years after the date of the alleged negligence. There are similar extending provisions where the claim is based on fraud, or where any fact relevant to the claim has been deliberately concealed from the claimant: in these cases there is no final cut-off point.

There is also the possibility that the accountant will be dragged into litigation to which he was not an original party. For instance, he may be sued for a contribution or indemnity by a party who has been ordered to pay damages. Such an action can be brought up to two years after the original judgment, arbitration award or settlement.[63]

In reality, however, most claims against accountants and auditors will be commenced within six years of the end of the engagement. Whilst proceedings might still be issued after this time, this is much less likely.

---

[62]Under the Limitation Act 1980, as amended by the Latent Damage Act 1986, the limitation period is extended to three years from the time when the damage was reasonably discoverable. This is, however, subject to a longstop of 15 years after the alleged act of negligence.

[63]Civil Liability (Contribution) Act 1978.

Index